Firaq Gorakhpuri

Surinder Deol is a poet, author and literary translator. Whether exploring the fields of fiction, non-fiction, poetry, or translations, his words captivate, enlighten and inspire, leaving an indelible impression on readers to immerse themselves in the literary treasures he carefully crafts. He lives in Maryland, United States.

By the same author

LITERARY NON-FICTION

The Treasure: A Modern Rendition of Ghalib's Lyrical Love Poetry

Sahir: A Literary Portrait

Faiz: From Passionate Love to a Cosmic Vision

Narang Reader: Selected Writings of Gopi Chand Narang

Hafiz: At My Beloved's Door (Forthcoming)

Gulzar's Cosmos: Verses that Make the Ordinary Extraordinary (Forthcoming)

FICTION

Endless Life

POETRY

A Moment in the Universe

TRANSLATED LITERARY WORKS

Ghalib: Innovative Meanings and the Ingenious Mind

The Urdu Ghazal: A Gift of India's Composite Culture

The Hidden Garden: Mir Taqi Mir

India's Freedom Struggle and the Urdu Poetry: Awakening

Rajinder Singh Bedi: Selected Short Stories

Firaq Gorakhpuri

The Poet of Indianness

Surinder Deol

RUPA

Published by
Rupa Publications India Pvt. Ltd 2026
161-B/4, Gulmohar House,
Yusuf Sarai Community Centre,
New Delhi 110049

Sales centres:
Bengaluru Chennai
Hyderabad Kolkata Mumbai

P-ISBN: 978-93-5352-028-1
E-ISBN: 978-93-5352-515-6

First impression 2026

10 9 8 7 6 5 4 3 2 1

Printed in India

nigaah o gosh ki purkaif tashnagi ko n puuchh
ik adh khili si kali adh suna sa raag hai tu

निगाह ओ गोष की पुरकैफ़ तश्नगी को न पूछ
इक अध् खिली सी कली अध् सुना सा राग है तू

Don't ask me about the intoxicating upshot
of your eyes and ears.
The one is like a half-opened bud
and the other a half-heard melody.

—Firaq

CONTENTS

FOREWORD

The Ecstasy of a Heart on Fire

Gopi Chand Narang

> *In the deaths of Firaq and Josh Malihabadi a few days ago, Urdu and Hindustani have suffered two grievous blows... Firaq Gorakhpuri appealed to and affected our people at many layers of consciousness. It was a privilege for me to have known Firaq for many years. He wrote to me now and then as he wrote to my father...In recent months, one could see from his letters that he was feeling that his end was near. Yet, when I last saw him, I was told he was much better and would soon be discharged. Such are the ways of life and death.*
>
> Indira Gandhi
> Prime minister of India

> *Firaq was a master of Urdu poetry and Ghazals and won lasting admiration from the students of Urdu literature in and outside India. He has left behind many friends and admirers, including myself, to mourn his death.*
>
> Zia-ul-Haq
> President of Pakistan

The leaders of India and Pakistan don't seem to agree on many things. Yet Firaq's death in 1982 was an event where they openly expressed the same sentiments and words of praise for the deceased poet and his literary contributions.

Firaq was one of those poets who, as he stated, appeared only once in many centuries. His poetry resonated completely with the mystery-filled music of the universe. Not many poets can weave the beauty and elegance that he does so easily into his words. The Indian archetypal voice was always present in Urdu poetry, but Firaq's feat was that he resurrected it from Mir Taqi Mir (1723–1810), the god of Urdu poesy. He breathed new life into the ancient Aryan spirit and the concept of love and made it the heartthrob of millions of readers. Although his life was filled with tragic events like estrangement from his wife and the suicide of his only son, Firaq continued to write ecstatic poetry while the fire in his heart continued to burn.

Firaq lent a sensuous, transcendental echo to Urdu romantic poetry. His ghazal (pronounced guzzle) resounds with the same spirit that inspired the *rishis* (sages) of ancient India to unprecedented heights of metaphysical thought. On the one hand, he was roused by the English Romantic poets such as Wordsworth (1770–1850), Shelley (1792–1822), and Keats (1795–1821), while on the other, his sense of aesthetics was deeply rooted in the tradition of Sanskrit poetics. He once said that the lyrics of a poet are the hands that ring the bells of the temple of the universe. His essential themes are love and beauty, the mystery of the web of relationships, and the nature of aesthetics. He is a poet of the labyrinths of emotions, sensuousness, the transcendence of beauty, and the merging shades of pain and ecstasy.

In this foreword, I plan to discuss the most innovative elements of Firaq's poetry. Let us begin with a few randomly chosen verses.

maa'il-e bedaad vo kab tha Firaq
tu ne us ko ghaur se dekha nahien

माइले बेदाद वो कब था 'फ़िराक़'
तू ने उस को घौर से देखा नहीं

When was she inclined to harshness, Firaq?
You have yet to observe her.

In this couplet, Firaq challenges the traditional view that the beloved is harsh and indifferent. Addressing the conformist, he says you have not given enough thought to the beloved's nature, suggesting she is usually responsive. If you have found her otherwise, it is because she has no control over some forces. Note the phrase 'inclined to harshness' in the first line, which implies that 'harshness' is not the nature of the beloved. The optimistic tone suggests that love is not merely an abstraction in this case, but a profound experience. Consider how Firaq, starting from a traditional concept, weaves his delicate idea into the fabric of the verse, deviating markedly from the beaten track. On the formal level, he has not introduced a single change in the ghazal. He has retained the traditional masculine gender in this verse by using the auxiliary verb *tha* (he was) instead of *thi* (she was). This helps to preserve the universality of the ghazal and the sense of decorum—a cherished value of composite Indian culture.

sitaare jaagte hain raat lat chhatkaaye soti hai
dabe paaon ye kis ne aa ke khwaab-e zindagi badla

सितारे जागते हैं रात लट छटकाये सोती है
दबे पाऊँ ये किस ने आ के ख़्वाब-ए ज़िंदगी बदला

The stars keep vigil;
a night with flowing tresses sleeps.
Who, coming on soft footfalls,
has changed the dream of life?

In this couplet, the poet is referring to an experience. The first line is in the present tense, rather unusual for the classical ghazal. The poet does not say, 'This happened,' but rather, 'This is so' or 'This seems to be so.' *Sitaare* (stars) and *raat* (night) metaphorically stand for the male and the female, further established by their grammatical nature, for *sitaara* is a masculine and raat a feminine noun. S*oti* (asleep) and raat suggest the physical presence. Its intensity is revealed in the second line, 'Who, coming on soft footfalls, has changed the dream of life?' The impact of the 'coming' of a third person is such that it has changed a lover's life. Therefore, the past looks unreal, like a dream. Or the present itself is a dream. Also, note the beautiful use of *ri'aayat-e lafzi* (morphologically linked images)[1], such as stars, night, dream, sleep, and vigil.

zara visaal ke baa'd aaiina to dekh ae dost
tere jamaal ki doshiizgi nikhar aaii

ज़रा विसाल के बा'द आईना तो देख ऐ दोस्त
तेरे जमाल की दोशीज़गी निखर आई

Examine the mirror,
O friend!
After the consummation of love,
your virginal youth
has blossomed beyond belief.

Moralists have often criticized this verse as obscene. The *visaal* (union) is nothing new in the ghazal. The difference, however, is that the couplet suggests a meeting where lovers are in a state of intimacy that some people consider

[1]Morphology, from the Greek, is the study of shapes and forms. The terms morphology and archaeology are often used interchangeably.

obscene. The poet refers to an experience that both the lover and the beloved share. Paradoxically, the poet demolishes the conventional idea of chastity by implying that it is more a state of mind than a state of the body. He also emphasizes that the consummation of love does not lessen the charm of beauty but rather enhances it.

Firaq's strength lies in his ability to clothe the traditional imagery of classical ghazal with a new awareness and sensibility. He possesses a 'historical sense' like that of T.S. Eliot. Such a poet, Eliot wrote, 'lives in what is not merely the present, but the present moment of the past ... not merely with his generation in his bones, but with a feeling that the whole of the literature has a simultaneous existence.' Firaq's ghazal shows that he first assimilated the tradition he inherited and then introduced it into a new lyrical dimension.

This is not a big jump from the classical ghazal to Firaq. The modernization of the ghazal began with Altaf Husain Hali (1837–1914) and was continued by Iqbal, Hasrat, Asghar, Fani and Jigar. Some of them, especially Hasrat and Jigar, spoke of humanistic love. Still, it was left to Firaq to speak of love in its totality, tenderness, coarseness, significance and meaninglessness. He offered a full-blooded response to love in its bewildering complexity.

This totality may need some elaboration. Firaq speaks of timeless human relationships, with their joys and sorrows, their union and separation. He can capture the intense excitement of love. He speaks of it in a state of heightened sensibility. His poetry is therefore not bound to the temporal but characterized by the universal. He added no new emotions in the Urdu ghazal, but he writes about some old ones with a new feeling. The lovers of Firaq's ghazal are deeply conscious of the complexity and anxiety of their age. Things for them are not as straightforward as they are for classical poets. Let us look at some more verses.

kis liye kam nahien hai dard 'Firaq'
ab to vo dhyaan se utar bhi gaye

किस लिए कम नहीं है दर्द 'फ़िराक़'
अब तो वो ध्यान से उतर भी गए

Why does the pain not lessen, Firaq?
Now that she has gone away
from my thoughts.

In this verse, 'she has gone away from my thoughts' alludes to the traditional view that the memory of an unattainable ideal brings one pain. The first line, in which the poet claims that despite forgetting the beloved, the pain is no less, suggests that life is about much more than mere haunting and painful memories. Observe, too, the subtle ambiguity of the verse. Firaq takes an unconventional or startling position after mentioning a common belief here and elsewhere, prompting the reader to think. He does not narrate, but only hints, for there is much in the emotional conflicts of modern humans or problems that have no definable nature. In such verses, his images are often fused. Although he points his finger, he never says, 'This is a vague feeling,' but suggests a situation where the impact of this vague feeling is deeply felt. This imprecise, amorphous feeling, an indefinable element, forms the third element of the traditional love triangle in Firaq's poetry. It does not make any allowance for the conventional *raqiib* (rival) or *mohatasib* (censor, ascetic or shaikh). He suggests that the free flow of love in its fullest expression is perhaps obstructed by the anxiety of the age, the very consciousness of the burden of life itself.

tujhe to haath lagaaya hai baar-ha lekin
tere khayal ko chhuute hue main darta huun

तुझे तो हाथ लगाया है बारहा लेकिन
तेरे ख़याल को छूते हुए मैं डरता हूँ

My hands have touched you so
many times.
But I am afraid to lay my hand
on the thought of you.

This couplet suggests that lovers were friendly some time ago, but now the mere thought of the beloved is sheer torment. The reason for this change is not mentioned. Perhaps it reminds the lover of problems that cannot be solved or are not easily understood.

faza tabassum-e sub-h-e bahaar thi lekin
pahunch ke manzil-e jaanaan pe aankh bhar aaii

फ़ज़ा तबस्सम-ए सुबह-ए बहार थी लेकिन
पहुँच के मंज़िल ए जानां पे आँख भर आई

It was like the smile of a spring morning.
But when I reached my beloved's abode,
tears filled my eyes.

◆

bataayein kya dil-e muztar udaas kitna tha
ke aaj to nigaah-e naaz ne bhi samjhaaya

बताएं क्या दिल-ए मुज़तर उदास कितना था
के आज तो निगाह-ए नाज़ ने भी समझाया

How can I explain
why the restless heart was so sad?
Today even the one with the unique flair
tried to console me.

In the above two couplets, the poet juxtaposes two opposites. Note the word 'smile' in the first couplet, followed by 'tears.' Conventionally speaking, the lover is expected to feel happy when he gets to the abode of his beloved. But 'love,' as we know, is 'many splendored things'. Who can tell what these tears are about? Perhaps they are of relief, anguish, excitement, or another feeling that cannot be precisely defined. The second couplet is about the heart of the lover. Despite all the assurances, it is as restless as ever. This, again, is both a negation of a traditionally held view and an allusion to the complexity of the nature of love and life.

tum mukhaatab bhi ho qariib bhi ho
tum ko dekhein k tum se baat karein

तुम मुख़ातिब भी हो क़रीब भी हो
तुम को देखें के तुम से बात करें

You are attentive,
and you are close.
Do I look at you
or speak to you?

This couplet is a marvel of simplicity and suggestive clarity of expression. The beloved's figure and speech are equally fascinating and absorbing. The poet avoids direct compliments and speaks of his realization of the beloved's beauty, implying that each aspect is as innately fascinating as the wholeness of beauty.

As mentioned earlier, Firaq is the poet of the totality of love, which implies that the beloved we find as the subject of his poetry is truly human, vivacious, and even voluptuous. Conversely, while the traditional poets also talked of the beloved, it was more of an idea, an image, an illusion than a physical reality. We read much of the ruby lips, almond eyes, night-black tresses, rosy face and darting gestures, but all these expressions were, at best, two-dimensional, lacking a third, more human dimension. They were inevitably flat, if colourful. But Firaq is different. His poetry is deep, sensuous, perhaps the most sensual in the Urdu language. Like Keats, it is a riot of sounds and colours. Firaq achieves this effect not so much by merely enumerating words such as touch, feeling, form, warmth, glow, fragrance and melody, but through a more ingenious use whereby they are filled with life, giving the reader a living sensation of being close to someone's vital, intimate presence, the one that is charged and tense with emotions, filled with the gently swaying figure of a youthful form that can almost touch. It is a fragrance that one can drink in deeply. Such is the effect of Firaq's language.

Firaq achieved distinction not only as a ghazal poet, but his quatrains are also noteworthy contributions to Urdu literature. We examine three quatrains in which he presents three facets of womanhood—as a virgin (daughter), as a wife, and as a mother.

doshiiza faza mein lahlahaaya hua ruup
aaiina-e sub-h mein jhalakta hua ruup
ye narm nikhaar ye sajal dhaj ye sugandh
ras mein hai kunvaare-pan ke duuba hua ruup

दोशीज़ा फ़ज़ा में लहलहाया हुआ रूप
आईना-ए सुबह में झलकता हुआ रूप
ये नरम निख़ार ये सजल धज ये सुगंध
रस में है कुंवारेपन के डूबा हुआ रस

Against the immaculate air, the surging beauty.
In the mirror of dawn, the shimmering beauty.

The soft glow, the elegant figure, the fragrance—
imbued with the elixir of virginity, the beauty.

And this one:

dhalka aanchal damakte hal pe alak
palkon ki muskurahat ki jhalak
vo maathe ki kahkashaan vo moti bhari maang
vo god mein nanha sa humakta baalak

ढलका आँचल दमकते सीने पे अलक
पलकों की मुस्कुराहट की झलक
वो माथे की कहकशाँ वो मोती भरी मांग
वो गोद में नन्हा सा हुमकता बालक

The edge of the scarf shines on her visible bosom.
A foretaste of pleasure is concealed
behind the disguise of the eyelashes.
A rainbow on her forehead,
the crown of her hair set with pearls,
and in her lap a bouncing child.

Firaq's use of language is also worth mentioning. He was a great advocate of Khari Boli Hindustani, which forms the everyday basis for Hindi and Urdu. The more one deviates from it by using *tatsama* forms in Hindi and pure Persian-Arabic forms in Urdu, the more one is removed from the common usage. Firaq's language attempts a happy blend of forms drawn from both sources, trying to stay as close to the base as possible. Each of his above-quoted verses, for instance, his second quatrain, demonstrates this fact.

On the phonological level[2], he employs three retroflex sounds, *dh* in *dhalka*, *t* in *ot*, and again *t* in *muskurahat*;

[2]Relating to the system of contrastive relationships among the speech sounds that constitute the fundamental components of a language.

and three aspirate sounds, *dh* in dhalka, *th* in *maathe, bh* in *bhari,* but not a single glottal or spirant velar sound from the Persian-Arabic stock. This is not to say that he avoids their use altogether. Instead, he uses them where they are naturalized in Urdu. On a lexical level, there is a Persian word in each of the first, second and third lines, and none in the fourth. In each line, the foreign word is semantically tied to an indigenous word.

siina	to	*aanchal*
palak	to	*ot*
kahkashaan	to	*maatha*

The quatrain opens with dhalka and closes with *baalak,* both native words. In this quatrain, there is no significant Persian *izafat,* although the meter and rhyme scheme are of Arabic origin. Izafat is not entirely avoided, however, but where it is used, Firaq ensures that it blends with the rest of the language. Let us note that all this is not programmed, but natural to Firaq's language.

Not many people are aware of this, but it is worth mentioning that Firaq also distinguished himself in the field of literary criticism. In a slim volume titled *Andaazey* ('Conjectures'), he offered critical commentary on the Urdu poets of the eighteenth and nineteenth centuries. A collection of his letters, *Man Aanam* ('I Am'), was published in Pakistan. Although they never met, Nasir Kazmi (1925–1972), the renowned Pakistani poet of the new ghazal, was greatly inspired by Firaq. Thanks to Nasir Kazmi's creative work at Lahore's 'Halqa-e Arbaab-e Zauq,' Firaq's influence ushered in a surge of modernism in Urdu poetry all over Pakistan and India.

Firaq had a distinct perspective on language. His poetry had drawn its essence from the old tradition of Indian literature through the route of Khari Boli and Mir Taqi Mir. He knew Farsi well, and his poetry was sprinkled with the naturalized element of Farsi words. Still, he was very fond of the Indianness of both Khari Boli and sophisticated Urdu, which emerged from the historical confluence of civilizations and cultures. Firaq was against artificiality or formalistic programming of the language. He wanted Hindi speakers to appreciate the grace and beauty of the naturalized, free-flowing style of Urdu, a developed Indian language, and take advantage of its indigenized vocabulary and idioms for the reconstruction and promotion of India's national language, modern Hindi. Firaq believed Urdu's sophistication and communicative capacity were a result of cultural and historical synthesis that took many centuries to flourish. Official commands do not create languages; they are the by-products of cultural growth over long periods. They are not born or produced overnight. In Firaq's opinion, defying the norms and currency of Urdu was not in the national interest. His Urdu transcends the boundaries of Urdu and Hindi as we know them. Firaq introduced a new tenderness and intimacy to Urdu lyric poetry, and his sensuousness reminds one of Sanskrit literature. He seems to have the mind of a modern human being, but deep within, he has the heart of an ancient Aryan. He repeatedly mentioned that he wants his poetry to be the voice that rises from the very soul of India. Thanks to Firaq, the Urdu language, especially poetry, gradually became conscious of its Indian heritage coupled with a modern sensibility, and its concrete manifestations are found in generation after generation of poets like Nasir Kazmi, Munir Niazi, Shakeb Jalali, Jaun Elia, Parveen Shakir, Nida Fazli, Gulzar and Javed Akhtar.

When I took over as president of Sahitya Akademi in

2003, Firaq's centenary had already been celebrated a few years ago. Still, given Firaq's stature as the leading Urdu poet of the twentieth century, I felt that what had been done was grossly insufficient. I was therefore instrumental in organizing a week-long national seminar on Firaq in March 2007, in which scholars from India, Pakistan, and many other parts of the world participated and presented their papers. The seminar, coinciding with the twentieth death anniversary of Firaq's death, ended with a musical evening at the India International Centre in New Delhi. I also enjoyed meeting Ajai Mansingh, the poet's nephew, a United Nations official posted in Jamaica. As there was a web of misunderstandings about Firaq's persona, I encouraged Ajai to write an authentic biography of the poet, providing a firsthand family account. I contributed a foreword, but he didn't live to see the book's launch.

Surinder Deol, the author of this book, is no newcomer to translating works of Urdu poets. His translations of Mirza Ghalib, Mir Taqi Mir, Faiz Ahmed Faiz, Sahir Ludhianvi and many others have been widely acclaimed by readers and critics. Unlike other ghazal poets, Firaq's work has not received much attention from translators. Surinder changes this equation, and his selection of Firaq ghazals and ruba'is is superb, as is his translation. A great poet transcends the boundaries of language; if the work touches the reader's heart, one will enjoy the verse in any language. This is why in today's interconnected world, we read Persian poets like Rumi and Hafiz, Spanish poets like Pablo Neruda, and Urdu poets like Ghalib, Faiz, and Sahir in English. We can now add Firaq's name to this list. The deep-rooted pathos in Firaq's ghazals leaves a strong impression on our emotional state as we read them. Surinder makes a valiant effort to sustain and express this feeling concealed in the poet's words. This book will be a good companion to the readers on pensive rainy evenings and cheerful sunny days. Firaq's work has a timeless quality that, thanks to Surinder's ingenious translation, is now preserved in English, in addition to its original Urdu.

◆

Gopi Chand Narang (1931–2022) was a leading Urdu scholar and critic who made seminal contributions to literature, literary criticism and linguistics. He was president of the Sahitya Akademi (2003–2007) and was honoured with Padma Bhushan in 2004. He wrote this foreword a few months before his death in June 2022.

INTRODUCTION

Think of Life and Be Sad

My poetry reflects the aesthetic aspect of existence and action, where the influence of ancient Sanskrit literature and the world's finest literature is evident. In my art and use of language, I have attempted to create a new symphony, one that gives new melodies to words and synchronizes poetry with the voice of humanity. Life cannot be understood in terms of relations, actions and systems. I wish life to become a synthesis of instinct and sublime cognition.[3]

—Firaq

Raghupati Sahai Firaq Gorakhpuri was born in 1896 at the end of a tumultuous nineteenth century that saw the end of the Mughal reign and the beginning of the enslavement of the country and its people by the British. His father, Babu Gorakh Prasad, was a leading civil lawyer and a highly respected figure in the community. Even at a young age, Firaq showed signs that he was an unusual lad. If there is one word to describe his childhood, it is 'love'. He loved the other boys in school and almost everyone on the street where he lived. He loved not only the people, but also everything in his home—the bed he slept on, the water pitchers, the furniture, the doors and

[3]Mansingh, Ajai, *Firaq Gorakhpuri: The Poet of Pain and Ecstasy*, Roli Books, New Delhi. The text was edited for clarity.

windows, and the rooms filled with things. The objects of his fascination included the streets, the neighboring homes, trees, milk-yielding cows, and birds big and small. He liked it when people sang songs at weddings or festivals, and the recitation of Tulsi Das's Ramayan moved his heart deeply. He didn't talk much, but every little thing influenced him. He didn't get much sleep. From his bedroom window, he could see fields and age-old trees. He was mystified by the darkness, the shimmering of the stars, the play of light, and the shadows. His mood swung from happy to sad, and he thought about matters that should rarely bother young boys.

Firaq was captivated by the changing of the seasons. The rainy season, winter, sweltering summer, spring and autumn were parts of nature's play that occupied his mind with many questions but no answers. He often had the feeling that a tree had a heart like a human being. The beauty of crops and greenery signalled to him that life was not simply pain and suffering but also contained hidden beauty and grace to be explored. When he saw a beautiful landscape, he would stop at that spot, try to fully grasp the elements, and preserve the memory for the unknown future. Many years later, he expressed these early impressions of his childhood in a mythical poem, *Hindola,* a multifaceted history of India, which he presented in memorable words.

At school, Firaq paid particular attention to the languages, such as Sanskrit, Hindi and Urdu. He noticed how the words sounded, how the sentences were structured, and how some words touched the reader's core more than others. He explored the primeval forms of Khari Boli, the mother tongue of Hindi and Urdu. It didn't take him long to understand that Urdu had absorbed the best aspects of Khari Boli better than Hindi. Urdu had a greater depth, a richness of expression, and an inner rhythm that facilitated the composition of ghazal. He coined a word for this, *bandish ki chusti* (dexterity of binding words together), which he found in Urdu. Hindi poetry lacked the splendour and marvel of Khari Boli, and it sounded lifeless and arcane. It was, therefore, a logical choice for Firaq to become an Urdu poet.

After completing high school in 1913, Firaq was admitted to the prestigious Muir College in Allahabad (now Madan Mohan Malviya College) and lived in the hostel. Moving to Allahabad was Firaq's journey to his 'promised land,' as he called it. He exposed himself to the broader use of English in his study. Thanks to Firaq's efforts in learning languages at school, his knowledge of English was as good as Hindi or Urdu. He could boast that he had not made a single mistake in grammar, syntax and sentence structure in English from class sixth to college. He was drawn to studying logic, ethics, philosophy, history and English literature. He also read Urdu poetry without venturing to write anything of his own.

He was still in the second year of his studies when his family was duped, and Firaq was forced to marry a girl named Kishori in 1914, who was not suitable as his wife. Firaq always described his marriage as the greatest tragedy of his life. This was nothing short of a destructive hurricane that hit him, or an exploding volcano that spewed lava and covered his entire body with a sulphur cloud. This fire burnt him practically all his life, and the pain inflicted by this unfortunate event never subsided. The idea of having a life partner whom he could love and with whom he could start a family vanished into thin air. Yet he accepted the inevitable and focused on other things, like writing Urdu verses to express his heart's anguish. No wonder he compared his poetry to a lotus flower that grows in dirt and grime. He did not sleep for a whole year—neither during the day nor at night. Firaq was a dead-man-walking. He became ill and missed a year before completing his undergraduate degree. He put a veil over himself to show the world that there was nothing wrong with him, but inside, his ability to feel pain was lost forever. So when his parents and other relatives passed away, he couldn't shed a tear.

Soon after completing his studies, Firaq was selected for the prestigious Imperial Civil Services (ICS). For Firaq's patriotic mind, this career path was unacceptable. In 1920, he resigned from the service, entered the freedom movement, and was imprisoned for eighteen months. As he exited the prison, Jawaharlal Nehru, Secretary of the Indian National Congress, selected Firaq as an undersecretary of the party. This ten- or twelve-year period was of great economic hardship for Firaq's family. He didn't shy away from meeting his obligations, as his father and elder brother had already passed away by this time. In this despairing night of great sorrow and struggle, something good sustained him: his relationship with Jawaharlal Nehru and his father, Motilal Nehru, and the time he spent in their company at Anand Bhavan. With Jawaharlal Nehru, he shared a vision for India—a modern nation based on the fusion of science, Indian philosophy, and culture.

When Pandit Nehru went to Europe for an extended period, Firaq gave up his job as an undersecretary and became a teacher. As a private student, he applied for an MA in English at Agra University, where he topped the list of successful candidates. A post as a lecturer in English at Allahabad University was the immediate reward. He stuck with this job until his retirement in 1957. While working at Allahabad University, Firaq concentrated entirely on mastering English literature, especially English Romantic poetry, and writing poetry in Urdu. His aim was to rediscover the spirit of Khari Boli and the conscious blending of his Urdu diction with Hindi and Sanskrit vocabulary to create something new and highly refreshing for Urdu readers. Firaq published several poetry collections, including *Ruuh-e Kaayenaat, Ghazalistaan, Shabnamistaan, Gul-e Naghma* and *Roop*.

Another passion that occupied Firaq's mind was Indian mythology and the discovery of a deep humanism in the core scriptures of Hinduism. He found that love, which he had discovered in his childhood, was the guiding principle of the universe. At the lowest level, love was the bond between a man and a woman, the meeting of their bodies and sexual union. On a broader level, love sustains everything beautiful—rivers, seas, mountains, fields, gardens, fire, air, moon and sun, stars, and the ever-changing procession of seasons. These entities and elements were as sacred as any religious scripture. The manifest was as alluring as the hidden. It was a poet's job to make apparent what the eye could not see or the senses could not feel. For this reason, Firaq was fascinated by the *rasa* tradition in Sanskrit poetry, which aimed to make the hidden visible.

Firaq strongly believed that poetry should never serve as a mouthpiece for politics or religious propaganda. Poetry can however, benefit from major political events or religious revival movements. Poetry concerns our awareness, transcending our self for something greater. Firaq was impressed by George Bernard Shaw's question in one of his plays: What does man gain by attaining the highest state of development and progress? Shaw said that in this case, the human being would think of issues beyond commerce, politics, economics and religion. Such a person would try to find unity in diversity, and literature would be a helpful tool in this endeavor. Firaq sought to promote creative consciousness beyond blind faith and religious rituals. However, he made an exception in this case. In his view, the Hindu way of life, if understood correctly, is not communal. Its philosophy doesn't promote division among humans. However, the way a particular faith is preached and practiced can be problematic.

These considerations didn't stop Firaq from writing poems about political and societal awareness, but he never lost sight of the creative aspects that improve living conditions. Poetry is the language of life; good poetry can't be created from words buried in dictionaries. It emerges and blooms from the daily concerns of real people. Words can be simple, but when they touch the veins of thought that depict worries of daily life, they can become the foundation of aesthetic and energizing verses.

Firaq felt hurt and insulted when Niaz Fatehpuri called him a 'Hindu poet of Urdu'. Niaz perhaps did not realize that he was putting a communal label on Firaq, implying that Urdu was a language of Muslims. Firaq faced discrimination in his younger years when some literary journals did not review his work objectively because of his religious identity. The poetry of Iqbal, when it assumed a communal flavor, and the politics of hatred preached by the Muslim League posed unique challenges for non-Muslim Urdu writers. Firaq suffered even more than others because he drew his inspiration from the Vedas, the Upanishads, the rasa theory and Hindu mythology. Firaq learned to live with the reality of communal politics and focused on his work rather than wasting energy writing rejoinders to baseless characterizations.

Firaq was greatly influenced by Mir Taq Mir (1723–1810). Like Mir, Firaq brings the magic of spoken language to his ghazals, which appear simple on the surface but conceal layers of complexity beneath. Mir witnessed the destruction of his dream city, Delhi, while Firaq witnessed the horrors of Partition and the loss of numerous close friends who migrated to Pakistan. Despair is like a deep wound that doesn't heal, and Firaq inherited this wound from Mir.

ghazal ke saaz uthaao bari udaas hai raat
nava-e mir sanaao bari udaas hai raat

ग़ज़ल के साज़ उठाओ बड़ी उदास है रात
नवा-ए मीर सुनाओ बड़ी उदास है रात

Pick up the musical instruments of the ghazal,
for the night is too despairing.
Tune the melodies of Mir,
because the night is too despairing.

Firaq was the recipient of some of the highest national and literary awards by the Sahitya Akademi (1960), Padma Bhushan (1968) and the Bharatiya Jnanpith (1969). He passed on the flame of ghazal to the next generation of younger poets, even before he died.

ab tum se rukhsat hota huun aao sambhaalo saaz-e ghazal
naye taraane chhero mere naghmon ko niind aati hai

अब तुम से रुखसत होता हूँ आओ सम्भालो साज़-ए ग़ज़ल
नए तराने छेड़ो मेरे नग़मों को नींद आती है

I bid you farewell.
Come and take control of the instruments of the ghazal.
Begin new melodies and verses.
My melodies will now rest and take a nap.

Firaq died in March 1982 after a long illness. After he was discharged from the All India Institute of Medical Sciences, Firaq moved into the home of R.K. Garg, a lawyer and one of his former students. Garg asked him if the doctor should give him a sedative to ease his pain as the end was near. Firaq replied, 'Yes, this pain will go away, but what about the pain in my heart?' With a loud wail, the poet collapsed and breathed his last. There was no blood-relative in the room at that time. Allahabad, the city where the poet spent most of his life, was plunged into deep mourning by the news of his death, and he was given a funeral worthy of a celebrity or a political figure.

I first saw and heard Firaq in the 1970s at the Shankar-Shad Mushaira in New Delhi. One scene I remember was often repeated: When it was Firaq's turn to recite his verses, it was late at night, often past midnight, and by that time, he was either sleepy or was hungover due to the drinks he had consumed the night before. He was thus unable to recite a complete ghazal. He uttered a few words, and the poet, who was sitting next to him on the stage, completed the couplet. However, there were also moments when he spoke either about his life or matters of general interest to the audience or cracked unusual jokes. I remember him saying once: 'The poet's beloved, for whom he composes ghazals, is not present in this world. She lives only in his dreams. He is the one who created her. He is the one who speaks on her behalf. When a poet writes about the beauty and charms of his girlfriend or life partner, take off your shoe and pound the poet's work with that.' He had an overpowering personality and a charged way of speaking in a thunderous style with eyes wide open and circling pupils. He made fun of artificial poets; if anyone dared to raise an eyebrow at him, he would make ruinous remarks and tear that person apart.

I vividly recall the colourful function at the Vigyan Bhavan in 1969 when Firaq received the Jnanpith Award from Prime Minister Indira Gandhi. One of my most prized possessions is a copy of the commemorative volume *Bazm-e Zindagi Rang-e Shaa'yiri,* signed by Firaq.

While I enjoyed reading Firaq's ghazals, I wondered whether their innate beauty and profundity could be retained by translating them into another language. A few years ago, I was invited to speak about Urdu poetry at a literary gathering attended by people who did not understand Urdu. The organizers asked me to bring English translations of four to five poems or ghazals by a leading Urdu poet. I decided to focus on Firaq's ghazals. My presentation was well-received. Over the next few years, I translated Firaq whenever I found time. It took a long time to complete this work, but when I look back, I can draw great satisfaction in selecting eighty ghazals and sixty ruba'is and giving them a new identity in another language. I can say that I have savoured every moment I spent in Firaq's company. Sometimes he is easy, but most of the time he is not. Sometimes, I struggled and even considered giving up the effort, but something motivated me to keep going, and here I am, at a stage where I'm presenting my finished work to readers. Firaq will never fail to move you, that much I can guarantee. We can envy the people who saw Firaq in action, as the poet alluded to this possibility.

aane vaali naslein tum par rashk karein gi ham-a'sro
jab ye dhyaan aaye ga un ko tum ne 'Firaq' ko dekha tha

आने वाली नस्लें तुम पर रश्क करें गी हम-असरो
जब ये ध्यान आये गा उन को तुम ने 'फ़िराक़' को देखा था

The future generations will be envious,
dear contemporaries,
when they realize
that you saw Firaq in person.

To highlight the deep and enduring connection of the ghazal with the Indian system of ragas, the chapter headings in *Ghazaliaat-e Firaq* (Part I) are taken from the North Indian system of ragas. The chapter headings in *Ruba'iaat-e Firaq* (Part II)—Beauty (*Sundaram*), Truth (*Satyam*), and Action (*Shivim*)—were taken from a classification system presented in the commemorative volume titled *Bazm-e Zindagi: Rang-e Shaa'yiri* issued at the Jananpith Award ceremony.

Surinder Deol
Potomac, Maryland
May 2025

Part I

GHAZALIAAT-E FIRAQ

One

SHADJA (SA)

Svara (musical scale), a word originating in the Vedas, has several meanings besides a musical note and tone. Sa is the basic svara in the Indian musical system, giving birth to the next six svaras—re, ga, ma, pa, dha and ni. *Each svara is associated with a sound produced by a bird or an animal. A ghazal singer must master all svaras, even if he or she doesn't have to adhere strictly to the rules of classical music. What good is a ghazal if it is not heard in the melodious voice of a singer? To recognize the close connection between ghazal writing and singing, the first seven chapters of the book are named after seven savaras of the Indian musical system.*

◆

Poetry can be like the Taj Mahal or Jam'a Masjid. Or it can be like an exquisite haveli. It can hit you hard. You can admire it. You can do your vah vah. But you can't absorb yourself in this. I take pride in the ordinariness of my existence. The verse of a great poet is like Taj Mahal or Jam'a Masjid. Or Red Fort. It gives you a feeling of loftiness. I like to give my readers a sense of intimacy and oneness with me. The total effect of my verse is wise passiveness.[1]

—Firaq

[1] *Firaq: Dayar-e Shab Ke Musafir,* 'Interview with Zoe Ansari', Suhail Ahmad Farooqi and Shamim Hanafi (eds), Maktaba Jamia Limited, New Delhi, 1996,p.43.

SOMEONE STARTED A MELODIOUS GHAZAL

Firaq wrote poems in various poetic sub-genres but was primarily a ghazal poet. Ghazal is a short lyrical form with deep roots in Persian and Urdu poetry. Two rhymed lines of a ghazal, *she'r* (couplet), have a self-contained thought. The ghazal must have unity of form, as it follows a rhyme scheme: AA, BA, CA, DA, EA, and the rest. We need to recall a few key technical terms related to the ghazal's poetic form. The first couplet in a ghazal is known as a *matl'a.* The first line of the matl'a and the second lines of all subsequent couplets must end with the same refrain. This is called the *radif.* The radif is preceded by words or phrases with the same end rhyme scheme, called the *qafiya.* The last couplet of the ghazal is the *maqt'a,* which by convention contains the poet's *takhallus* or nom de plume. To preserve its lyrical quality, the ghazal must follow the same metrical pattern and syllabic count. This is known as *behr.* Each couplet of a ghazal may contain several themes or ideas, although in practice the couplets generally tend to describe the beloved's beauty and the endless frustrations of the lover. Sometimes a thematic unity can be found in a ghazal, but this is the exception and not the rule. The length of a ghazal can vary.

The following words come to mind when we think of the ghazal: elegance, mindfulness, subtle mystical feelings, the density of thought, passionate imagery, innate musicality, and richly evocative meaning. Each couplet tells an imaginative story—a condensed, existential and universal narrative of love. The world of the ghazal is rich in creativity and metaphorical language. Brevity is the soul of the structure of the ghazal. Everything is mystical, everything is the stuff of dreams. It represents a state in which everything is mysterious, magical, dens and complex, like a web of a mythical dream, a play of love in a meditative state of superconsciousness.[2]

The ghazal's origin can be traced back to the Arabic *qasida*, a long poem that celebrates the victory of a tribe or a ruler in battle. Although some parts of the poem could be considered romantic, love was not the central theme in a qasida. The ghazal borrowed the verse structure of the qasida in Persian and added love and physical attributes of beauty such as the beloved's hair, lips, height and cheeks. Muhammad Rudaki was the first major Persian poet to use the ghazal form. He was followed by several poets who perfected the form and structure of the ghazal as we know it today. The list includes poets such as Sana'i (1080–1131), Attar (1145–1221), Khaqani (1120–1186), Anvari (1126–1189), Nizami (1141–1209) and the highly regarded poets Rumi (1207–1273) and Hafiz (1325–1390). Since Hafiz wrote exclusively ghazals, his mastery of the genre was exceptional and a source of inspiration for future ghazal poets in many languages, including Urdu. Two of the greatest Urdu ghazal poets, Mir Taqi Mir (1723–1810) and Mirza Ghalib (1797–1869), acknowledged their debt to Hafiz, for he was a master guide and motivator.

The British actively discouraged the form of ghazal poetry as they believed it turned people into lazy hallucinators. They encouraged poets to write on natural themes, following the lead of British poets like Wordsworth. Many people believed that the era of ghazal writing had come to an end with the deaths of great ghazal poets like Maulana Hali and Daagh Dehlvi in the early twentieth

---

[2]Narang, Gopi Chand, *The Urdu Ghazal: A Gift of India's Composite Culture.* pp. 3-4.

century. Three poets who appeared on the scene in the early 1920s, namely Josh Malihabadi, Hasrat Mohani, and Firaq Gorakhpuri, picked up the threads and revived the art of ghazal-writing. Firaq was not just a ghazal poet, but elevated the craft by adding great musicality and vocabulary that drew on the richness of the spoken language, much like Mir Taqi Mir before him. Firaq drew from India's rich and diverse cultural heritage, including Sanskrit poetics and Hindu mythology. It is essential to mention this as Arabic and Persian were once favoured sources of Urdu poets.

In Firaq's poetry, we find an echo of Mir because of their stylistic similarities. Mir knew Persian well, but he often used the vernacular of Delhi and Agra, where he had spent his early years. However, as Abul Kalam Qasmi noted, there were noticeable differences in their approaches. While Mir was ready to accept the beloved despite all her strengths and weaknesses, Firaq extended to his beloved a distinctive place that conferred on her freedom of choice and made her a person in her own right.[3]

We can confidently say that Firaq's ghazal poetry postulates a triangle of meaning, feelings, and musicality. While he respects tradition, he is not afraid to criticize old customs and blaze new paths. He uses novel metaphors and similes to create imagery that complements his lyrical tone. His poetic expression is full of courage and novelty, sustaining freshness. His range of themes is vast, and he draws from Indian classicists like Kalidasa, iconic English romantic poets, and Persian master poets. His ghazal poetry is the high road that transcends the boundaries of enlightenment, mystical experiences, and deep-seated

[3]Narang, Gopi Chand, *Firaq Gorakhpuri: Shaa'yir, Naqqaad, Daanishvar.* p. 16.

humanism. The peace and serenity found in India's enlightened souls of antiquity provide a shining light to his ghazals.[4]

ROSES AND THORNS IN THE TAVERN OF LIFE

Firaq's early childhood memories were associated with the family's ancestral home in Banwarpar, with its large courtyards, high-ceilinged rooms, and expansive corridors. The Sahai family could look back with pride at its roots, which dated back to the Mughal Empire and the title of 'panchgaon kayastha' (a Kayasth family that owned five villages), which they held. Banwarpar was one of these villages. As a child, Firaq breathed in the air of this village, and when he walked through its dusty lanes, he felt blessed. The vast plains stretching across the foothills of the Himalayas introduced this inquisitive child to the wonders of Mother Nature and captured his feelings about the landscape, the nearby forests, and the adjacent rivers like Rapti, Ghagra, Saryu and Ganga in his verses. In her sublime role as a teacher, nature taught him virtues of patience, kindness and love in its manyfold manifestations. He also learnt that love is the founding principle of all religions and that faith has no divine significance if it is practiced without love as its central core.

Gorakh Prasad, Firaq's father, was born in 1865 as the Mughal Empire was coming to an end and a new era of slavery was beginning under British rule. He knew that to prosper in this time of transition, he would need a professional qualification, such as law, and a command of languages that mattered—English, Hindi, Urdu, Sanskrit,

[4]Ibid., pp. 77–78.

Persian and Arabic. This love of languages and literature, passed on to his son by his caring father, bore fruit, and he could be found in his teens discussing the complexities of the works of poets such as Mir Taqi Mir.

The father had the good fortune to build a professional career as a lawyer and to gain a reputation as a gifted poet, but he was not so lucky in his personal life. He lost his first wife; he remarried, but soon after the marriage, he lost his second wife and a five-year-old son. These tragedies crippled him emotionally, but he didn't give up his dream of a great nuclear family. He married a third time, and it was his third wife, Dulari Devi, who bore him five sons and three daughters, becoming the pillar of the entire clan. The family built and moved into a new mansion called Lakshmi Bhavan with sixteen large rooms, several courtyards, servants' quarters, and sheds for horses and cows on the outskirts of Gorakhpur. The new estate had many distinguished guests, poets and politicians, including Nehrus. Gorakh Prasad was proud of his list of clients, which was headed by Motilal Nehru.

Life is deceptive, and when things seem to be headed in the right direction, unexpected events disturb the equilibrium. The eldest son, Ganpati, was diagnosed with tuberculosis and had to be admitted to a sanatorium in Nainital. The family was desperate to arrange the son's wedding, but with Ganpati's illness, the burden fell on Firaq, who was next in line. He was forced to marry a girl named Kishori Devi in 1914, when he was eighteen years old, through an act of deception that changed the arc of his life for years to come.[5] This marriage was a tragedy,

[5]According to an account of this deception, Firaq's aunt visited the girl's family. She saw a young, good-looking girl who was homeschooled

like a lightning strike from which Firaq never recovered. Firaq could have ended the marriage thrust upon him, but he accepted it as an act of karma and decided to stay in this relationship that did not bring him happiness. Firaq concentrated on his education and joined Allahabad University to study English, History and Logic for his undergraduate degree. In 1916, his daughter, Prabha, was born, and in 1920, his son, Govind,[6] Another tragedy struck the family when Gorakh Prasad died suddenly in 1918, presumably of a heart attack. The family was devastated, but more importantly, Firaq, fresh out of college, was now the head of the Sahai family and their financier. A few months later, his elder brother passed away. His emotional distress knew no bounds.

Firaq was offered the post of deputy collector by the British government because of his academic performance and brilliant mind. For any educated Indian, this was the biggest dream job, but not for Firaq. Joining the freedom movement was an incredible honour compared to serving

---

and interested in good literature. Impressed by what she saw, the aunt recommended the alliance. The girl the aunt had seen was not Kishori Devi. Tragically, not even the bride realized that her parents had played this trick on her. Firaq captured his frustration in a few stanzas of his historical poem *Hindola.* The problem with Kishori Devi was not limited to her lack of beauty and grace; she was intellectually deficient and no match for a man of Firaq's calibre.

[6]Firaq told an interviewer about his marriage, 'Yes, my family life has been better than that of many of my critics. But it was never emotionally fulfilling, physically satisfying, metaphysically happy and blissful...My marriage made me a victim of loneliness. I have expressed this thought in one of my couplets. *gham-e firaq to us din gham-e firaq hua/ jab unko pyaar kiya main ne jin se pyaar nahien* (My sadness was born the day I was forced to love someone for whom I had no love in my heart).' (Amir Ahmad Siddiqi, Naya Daur, Firaq Number 1, 1983.)

the foreign rulers in a high position. Firaq became director of the Government Model School, a job that brought little financial gain. But a richer reward awaited him when he became friends with Munshi Premchand, a pioneer of modern Indian fiction, and published his ghazals and poems in literary magazines. Firaq's participation in the freedom movement soon landed him in prison, where he served an 18-month sentence. During his time in prison, Firaq met Jawaharlal Nehru, who later appointed him undersecretary of the Indian National Congress in 1923. This job paid a good salary and allowed Firaq to deepen his relationship with Motilal Nehru and his son Jawaharlal Nehru. As he stayed at Ananda Bhavan, the Nehru residence, he also met other visiting national leaders, such as Sarojini Naidu. Firaq remained in this job for four years. In 1927, he moved to Lucknow and Kanpur to work as a teacher, a profession he loved, but eventually landed a job at the University of Allahabad's English department. To prepare for a job as a college teacher, Firaq earned a master's degree in English from Agra University as a private candidate, meaning he took the exams but studied independently. Despite this limitation, Firaq topped the list of successful candidates in 1930. Facing the ravages of time and amid many other family tragedies, the family mansion in Gorakhpur was finally sold in 1949 for a paltry sum of ten thousand rupees.

◆

The ghazals included in this book have been arranged chronologically to demonstrate how Firaq's poetic talent evolved from his early years to the 1970s. However, we were disappointed in our endeavor. Firaq was born and died a master poet. The first ghazal in this collection, which he wrote in 1919 (Inside Your Seeing: *diidaar mein ik turfa diidar nazar aaya),* doesn't look like the work of a poet in his early twenties. It looks and feels like a masterpiece—each couplet shows the poet's complete command of his craft.

Inside Our Seeing

diidaar mein ik turfa diidar nazar aaya

Firaq wrote this ghazal in his early twenties. He discusses how love and beauty are always present, regardless of the circumstances. Its special power can't be hidden or escaped. He begins by saying that even if someone tries to hide their beauty, it still manages to shine through. This idea sets the mood for the rest of the ghazal. Firaq strategically employs Majnun and Laila's poignant love story to underscore the profound impact of love's omnipresence. This narrative starkly illustrates the depths of despair to which a broken heart can plunge. Majnun's anguish is so intense that in his eyes, even a thorny wilderness is transformed into a beautiful rose garden. Firaq's verses also warn against seeking solace or answers in love in moments of desolation. He poignantly reminds us of the brevity of life and the insignificance of many of our worries in the grand tapestry of life. In the final part of the ghazal, Firaq summarizes the main idea by stating that even the pain of being separated from a loved one and the passage of time are ultimately meaningless. So, if we look at the entire ghazal, the point is that love and beauty are powerful forces that cannot be avoided and can cause much pain, which might seem important in the moment, but has no meaning in the grand scheme of things.

diidaar mein ik turfa diidar nazar aaya
har baar chhupa koi har baar nazar aaya

दीदार में इक तुर्फ़ा दीदार नज़र आया
हर बार छुपा कोई हर बार नज़र आया

Inwardly, the vision was a rare spectacle.
Every time she tried to hide,
she revealed herself.

◆

chhaalon ko biyabaan bhi gulzaar nazar aaya
jab chher par aamaada har khaar nazar aaya

छालों को बयाबाँ भी गुलज़ार नज़र आया
जब छेड़ पर आमादा हर ख़ार नज़र आया

The blisters saw the wilderness
as a garden of roses.
When every thorn was destined
to cause mischief.

◆

ho sabr k betaabi ummid k maayuusi
nairang-e mohabbat bhi bekaar nazar aaya

हो सब्र कि बेताबी उम्मीद कि मायूसी
नैरंग-ए मोहब्बत भी बे-कार नज़र आया

Whether it is the despair of patience
or the distress of hope,
the magic of love was of no avail.

◆

tu ne bhi to dekhi thi vo jaati hui duniya
kya aakhri lamhon mein biimaar nazar aaya

तू ने भी तो देखी थी वो जाती हुई दुनिया
क्या आख़री लम्हों में बीमार नज़र आया

You too saw the world
as it faded away,
and how the dying looked
in his final moments!

◆

zarra ho k qatra ho khum-khaana-e hasti mein
makhmuur nazar aaya sarshaar nazar aaya

ज़र्रा हो कि क़तरा हो ख़ुम-ख़ाना-ए हस्ती में
मख़मूर नज़र आया सरशार नज़र आया

In the tavern of life,
it doesn't matter
whether it is an atom or a dribble,
it appeared inebriated
and ecstatic.

◆

kya kuchh n hua gham se kya kuchh n kiya gham ne
aur yuun to hua jo kuchh be-kaar nazar aaya

क्या कुछ न हुआ ग़म से क्या कुछ न किया ग़म ने
और यूँ तो हुआ जो कुछ बे-कार नज़र आया

Grief did its best,
and sorrow also did well.
Whatever happened—
all was fruitless.

◆

shab kat gaaii furqat ki dekha n 'Firaq' aakhir
tuul-e gham-e hijraan bhi be-kaar nazar aaya

शब कट गई फ़ुर्क़त की देखा न 'फ़िराक़' आख़िर
तूल-ए ग़म-ए हिज्राँ भी बे-कार नज़र आया

Firaq, behold,
even the night of separation
ended its course.
In the end, even the weight of
the sorrow didn't matter.

Love Changes Everything

vaqt-e ghuruub aaj karamaat ho gaaii

Firaq discusses how powerful love can be and how the person you love can change your whole world just by being who they are. He begins by illustrating the transformative power of his beloved's beauty by comparing it to her ability to turn day into night when she lets her hair down. He says that his beloved's eyes have suddenly become like a sacred place where all his prayers and wishes come true, even though they didn't have this power before. Then he talks directly about love itself, saying that it makes him feel so profoundly that every breath feels like a prayer as he constantly thinks of his beloved. He even treasures his beloved's brief, not-so-nice glance as if it were the most precious thing in the world, like a poor man receiving a wonderful gift. Just the thought of his beloved's curly hair darkens his whole world, showing how much he misses her and how much she means to him. Firaq marvels at himself for staying so calm and composed, being far away from his home and his beloved, as if it's a miracle he can handle it. The ghazal is ultimately about how love transforms the lover and beloved, and everything else in life.

vaqt-e ghuruub aaj karamaat ho gaaii
zulfon ko us ne khol diya raat ho gaaii

वक़्त-ए घरऊब आज करामात हो गई
ज़ुल्फ़ों को उस ने खोल दिया रात हो गयी

As the sun was setting,
a miracle happened.
She opened her locks,
and behold, it was night.

◆

kal tak to us mein aisi karamaat n thi koi
vo aankh aaj qibla-e haajaat ho gaaii

कल तक तो उस में ऐसी करामत न थी कोई
वो आँख आज क़िबला-ए हाजात हो गई

Until yesterday,
there was no such miracle in her.
Today, that eye has become the sanctum of desires.

◆

ae soz-e i'shq tu ne mujhe kya bana diya
meri har ek saans munajaat ho gaaii

ऐ सोज़-ए इ'श्क़ तू ने मुझे क्या बना दिया
मेरी हर एक साँस मुनाजात हो गई

O lovesickness!
See what you have made of me.
Every breath I take
is like a prayer.

◆

ochhi nigaah daal ke ik samt rakh diya
dil kya diya ghariib ki saugaat ho gaaii

ओछी निगाह डाल के इक सम्त रख दिया
दिल क्या दिया ग़रीब की सौग़ात हो गई

After giving a mean glance,
she turned away.
The rejected heart
became the poor man's
precious treasure.

◆

kuchh yaad aa gaaii thi vo zulf-e shikan-shikan
hasti tamaam chashma-e zulmaat ho gaaii

कुछ याद आ गई थी वो ज़ुल्फ़-ए शिकन-शिकन
हस्ती तमाम चश्मा-ए ज़ुल्मात हो गई

It was a thought
of her tangled tresses.
My whole existence was transformed
into a fountain-spring of darkness.

◆

ahl-e vatan se duur judaaii mein yaar ki
sabr aa gaya 'firaq' karamaat ho gaaii

अहल-ए वतन से दूर जुदाई में यार की
सब्र आ गया 'फ़िराक़' करामात हो गई

Away from fellow-countrymen
and the one who is much loved,
your state of composure, Firaq,
is simply powerful and magnificent.

Love and the World of Mysteries

tuur tha kaa'ba tha dil tha jalva-zaar-e yaar tha

Firaq explores the transformative power of love in this ghazal, using colourful imagery and religious symbolism to convey its sacred and all-consuming nature. He compares the yearning for his beloved and the pain of separation to intoxication, emphasizing love's ability to alter one's perception of reality. Firaq suggests that love transcends the physical domain, with tears turning into jewels and life reduced to dust in the path of the beloved. The poet also touches upon the timeless aspect of love when the beloved enquires about past affections, and the lover's heart aches near the beloved's home. The world becomes a reflection of the beloved, as glittering dust and particles mirror their presence. Firaq's ghazal ultimately portrays love as a catalyst for spiritual change, with the beloved's presence profoundly impacting the lover's soul.

tuur tha kaa'ba tha dil tha jalva-zaar-e yaar tha
i'shq sab kuchh tha magar phir aa'lam-e asraar tha

तूर था का'बा था दिल था जल्वा-ज़ार-ए यार था
इ'श्क़ सब कुछ था मगर फिर आ'लम-ए असरार था

There was Mount Sinai,
there was the Sanctum,
there was the heart,
and there was a place for her
to make her mystical appearance.
Love was everything,
and then there was a world
of mysteries.

◆

nash-sha-e sad-jaam kaif-e intizaar-e yaar tha
hijr mein thahra hua dil saaghar-e sarshaar tha

नश्शा-ए सद-जाम कैफ़-ए इंतिज़ार-ए यार था
हिज्र में ठहरा हुआ दिल साग़र-ए सरशार था

The longing for the beloved
felt like a never-ending intoxication.
In the pain of separation,
the heart was a vessel brimming with emotion.

◆

jauhar-e aaiina-e aa'lam bane aansu mere
yuun to sach ye hai k rona i'shq mein bekaar tha

जौहर-ए आईना-ए आलम बने आँसू मिरे
यूँ तो सच ये है कि रोना इ'श्क़ में बेकार था

My tears became jewels
of the mirror of the world.
Though the truth is that
crying in love was in vain.

◆

shokhi-e raftaar vajah-e hasti-e barbaad thi
zindagi kya thi ghubaar-e rahguzaar-e yaar tha

शोख़ी-ए रफ़्तार वज्ह-ए हस्ती-ए बर्बाद थी
ज़िंदगी क्या थी ग़ुबार-ए रहगुज़ार-ए यार था

The audacity of speed
was the reason
for the destruction of existence.
What was life?
It was nothing
but the dust of the path of the beloved.

◆

ulfat-e diriina ka jab zikr ishaaron mein kiya
muskara kar mujh se puuchha tum ko kis se pyaar tha

उल्फ़त-ए देरीना का जब ज़िक्र इशारों में किया
मुस्कुरा कर मुझ से पूछा तुम को किस से प्यार था

When I gestured
about the love of a long-standing love,
she smiled and asked—
Who did you love back then?

◆

dil dukhe roye hain shaayad is jagah ae kuue dost
khaak ka itna chamak jaana zara dushvaar tha

दिल-दुखे रोए हैं शायद इस जगह ऐ कू-ए-दोस्त
ख़ाक का इतना चमक जाना ज़रा दुश्वार था

My heart aches
and weeps near the beloved's lane.
The dust could not glitter
so much otherwise.

◆

zarra zarra aaiina tha khud-numaayi ka 'Firaq'
sar basar sahra-e aa'lam jalva-zaar-e yaar tha

ज़र्रा ज़र्रा आइना था ख़ुद-नुमाई का 'फ़िरा'
सर-ब-सर सहरा-ए आलम जल्वा-ज़ार-ए यार था

Every particle was a mirror of self-revelation, Firaq.
The vast desert of the world
showcased the essence of the beloved.

Hidden Passion

i'shq ki maayuusion mein soz-e pinhaan kuchh nahien

Firaq explores the transformative nature of love, emphasizing that the hardships and heartache that accompany it are integral to the experience. He suggests that love transcends the physical and ordinary aspects of life, rendering them insignificant in comparison to the intense emotions felt by those who love deeply. Firaq uses imagery such as storms and lamps, conveying the tumultuous and all-consuming nature of love, highlighting that its true essence lies in the struggles and heartbreak it brings. He also touches on the transience of physical beauty, implying that genuine love transcends superficial attraction and is rooted in a deeper, spiritual connection. The recurring themes of the 'ruined heart' and forgetful lovers underscore how love can transform individuals and disconnect them from their former selves. Firaq also explores the contradictory nature of love, where insufficiency and abundance coexist, and the willingness of lovers to endure any hardship for their beloved. The ghazal conveys the notion that true love is a profoundly personal passion that transcends the boundaries of the material world and external influences.

i'shq ki maayuusion mein soz-e pinhaan kuchh nahien
is hava mein ye charaagh-e zer-e daamaan kuchh nahien

इ'श्क़ की मायूसियों में सोज़-ए पिन्हाँ कुछ नहीं
इस हवा में ये चराग़-ए ज़ेर-ए दामाँ कुछ नहीं

In the failures of love,
the concealed passion
is not a material factor.

In this tempest,
the lamps flickering beneath
are insignificant.

◆

i'shq ki hai khud-numaaii i'shq ki aashuftagi
ru-e taabaan kuchh nahien zulf-e pareshaan kuchh nahien

इ'श्क़ की है ख़ुद-नुमाई इ'श्क़ की आशुफ़्तगी
रू-ए ताबाँ कुछ नहीं ज़ुल्फ़-ए परेशाँ कुछ नहीं

It is the self-manifestation of love,
and it is love's torment.
The dazzling, beaming face means nothing,
and disheveled tresses mean nothing.

◆

yaad aa hi jaati hai aksar dil-e barbaad ki
yuun to sach hai chand zarraat-e pareshaan kuchh nahien

याद आ ही जाती है अक्सर दिल-ए बर्बाद की
यूँ तो सच है चंद ज़र्रात-ए परेशाँ कुछ नहीं

The memory
of the ruined heart
comes back often.
While it is true
some chaotic particles
put together
mean nothing.

◆

aur un ki zindagi hai aur u'nvaan-e hayaat
khud-faraamoshon ko tere a'hd o paimaan kuchh nahien

और उन की ज़िंदगी है और उ'नवान-ए हयात
ख़ुद-फ़रामोशों को तेरे अ'हद ओ पैमाँ कुछ नहीं

And this is how they live.
And this is the masthead of their existence.
For those who are forgetful,
your promises and pledges
mean nothing.

◆

jo n ho jaaye vo kam hai jo bhi ho jaaye bahut
kaar-zaar-e i'shq mein dushvaar o aasaan kuchh nahien

जो न हो जाए वो कम है जो भी हो जाए बहुत
कार-ज़ार-ए इ'श्क़ में दुश्वार ओ आसाँ कुछ नहीं

That which does not happen is insufficient.
What happens is enough.
On the battlefield of love,
there is no such thing as easy or difficult.

◆

kaash apne dard se betaab hote ae 'Firaq'
duusre ke haathon ye haal-e pareshaan kuchh nahien

काश अपने दर्द से बेताब होते ऐ 'फ़िराक़'
दूसरे के हाथों ये हाल-ए परेशाँ कुछ नहीं

Firaq would have wished for unrest
if it were self-inflicted.
The travails at the hands of others
mean nothing.

Two

RSABHA (RE)

The introspective and intoxicating nights appear to create such an atmosphere in my verses as can be sought nowhere else but the night. There is a great section of my poetic volume that can qualify me as the bard of midnight.[7]

—Firaq

BARBS AND BRISTLES

When Firaq joined the English faculty at the University of Allahabad in 1930, he fulfilled an intense inner longing to become a college professor. The decade of the 1930s started well with the addition of a family member, a fourth child, a girl named Pushpa, born in 1932. Firaq had a loving relationship with all his children, but felt a special connection with his firstborn, Prabha, a very intuitive child.

Having established himself in his job at the university with a regular income, Firaq wanted to live his life in style. He bought a red Austin car in 1934 and hired a chauffeur to drive it. But misfortune is never far away, and there is no way to prepare for the loss that suddenly befalls you. As the talk of Prabha's wedding was gathering momentum, she

[7]Gorakhpuri, Firaq. Man Anam: Mudir-e-Nuqush Ke Nam Khutut. Saqi Buk Dipu, 1997.

fell ill and was diagnosed with typhoid. Despite reasonably good medical care in Allahabad, she could not be saved. This tragedy was too much for Firaq to bear, although life marched on at its uneasy pace.

The family moved into the Bank Road accommodation provided by the university, where Firaq lived for the rest of his life. Prabha's demise had impacted the whole family, but for Govind, who saw his elder sister as his mentor and protector, it was a great personal shock. The boy had severe psychological issues; he was concerned about his below-average school record. He felt the pressure of being the son of a distinguished poet and a highly respected academic. Govind was not doing well; his teachers and peers called him a disgrace to the family.

One summer's day in 1937, Govind threw himself in front of an incoming train and lost a leg. The blood loss was severe. Before his death on the fourth day after the accident, he told his mother, Kishori Devi, 'Mother, the sun has started to set. It doesn't have any brightness. Darkness is creeping.' Firaq was an inwardly broken man after the loss of his daughter, Prabha, but the death of Govind tore him apart. He started to ask some fundamental questions: What is life? What is the meaning of life? The 1930s thus ended on a very sad note for the family.

JOSH AND FIRAQ'S FRIENDSHIP

Josh Malihabadi and Firaq Gorakhpuri were Urdu's most significant poets who reached the peak of their creativity in the twentieth century. They were born two years apart (Firaq in 1896, Josh in 1898) but died in the same year (1982). They belonged to the same socio-cultural background. Josh came from a family of poets; Firaq's father was a well-respected poet. Both received a good English education; both attained proficiency in Urdu and Persian. Firaq said in an interview about his friendship with Josh,

> Josh, as a friend, is close to my heart. I consider him a great poet. He has lived in my house for months, like a family member. I'm a great admirer of his personality. But I've also absorbed several hundred negative influences of his personality. He saw a dream in his imagination and decided to leave India. It greatly saddened Indian Muslims. I wouldn't say I liked it either, but my disappointment with him is not limited to his migration. We had differences even before this event. Still, I dedicated the collection of my ruba'is, *Roop,* to him. In the preface I wrote, I referred to our differences. But I know we held no hard feelings on either side. He didn't even utter a single bad word about me and continued to admire my poetry.

Firaq added, 'Josh liked praise, but he didn't praise others… my differences with Josh are rooted in love…'[8]

Josh and Firaq started as ghazal poets, but their paths soon diverged. While Firaq stayed with the ghazal, Josh wrote nazms (poems) because he wanted to write about political issues, such as the freedom struggle. As a result, he earned the title of *shaa'yir-e inqilaab* (poet of the revolution). Firaq remained apolitical for most of his life. Stylistically, Josh's poetry had a lot of thunder, while Firaq was a poet of solitude, peace and tranquility. Although they were contemporaries and close friends, they had very

---

[8] *Firaq: Shakhsiaat, Shairi aur Shanaakhat,* Aziz Nabeel (eds), Majlis-e-Fakhr-e-Bahrain, 2014, pp. 628–629.

different personalities. These differences are also reflected in their poetry. Firaq was a better ghazal and ruba'i poet; Josh was quite effective in his nazm. Who was better is a futile question. The arcs of their competences crossed at some points, but they should be judged separately. Sadly, Josh made a wrong decision at the height of his career, for which he paid a heavy price. He faced rejection in Pakistan; only a handful of people attended his funeral, while Firaq was honoured as a hero upon his death. Josh would have received the same honour if he had stayed in India.

Intezar Husain, a famous novelist and story writer, best described the place of Josh and Firaq in Urdu literature when he wrote,

> Josh and Firaq, in their ways, were bright lights of their time, but there was a difference in their luminescence. Josh represented the end of a tradition. With Firaq, we see the start of a new era. Metrical poetry had run its course. It could not move ahead. The new nazm occupied its place. With Josh, the old nazm died. But with Firaq, the ghazal started its new journey. Firaq is the guardian angel of the new ghazal.

Love Is Transformative

tumhein kionkar bataayein zindagi
ko kya samajhte hain

Firaq explores the all-consuming nature of love, which blurs the lines between the physical and spiritual world, causing the lover to question the essence of life and its meaning. He portrays love's intensity by combining its transformative power with its potential for pain, equating breathing with self-destruction to underscore the agony and torment love can inflict. Firaq also addresses love's mystical aspect, suggesting that it grants the lover access to a realm beyond the tangible world, which may seem incomprehensible to those who have not experienced it. The poet explores fate and the lover's willingness to surrender to love's demands, even if it leads them into the treacherous terrain of love, symbolized by the desert. Firaq challenges societal norms and expectations, proposing that the essence of love lies in its simplicity and the lover's ability to transcend conventional notions of beauty and skill. He also explores love as a timeless and eternal force, capable of obliterating past grievances and forging unbreakable bonds. In the final couplet, Firaq compares love to the wild playfulness of waves that blur the distinction between existence and non-existence, suggesting that love operates beyond human understanding, making time and space irrelevant.

tumhein kionkar bataayein zindagi ko kya samajhte hain
samajh lo saans lenu khudkushi harna samajhte hain

तुम्हें क्यूँकर बताएँ ज़िंदगी को क्या समझते हैं
समझ लो साँस लेना ख़ुद-कुशी करना समझते हैं

How do I explain
how I interpret
the meaning of life?
To put it simply—
breathing for me
is the same
as killing myself.

◆

bas itne par hamein sab log diivaana samajhte hain
k is duniya ko ham ik duusri duniya samajhte hain

बस इतने पर हमें सब लोग दीवाना समझते हैं
कि इस दुनिया को हम इक दूसरी दुनिया समझते हैं

People think I'm crazy
just because
I confused this world
with the world
that unfolds
in my imagination.

◆

kahaan ka vasl tanhaaii ne shaayad bhes badla hai
tere dam bhar ke mil jaane ko ham bhi kya samajhte hain

कहाँ का वस्ल तन्हाई ने शायद भेस बदला है
तिरे दम भर के मिल जाने को हम भी क्या समझते हैं

It is no union.
It is another manifestation
of loneliness.
When I meet you
for a short while,
multiple interpretations come to mind.

◆

yahi zid hai to khair aankhein uthaate hain ham us jaanib
magar ae dil ham is mein jaan ka khatka samajhte hain

यही ज़िद है तो ख़ैर आँखें उठाते हैं हम उस जानिब
मगर ऐ दिल हम इस में जान का खटका समझते हैं

If you insist,
I will lift my gaze

and look in that direction.
But my heart,
please be aware
that it poses a risk
to my existence.

◆

kahien hon tere diivaane thahar jaayein to zinda hain
jidhar ko munh utha kar chal pare sahra samajhte hain

कहीं हों तेरे दीवाने ठहर जाएँ तो ज़िंदाँ है
जिधर को मुँह उठा कर चल पड़े सहरा समझते हैं

It's irrelevant
where your crazy lovers live.
If they stop their motion,
it is proof that they are alive.
Unknowingly,
wherever they go,
they believe they are heading
to the desert.

◆

jahaan ki fitrat-e be-gaana mein jo kaif-e gham bhar dein
vohi jiina samjhte hain vohi marna samajhte hain

जहाँ की फितरत-ए-बेगाना में जो कैफ़-ए ग़म भर दें
वही जीना समझते हैं वही मरना समझते हैं

Given the innate
nature of being,
both life and death
add excitement
to its sadness.

◆

hamaara zikr kya ham ko to hosh aayaa mohabbat mein
magar ham qais ka diivaana ho jaana samajhte hain

हमारा ज़िक्र क्या हम को तो होश आया मोहब्बत में
मगर हम क़ैस का दीवाना हो जाना समझते हैं

Don't talk about me.
I gained consciousness in love.
Yet I do understand
how someone like Qais
might have lost his mind.

◆

na shokhi shokh hai itni n purkaar itni purkaari
n jaane log teri saadgi ko kya samajhte hain

न शोख़ी शोख़ है इतनी न पुरकार इतनी पुरकारी
न जाने लोग तेरी सादगी को क्या समझते हैं

Your playfulness
is not very exuberant.
Your skillfulness
lacks artistry.
I don't know
what people see
in your lack of embellishment.

◆

bhula diin ek muddat ki jafaaein us ne ye kah kar
tujhe apna samajhte the tujhe apna samajhte hain

भुला दीं एक मुद्दत की जफ़ाएँ उस ने ये कह कर
तुझे अपना समझते थे तुझे अपना समझते हैं

She made me forget
tyrannies of a lifetime
as she shared with me
this beautiful thought:
You were mine before,
you're mine now.

◆

ye kah kar aabla pa raundte jaate hain kaanton ko
jise talvon mein kar lein jazb use sahra samajhte hain

ये कह् कर आबला-पा रौंदते जाते हैं काँटों को
जिसे तलवों में कर लें जज़्ब उसे सह्रा समझते हैं

Those who have blisters
say something
and then crush barbs and bristles.
Whatever falls below the surface
is a desert in their view.

◆

ye hasti nesti sab mauj-khezi hai mohabbat ki ham qatra samajhte hain n ham dariya samajhte hain

ये हस्ती नीस्ती सब मौज-ख़ेज़ी है मोहब्बत की
न हम क़तरा समझते हैं न हम दरिया समझते हैं

This existence,
this non-existence,
it is
but the wild playfulness
of love's waves.
We neither know
what a drop of water is
nor what a river is.

◆

'firaq' is gardish-e ayyaam se kab kaam nikla hai
sahar hone ko bhi ham raat kat jaana samajhte hain

'फ़िराक़' इस गर्दिश-ए अय्याम से कब काम निकला है
सहर होने को भी हम रात कट जाना समझते हैं

The motion of time, Firaq,
does not serve any purpose.
To me, dawn is nothing
but an end to the night.

Love's Impact

bastiyaan dhuundh rahi hain unhein viiraanon mein

Firaq uses personification (giving human qualities to non-human things) to convey love's intensity and all-consuming nature. 'Abodes' search for lovers in remote places, symbolizing how love can push individuals to the margins of society. The poet also uses the metaphor of burning passion and fire to illustrate the destructive potential of love. Firaq explores how the expressions of love change over time, with the once-vibrant signs of the lovers' world fading away. He touches on the theme of yearning for and missing the beloved, highlighting the deeply personal nature of love, which is shaped by the lover's own perceptions. He also considers the ambiguity of promises and the difficulty of finding solace in uncertain assurances, emphasizing the vulnerability and risk of opening oneself up to love.

bastiyaan dhuundh rahi hain unhein viiraanon mein
vahshatein barh gayii hadd se tere diivaanon mein

बस्तियाँ ढूँढ रही हैं उन्हें वीरानों में
वहशतें बढ़ गईं हद से तिरे दीवानों में

Abodes search for them
in deserted places.
The frenzy of those
who are in love with you
is uncontrollable.

◆

sair kar ujre dilon ki jo tabii'yat hai udaas
ji bahal jaate hain aksar inhiin viiraanon mein

सैर कर उजड़े दिलों की जो तबीअ'त है उदास
जी बहल जाते हैं अक्सर इन्हीं वीरानों में

In desolation,
look at the hearts
devastated.
These lonely places
are a source
of comfort sometimes.

◆

jis jagah baith gaye aag laga kar uthe
garmiyaan hain kuchh abhi sokhta-jaanon mein

जिस जगह बैठ गए आग लगा कर उट्ठे
गर्मियाँ हैं कुछ अभी सोख़्ता-सामानों में

Wherever they went,
they left
after burning the place.
Lovers burn
with such passion.

◆

jauhar-e guncha o gul mein hai ik andaaz-e junuun
kuchh biyabaan nazar aaye hain garebaanon mein

जौहर-ए ग़ुंचा ओ गुल में है इक अंदाज़-ए जुनूँ
कुछ बयाबाँ नज़र आए हैं गरेबानों में

In the beauty of flowers,
there is a frenzy.
Some deserted places
have shown up
at the edge of my collar.

◆

ab vo rang-e chaman o khanda-e gul bhi n rahe
ab vo aasaar-e junuun bhi nahien diivaanon mein

अब वो रंग-ए चमन ओ ख़ंदा-ए गुल भी न रहे
अब वो आसार-ए जुनूँ भी नहीं दीवानों में

There is no wild laughter
and a splash of colour in the flowers
of the garden.
Your lovers show.
fewer signs of madness.

◆

ab vo saaqi ki bhi aankhein n rahien rindon mein
ab vo saaghar bhi chhalakte nahien mai-khaanon mein

अब वो साक़ी की भी आँखें न रहीं रिंदों में
अब वो साग़र भी छलकते नहीं मय-ख़ानों में

The Saqi does not pay attention
to the addicts.
The wine cups don't overflow in the tavern.

◆

ab vo ik soz-e nihaani bhi dilon mein n raha
ab vo jalve bhi nahien i'shq ke afsaanon mein

अब वो इक सोज़-ए निहानी भी दिलों में न रहा
अब वो जल्वे भी नहीं इश्क़ के काशानों में

There is no more burning passion
in the hearts of lovers.
There is no splendor in places
where love once flowered.

◆

ab n vo raat jab ummiidein bhi kuchh thien tujh se
ab n vo baat gham-e hijr ke afsaanon mein

अब न वो रात जब उम्मीदें भी कुछ थीं तुझ से
अब न वो बात ग़म-ए हिज्र के अफ़्सानों में

The night doesn't arrive,
carrying any hope from you.
Something is amiss
in the stories of separation.

◆

ta-b-kai vaa'da-e mauhuum ki tafsiil 'firaq'
shab-e furqat kahien kat-ti hai in afsaanon mein

ता-ब-कै वा'दा-ए मौहूम की तफ़्सील 'फ़िराक़'
शब-ए फ़ुर्क़त कहीं कटती है इन अफ़्सानों में

I have a vague outline, Firaq,
of your ambiguous promises.
But how can I spend
the night of separation
with uncertain assurances?

Transformation

hijr o visaal-e yaar ka parda utha diya

Firaq uses the metaphor of the veil to represent the barriers separating lovers from each other from their true selves, highlighting love's intensity and all-encompassing nature. He explores love's contradictory aspects, where the beloved's presence can be comforting and painful, and how love can transform even the most ordinary aspects of life into something extraordinary. He also touches on the theme of faith, suggesting that love can turn moments of doubt into profound spiritual experiences. Firaq describes the lover's tears as rivers and the restless flashes as a sign of beauty's majesty, emphasizing love's ability to imbue deep meaning and significance to even the most fleeting and intangible aspects of existence. Throughout this ghazal, Firaq reflects on the nature of suffering and the role of love in shaping the human experience, recognizing the beauty inherent in the pain and sorrow that accompany love and suggesting that these experiences are necessary for the growth and self-discovery of the lover. He explores the idea of love as a force that can hide and reveal the true nature of the self, disrupting the very fabric of time and existence.

hijr o visaal-e yaar ka parda utha diya
khud barh ke i'shq ne mujhe mera pata diya

हिज्र-ओ-विसाल-ए-यार का पर्दा उठा दिया
ख़ुद बढ़ के इ'श्क़ ने मुझे मेरा पता दिया

I'shq removed the veil
of union and separation, and
revealed to me who I was.

◆

gard o ghubaar-e hasti-e faani ura diya
ay qiimiiya-e i'shq mujhe kya bana diya

गर्द ओ ग़ुबार-ए हस्ती-ए फ़ानी उड़ा दिया
ऐ कीमिया-ए इ'श्क़ मुझे क्या बना दिया

The dust storm of life and death
crushed me.
O alchemy of i'shq,
look what you have made me.

◆

vo saamne hai aur nazar ne chhupa diya
ay i'shq-e be-hijaab mujhe kya dikha diya

वो सामने है और नज़र से छुपा दिया
ऐ इ'श्क़-ए बे-हिजाब मुझे क्या दिखा दिया

She is standing face-to-face
but hidden from my sight.
O unveiled i'shq,
what did you show me?

◆

vo shaan-e khaamushi k bahaarein hain muntazir
vo rang-e guftguu k gulistaan bana diya

वो शान-ए ख़ामुशी कि बहारें हैं मुंतज़िर
वो रंग-ए गुफ़्तुगू कि गुलिस्ताँ बना दिया

Such grandeur of silence,
spring is agog,
such vibrancy of dialogue, an entire garden
flourished.

◆

dam le rahi thiin husn ki jab sehar-kaariyaan
in vaqfaa-ha-e kufr ko imaan bana diya

दम ले रही थीं हुस्न की जब सेहर-कारियाँ
इन वक़्फा-हा-ए कुफ्र को ईमाँ बना दिया

As the enchantment
of beauty unravelled,
the interludes of unbelief
turned into articles of true faith.

◆

maa'luum kuchh mujhi ko hain un ki ravaniyaan
jin qatra-ha-e ashk ko dariya bana diya

मालूम कुछ मुझी को हैं उन की रवानियाँ
जिन क़तरा-हा-ए-अश्क को दरिया बना दया

Only I know how fast they flowed,
The teardrops that coalesced into a river.

◆

ik barq-e beqaraar thi tamkiin-e husn bhi
jis vaqt i'shq ko gham-e sabr-aazmaa diya

इक बर्क़-ए बे-क़रार थी तम्कीन-ए हुस्न भी
जिस वक़्त इ'श्क़ को ग़म-ए-सब्र-आज़मा दिया

The restless lightning
was also the majesty of beauty
when i'shq learned to be patient
with its sorrow.

◆

saaqi mujhe bhi yaad hain vo tashna-kaamiyaan
jin ko hariif-e saaghar-o miina bana diya

साक़ी मुझे भी याद हैं वो तिश्ना-कामियाँ
जिन को हरीफ़-ए साग़र ओ मीना बना दिया

Saqi, I do remember
the days of my thirst
which you turned into rivals
of glass and goblet.

◆

maa'luum hai haqiiqat-e gham-ha-e rozgaar
duniya ko tere dard ne duniya bana diya

मालूम है हक़ीक़त-ए ग़म-हा-ए रोज़गार
दुनिया को तेरे दर्द ने दुनिया बना दिया

I know the reality of
ordeals and griefs
of making a living.
The sorrow you gave me
changed the world
into something else.

◆

ae shokhi-e nigaah-e karam muddaton ke baa'd
khwaub-e giraan e gham se mujhe kiyon jaga diya

ऐ शोख़ी-ए निगाह-ए करम मुद्दतों के बा'द
ख़्वाब-ए गिरान-ए ग़म से मुझे क्यूँ जगा दिया

The one with a compassionate yet carefree gaze,
Why did you awaken me up from
my sorrowful dream?

◆

kuchh shorshein taghaaful-e pinhaan mein thiin jinhe
hangaama zaar-e hashr-e tamanna bana diya

कुछ शोरिशें तग़ाफ़ुल-ए-पिन्हाँ में थीं जिन्हें
हंगामा ज़ार-ए हश्र-ए तमन्ना बना दिया

Commotions were hidden
in neglected places,
but you turned them into catastrophic desires.

◆

barhta hi ja raha hai jamaal-e nazar-fareb
husn-e nazar ko husn-e khud aara bana diya

बढ़ता ही जा रहा है जमाल-ए नज़र-फ़रेब
हुस्न-ए नज़र को हुस्न-ए ख़ुद-आरा बना दिया

The beauty of deception increases its grip.
Welcoming beauty is thus transformed
into a self-adorning beauty.

◆

phir dekhna nigaah lari kis se i'shq ki
gar husn ne hijab-e taghaaful utha diya

फिर देखना निगाह लड़ी किस से इ'श्क़ की
गर हुस्न ने हिजाब-ए-तग़ाफुल उठा दिया

See how i'shq falls in love
if the beauty carelessly
unveils
itself.

◆

jab khuun ho chuka dil-e hasti-e e'itbaar
kuchh dard bach rahe jinhe insaan bana diya

जब ख़ून हो चुका दिल-ए हस्ती-ए एतिबार
कुछ दर्द बच रहे जिन्हें इंसाँ बना दिया

When the heart of existence
was bloodied,
there were some leftover sorrows.
They were carved
into humans.

◆

gum karda-e vafuur-e gham-e intizaar huun
tu kya chhupa k mujh ko mujhi se chhupa diya

गुम-कर्दा-ए वफ़ूर-ए ग़म-ए इंतिज़ार हूँ
तू क्या छुपा कि मुझ को मुझी से छुपा दिया

I have lost the intensity of sorrow
but I'm waiting.
When you hid from yourself,
I hid from myself.

◆

raat ab hariif-e sub-ha-e qiyaamat hi kiyon n ho
jo kuchh bhi ho us aankh ko ab to jaga diya

रात अब हरीफ़-ए सुब्हह-ए क़यामत ही क्यूँ न हो
जो कुछ भी हो उस आँख को अब तो जगा दिया

The night has become a
rival of Doomsday.
So be it.
Whatever happens,
that eye is awake now.

◆

ab main huun aur lutf o karam ke taqalufaat
ye kiyon hijab-e ranjish-e be-ja bana diya

अब मैं हूँ और लुत्फ़ ओ करम के तकल्लुफ़ात
ये क्यूँ हिजाब-ए रंजिश-ए बे-जा बना दिया

Now it's me and the pretence of pleasure and grace.
But why did you turn it into a veil
of hostility?

◆

thi yuun to shaam-e hijr magar pichhli raat ko
vo dard utha 'Firaq' main muskara diya

थी यूँ तो शाम-ए हिज्र मगर पिछली रात को
वो दर्द उठा 'फ़िराक़' कि मैं मुस्कुरा दिया

Although it was an evening
of separation, but last night,
the pain was so intense
that Firaq let it go and smiled.

Portrait of Anguish

mai-kade mein aaj ik duniya ko izn-e aam tha

Firaq depicts the tavern as a place that beckons the whole world to immerse itself in its intoxication, emphasizing love's ability to transcend the boundaries of time and reality. He explores the destructive aspect of love, portraying it as a form of anguish that gradually erodes the lover. He suggests that beauty can also bring misfortune, disrupting the natural course of life and leading to profound suffering. The poet employs the metaphor of the evening lamp to symbolize how the pain of love can illuminate even the darkest parts of the soul, suggesting that the lover's suffering is a necessary catalyst for self-discovery and transformation. Firaq also views beauty as ephemeral and elusive, with the beloved's glances barely perceptible yet conveying the essence of beauty's message, underscoring the idea that love and beauty are often intangible but profoundly impact the human heart. He contrasts society's perception and treatment of love and beauty, implying that beauty usually escapes unscathed. In contrast, love faces criticism and condemnation. Ultimately, Firaq portrays lovers as a source of joy and light despite their suffering, suggesting that their contradictory attributes and experiences testify to the complexity and depth of the human experience and that true understanding can only be achieved through love.

mai-kade mein aaj ik duniya ko izn-e aam tha
daur-e jaam-e be-khudi begaana-e ayyaam tha

मय-कदे में आज इक दुनिया को इज़्न-ए आम था
दौर-ए जाम-ए बे-ख़ुदी बेगाना-ए अय्याम था

The whole world
had an open invitation
to come to the tavern today.
There were rounds
of wine drinking,
with people losing
the sense of time.

◆

ruuh larzaan aankh mahv-e diid dil ka naam tha
i'shq ka aaghaaz bhi shaaisṭa-e anjaam tha

रूह लर्ज़ां आँख महव-ए दीद दिल का नाम था
इ'श्क़ का आग़ाज़ भी शाइस्ता-ए-अंजाम था

The soul quivered,
the eyes were absorbed in seeing,
and the heart
was uselessly present.
The beginning of love was also its
gracious end.

◆

rafta rafta i'shq ko tasviir-e gham kar hi diya
husn bhi kitna kharaab-e gardish-e ayyaam tha

रफ़्ता रफ़्ता इश्क़ को तस्वीर-ए ग़म कर ही दिया
हुस्न भी कितना ख़राब-ए गर्दिश-ए अय्याम था

Slowly and gradually,
love became a portrait of pain.
Beauty was an unfortunate spoiler
of the movement of days.

◆

gham-kade mein dahar ke yuun to andhera tha magar
i'shq ka daagh-e siyaah-bakhti charaagh-e shaam tha

ग़म-कदे में दहर के यूँ तो अँधेरा था मगर
इ'श्क़ का दाग़-ए सियह-बख़्ती चराग़-ए शाम था

Although at the grief's centre,
there was nothing but darkness.
Love's stain of bad luck
was like an evening lamp.

◆

teri duzdiida-nigaahi yuun to na-mahsuus thi
haan magar daftar ka daftar husn ka paighaam tha

तेरी दुज़दीदा-निगाही यूँ तो ना-महसूस थी
हाँ मगर दफ़्तर का दफ़्तर हुस्न का पैग़ाम था

Your shifting glances were present,
Even if one could not feel
their presence.
Yet, all things considered,
that was the beauty's message.

◆

be-khata tha husn har jaur o jafa ke baa'd bhi
i'shq ke sar taa-abad ilzaam hi ilzaam tha

बे-ख़ता था हुस्न हर जौर ओ जफ़ा के बा'द भी
इ'श्क़ के सर ता-अबद इल्ज़ाम ही इल्ज़ाम था

One could not blame beauty
even after all those infidelities.
Love had one blame after another,
stretching into eternity.

◆

dekh husn-e sharmgiin dar-parda kaya laaya hui rang
i'shq rusva-e jahaan badnaam hi badnaam tha

देख हुस्न-ए शर्मगीं दर-पर्दा क्या लाया है रंग
इ'श्क़ रुस्वा-ए जहाँ बदनाम ही बदनाम था

Look what colour the bashful beauty
has brought forth behind the veil.
Love was infamous in the world,
thoroughly maligned and slandered.

◆

raunak-e bazm-e jahaan tha go dil-e gham-giin 'firaq'
sard tha afsurda tha mahruum tha naakaam tha

रौनक़-ए बज़्म-ए जहाँ था गो दिल-ए ग़म-गीं 'फ़िराक़'
सर्द था अफ़्सुर्दा था महरूम था नाकाम था

He was the joy of the gathering,
although Firaq was a great sufferer.
He was cold, depressed, abandoned,
and useless.

And I Am

januun-e kaargar hai aur main huun

Firaq embarks on a profound journey of self-reflection and self-discovery, exploring the complex and often contradictory nature of his inner world. The poet's identity is portrayed as multifaceted and deeply reflective, residing in various layers of consciousness and embracing the rational and irrational aspects of existence. The powerful refrain 'and I am' *(main huun)* affirms the poet's identity in the face of life's complexities and challenges, emphasizing that his true self combines seemingly disparate elements, from 'prolific craziness' to 'unconscious life'. Firaq delves deeply into the theme of his imaginative power, describing the ability to transcend physical boundaries and soar on the wings of creativity, while acknowledging the inherent difficulties and 'jinx' (a curse or spell) associated with this imaginative flight. He explores the idea of confinement and liberation, using the metaphor of prison to symbolize the limitations imposed by societal norms, while finding comfort in the walls and doors that seek to confine his unyielding spirit. Firaq also touches on vulnerability and the willingness to sacrifice his broken heart for the irreverent gaze of his beloved, underscoring his deep commitment to love and the transformative power of emotion.

januun-e kaargar hai aur main huun
hayaat-e be-khabar hai aur main huun

जुनून-ए कारगर है और मैं हूँ
हयात-ए बे-ख़बर है और मैं हूँ

My prolific madness
and I am.
My oblivious life,
and I am.

◆

kahaan main aa gaya ae zor-e parvaaz
vabaal-e baal o par hai aur main huun

कहाँ मैं आ गया ऐ ज़ोर-ए परवाज़
वबाल ए बाल ओ पर है और मैं हूँ

Where have you brought me,
my mighty flight?
The jinx of wings and feathers,
and I am.

◆

mubarakbaad aayaam-e asiiri
gham-e diivaar o dar hai aur main huun

मुबारकबाद अय्याम-ए असीरी
ग़म-ए दीवार ओ दर है और मैं हूँ

Congratulations on the days
spent in prison!

There is a grief
of walls and doors
and I am.

◆

nigaah-e be-muhaaba tere sadqe
kaii tukre jigar hai aur main huun

निगाह-ए बे-महाबा तेरे सदक़े
कई टुकड़े जिगर है और मैं हूँ

A glance of irreverence,
I make you an offering.
My heart is broken into pieces,
and I am.

◆

thikaana hai kuchh is u'zr-e sitam ka
teri niichi nazar hai aur main huun

ठिकाना है कुछ इस उ'ज़्र-ए सितम का
तिरी नीची नज़र है और मैं हूँ

Is there any excuse
for this tyranny?
Your eyes are cast
downward,
and I am.

◆

koi ho sust-paimaan bhi to yuun ho
ye shaam-e be-sahar hai aur main huun

कोई हो सुस्त-पैमाँ भी तो यूँ हो
ये शाम-ए बे-सहर है और मैं हूँ

Someone is late in coming.
That is the way it is.
There is the evening
without dawn,
and I am.

◆

'Firaq' ik ek hasrat mit rahi hai
ye maatam raat bhar hai aur main huun

'फ़िराक़' इक एक हसरत मिट रही है
ये मातम रात भर है और मैं हूँ

Firaq, each failed desire
is obliterating.
This grief will last
all night,
and I am.

Life, Death and Love

bahsein chhiri hui hain hayaat o mamaat ki

This ghazal explores the profound and paradoxical nature of life and death, with love at the centre. The poet suggests that these seemingly simple concepts are filled with countless layers of meaning and complexity, inviting endless debates and interpretations. He uses imagery and metaphors to convey the intricacy of these existential themes, describing the 'war of words' surrounding life and death, which creates a multitude of ideas and perspectives, each with its unique significance. Firaq touches on the theme of resilience and the human capacity to endure life's struggles, evoking respect for those who have maintained their dignity in the face of adversity. He explores the idea of the transience of existence using the metaphor of 'evening of doomsday' to symbolize the inevitability of death. Yet he encourages embracing the beauty and vitality of life, engaging with the ever-changing narrative of existence. Firaq examines the nature of love, describing it as a 'martyr' to the life-giving smiles of those who embody the dawn of life, suggesting that love willingly sacrifices itself for the sake of the beloved. That joy and ecstasy are closely linked to pain and suffering. Despite acknowledging love's inherent duality, Firaq affirms his identity as a 'portrait of the ecstasy of life,' suggesting that embracing and experiencing love, with all its complexities and contradictions, defines the human experience.

bahsein chhiri hui hain hayaat o mamaat ki
sau baat ban gaaii hai 'firaq' ek baat ki

बहसें छिड़ी हुई हैं हयात ओ ममात की
सौ बात बन गई है 'फ़िराक़' एक बात की

There is a war of words
over life and death.
Firaq, a straightforward matter,
has hundreds of offshoots.

◆

rakh li jinhon ne kashmakash-e zindagi ki laaj
be-dardiyaan n puuchhiye un se hayaat ki

रख ली जिन्हों ने कशमकश-ए ज़िंदगी की लाज
बे-दर्दियाँ न पूछिए उन से हयात की

Those who saved the honour
of life's struggles,
Would you mind not asking

about the cruelties of the life
they lived.

◆

shaam-e abad ko jalva-e sub-h-e bahaar de
ruudaad chher zindagi-e be-sabaat ki

शाम-ए अबद को जल्वा-ए सुब्ह-ए बहार दे
रूदाद छेड़ ज़िंदगी-ए बे-सबात की

Give the evening of doomsday,
the appearance
of a spring morning.
Begin a story and
grant it a transitory life.

◆

hai i'shq us tabassumm-e jaan-bakhsh ka shahiid
rangiiniyaan liye hai jo sub-h-e hayaat ki

है इ'श्क़ उस तबस्सुम-ए जाँ-बख़्श का शहीद
रंगीनियाँ लिए है जो सुब्ह-ए-हयात की

Love is a martyr
of life-giving smiles
of those who have
the embellishment
of the dawn of life.

◆

sau-dard ik tabassumm-e pinhaan mein band hain
tasviir huun 'Firaq' nishaat-e hayaat ki

सौ दर्द इक तबस्सुम-ए पिन्हाँ में बंद हैं
तस्वीर हूँ 'फ़िराक़' नशात-ए-हयात की

Hundreds of calamities
are embodied
in the hidden smiles.
Firaq, I am the portrait
of the ecstasy of love.

Endless Variations

nigaah-e naaz ne parde uthaaye hain kya kya

Firaq once again explores love's profound power, emphasizing its ability to penetrate the deepest recesses of the lover's being. He suggests that true love requires vulnerability and authenticity, as the beloved's gaze can see through any attempt at concealment. Firaq employs metaphors of flickering lamps in temples and mosques to symbolize the human endeavour to grasp the divine essence, acknowledging the inadequacy of these efforts in capturing the beloved's true magnificence. The poet also alludes to the mystical and spiritual dimensions of love, likening it to the story of Moses on Mount Sinai, where the divine is experienced as a gradual unveiling of reality's true essence. Through the repeated refrain 'in countless ways' or 'in scores of ways,' Firaq underscores the infinite complexity and variety of the experience of love, highlighting its ability to evoke a wide range of emotions, sensations and insights. Ultimately, he presents love as a path to self-discovery and revelation, capable of healing wounds, altering perceptions, and fundamentally transforming the lover's understanding of themselves and their world.

nigaah-e naaz ne parde uthaaye hain kya kya
hijaab ahl-e mohabbat ko aaye hain kya kya

निगाह-ए नाज़ ने पर्दे उठाए हैं क्या क्या
हिजाब अहल-ए मोहब्बत को आए हैं क्या क्या

Your deeply affectionate gaze
has lifted many veils.
Those who love you
had to cover themselves
in myriad ways.

◆

jahaan mein thi bas ik afvaah tere jalvon ki
charaagh-e dair o haram jhilmalaaye hain kya kya

जहाँ में थी बस इक अफ़्वाह तेरे जल्वों की
चराग़-ए दैर ओ हरम झिलमिलाए हैं क्या क्या

Rumours circulated
of your splendour
in this world.
Lamps have flickered
in temples and mosques
in myriad ways.

◆

nisaar nargis-e mai-guun ke aaj paimaane
labon tak aaye hue thar-tharaae hain kya kya

निसार नर्गिस-ए मय-गूँ कि आज पैमाने
लबों तक आए हुए थरथराए हैं क्या क्या

The narcissus-coloured wine
in goblets—
when it reached
my lips, they shivered
in myriad ways.

◆

vo ik zara si jhalak barq-e kam-nigaahi ki
jigar ke zakhm-e nihaan muskaraaye hain kya kya

वो इक ज़रा सी झलक बर्क़-ए कम-निगाही की
जिगर के ज़ख़्म-ए निहाँ मुस्कुराए हैं क्या क्या

That fleeting lightning of little glances
made the hidden wounds smile
in myriad ways.

◆

charaagh-e tuur jale aaiina dar aaiina
hijaab barq-e ada ne uthaaye hain kya kya

चराग़-ए तूर जले आईना दर आईना
हिजाब बर्क़-ए अदा ने उठाए हैं क्या क्या

The divine light of Mount Sinai
glows like mirrors reflecting mirrors
The beloved's lightning-like arrogance
has lifted myriad veils.

◆

kahien charaagh kahien gul kahien dil-e barbaad
khiraam-e naaz ne fitne uthaaye hain kya kya

कहीं चराग़ कहीं गुल कहीं दिल-ए बर्बाद
ख़िराम-ए नाज़ ने फ़ित्ने उठाए हैं क्या क्या

Sometimes light, sometimes a rose
Sometimes a ruined heart
Temptations were stirred
by beloved's tantalizing walk
in myriad ways.

◆

payaam-e husn payaam-e junuun payaam-e fana
teri nigaah ne fasaane sunaaye hain kya kya

पयाम-ए हुस्न पयाम-ए जुनूँ पयाम-ए फ़ना
तिरी निगह ने फ़साने सुनाए हैं क्या क्या

The message of beauty,
the message of frenzy,
the news of death.
Your eyes have told their story
in myriad ways.

◆

tughaaful aur barha us ghazaal-e r'aina ka
fasuun-e gham ne bhi jaadu jagaaye hain kya kya

तग़ाफ़ुल और बढ़ा उस ग़ज़ाल-ए र'अना का
फ़ुसून-ए ग़म ने भी जादू जगाए हैं क्या क्या

The indifference of gazelle-like beauty has grown,
Deceits of sorrow
have conjured magic
in myriad ways.

◆

'firaq' raah-e vafa mein subuk-ravi teri
bare-baron ke qadam dagmagaaye hain kya kya

'फ़िराक़' राह-ए वफ़ा में सुबुक-रवी तेरी
बड़े-बड़ों के क़दम डगमगाए हैं क्या क्या

You were impatient
in the path of loyalty, Firaq,
but that doesn't matter.

Even the steps of the great ones
have wavered in myriad ways.

Rejection and Acceptance

kuchh n kuchh i'shq ki taasiir ka iqraar to hai

This ghazal explores the intricate and often ambiguous nature of love, highlighting how it manifests through subtle signs, rejections, and affirmations. Firaq suggests that even the slightest indication of love's presence can be seen as a form of acknowledgment, even if it is accompanied by denial or rejection. This constant interplay between acceptance and rejection underscores the complexity of the love experience. The poet explores the theme of longing, illustrating how the desire for the beloved's presence persists, with lovers finding sustenance in the mere hope of a glance. Firaq also addresses the physical and emotional toll that love takes on the lover, using the metaphor of the lover's head smashing against the walls and doors of the beloved's house to symbolize the intensity and desperation of their experience. Echoing Mirza Ghalib's favourite metaphor, Firaq brings the walls and doors to life as they feel the beloved's presence while witnessing the lover's pain and suffering. The poet suggests that love can be expressed through various means, from subtle glances to heartfelt expressions of gratitude, with even the smallest gesture serving as a form of communication between the lover and the beloved. Firaq emphasizes the robust emotional response evoked by the mere mention of the beloved's name, underlining love's pervasive and undeniable nature.

kuchh n kuchh i'shq ki taasiir ka iqraar to hai
us ka ilzaam-e tughaaful pe kuchh inkaar to hai

कुछ न कुछ इश्क़ की तासीर का इक़रार तो है
उस का इल्ज़ाम-ए तग़ाफ़ुल पे कुछ इंकार तो है

There is a certain acceptance
of love's presence.
When I say, 'You have snubbed me,'
she rejects the statement.

◆

dekh lete hain sabhi kuchh tere mushtaaq-e jamaal
khair diidaar n ho hasrat-e diidaar to hai

देख लेते हैं सभी कुछ तिरे मुश्ताक़-ए जमाल
ख़ैर दीदार न हो हसरत-ए दीदार तो है

The admirers of your beauty
understand it.
Even if they can't see you,
they sustain the desire
to catch a glimpse of you.

◆

sar patakane ko patakta hai magar ruk ruk kar
tere vahshi ko khayaal-e dar o divaar to hai

सर पटकने को पटकता है मगर रुक रुक कर
तेरे वहशी को ख़याल-ए दर ओ दीवार तो है

My head smashes itself,
but with suitable pauses.
The wild one is careful
about not damaging
your doors and walls.

◆

tujh se himmat to pari i'shq ko kuchh kahne ki
khair shikva n sahi shukr ka izhaar to hai

तुझ से हिम्मत तो पड़ी इ'श्क़ को कुछ कहने की
ख़ैर शिकवा न सही शुक्र का इज़हार तो है

At last, love found the courage
to say something.
It's not whining,
It's an expression of gratitude.

◆

kiyon jhapak jaati hai rah rah ke teri barq-e nigaah
ye jhijhak kis liye ik kushta-e diidaar to hai

क्यूँ झपक जाती है रह रह के तिरी बर्क़-ए निगाह
ये झिजक किस लिए इक कुश्ता-ए दीदार तो है

Why does your electrifying gaze
blink at the end?
Why does this hesitation
become a victim
of your sight?

◆

chonk uth-te hain 'firaq' aate hi us shokh ka naam
kuchh sara-siimgi-e i'shq ka izhaar to hai

चौंक उठते हैं 'फ़िराक़' आते ही उस शोख़ का नाम
कुछ रारासीमगी-ए इ'श्क़ का। इक़रार तो है

Firaq is surprised and bewildered
when he catches the name
of a vividly cheerful person.
Undoubtedly, there is some frenzy of love.

Trickery of the Tumult of Time

ho ke sar-ta-b-qadam aa'lam-e asraar chala

Firaq explores the bittersweet nature of love as it awakens in the lover a deeper understanding of the self and the universe. The image of the lover leaving the tavern of love intoxicated and ecstatic highlights the idea that love can alter one's perception of reality. The poet suggests that even the most fulfilling experiences of love are often accompanied by a sense of burden, as lovers carry the weight of their love with them, forever changed by their experiences. Firaq also touches on the beloved's unchanging nature and the ambiguity or indifference often encountered in the lover's efforts to win their affection, emphasizing that love is rarely straightforward or easily resolved. The metaphor of the 'trickery of the tumult of time' implies that love can transcend even the most potent and uncontrollable aspects of existence, such as death and the passage of time, with the lover's willingness to surrender to this force serving as a testament to love's enduring power. In the end, Firaq reflects on how the experience of love can leave the lover perpetually yearning for more even after witnessing the beloved's glory, suggesting that love is an insatiable and unending experience that can never be fully satisfied or resolved.

ho ke sar-ta-b-qadam aa'lam-e asraar chala
jo chala mai-kada-e i'shq se sarshaar chala

हो के सर-ता-ब-क़दम आ'लम-ए असरार चला
जो चला मय-कदा-ए इश्क़ से सरशार चला

The world of mysteries
began to stir and shift

from head to toe.
Those who walked away
from the tavern
were intoxicated and ecstatic.

◆

n hua raah-e mohabbat mein koi ohda bara
jo subak-dosh hua vo bhi giraan-baar chala

न हुआ राह-ए मोहब्बत में कोई ओहदा-बरा
जो सुबुक-दोश हुआ वो भी गिराँ-बार चला

Walking the road of love
did not elevate anyone to prominence.
Even the ones who retired
walked away with a great burden.

◆

un ka jo haal k pehle tha vohi haal raha
tere gham-kushton se iqraar n inkaar chala

उन का जो हाल कि पहले था वही हाल रहा
तेरे ग़म-कुश्तों से इक़रार न इंकार चला

Their condition
remained unchanged.
The victims of grief
could neither say yes nor no.

◆

aasmaan ho k qiyaamat ho k ho tiir-e qaza
chaal us fitna-e dauraan se har ik baar chala

आसमाँ हो कि क़यामत हो कि हो तीर-ए क़ज़ा
चाल उस फ़ित्ना-ए दौराँ से हर इक बार चला

Whether it's sky or doomsday
or the arrow of death.
The trickery of the tumult of time
worked each time.

◆

zauq-e nazzaara usi ka hai jahaan mein tujh ko
dekh kar bhi jo liye hasrat-e diidaar chala

ज़ौक़-ए नज़्ज़ारा उसी का है जहाँ में तुझ को
देख कर भी जो लिए हसरत-ए दीदार चला

The pleasure of your spectacle
in the arena of this world
belongs to the one who saw it,
yet he too left carrying the longing
to see you.

◆

husn-e kaafir se kisi ki n gaii pesh 'firaq'
shikva yaaron ka n shukraana-e aghayaar chala

हुस्न-ए काफ़िर से किसी की न गई पेश 'फ़िराक़'
शिकवा यारों का न शुकराना-ए अग़यार चला

No one was able to manage
the beauty of that non-believer.
Neither the complaints of friends
nor a sense of gratitude
to others worked.

The Flare of Love

daur-e aaghaaz-e jafa dil ka sahaara nikla

In Firaq's poetry, love is portrayed as a force that can sustain and destroy the lover, with the journey of love fraught with uncertainty, deceit and heartbreak. The heart becomes a source of support in times of infidelity, as the lover must rely on their inner strength and resilience to navigate the challenges of love. However, the deceptions of the heart can also lead lovers astray, leaving them lost and adrift in a world of hidden mysteries and veiled gestures. The image of the heart that is forever lost and unable to find its place emphasizes the isolation and despair accompanying the experience of love. Firaq also explores the heart's inadequacy and how it can fail the lover even as it continues to pursue its desires, with the heart's painful, slow death, which in the end belongs to no one, suggesting that the journey of love can ultimately leave the lover empty and alone. The metaphor 'flare of love' illustrates the intensity and destructive power of the experience of love, which is capable of burning the wings of angels and rivalling the sun on the Day of Judgment. Firaq reflects on how the experience of love can leave the lover feeling like an outcast or a vagrant, subject to the mockery and ridicule of others, underscoring the sense of isolation and alienation that can accompany the journey of love.

daur-e aaghaaz-e jafa dil ka sahaara nikla
hausla kuchh n hamaara n tumhaara nikla

दौर-ए आग़ाज़-ए जफ़ा दिल का सहारा निकला
हौसला कुछ न हमारा न तुम्हारा निकला

The beginning of infidelity
turned out to be
a manner of support.
Your courage or mine—
it didn't matter in the end.

◆

hosh jaata hai jigar jaata hai dil jaata hai
parde hi parde mein kya tera ishaara nikla

होश जाता है जिगर जाता है दिल जाता है
पर्दे ही पर्दे में क्या तेरा इशारा निकला

The senses are lost,
the heart is lost,
everything I had is lost.
What was the gesture
that remained hidden
beneath the layers of veils?

◆

hai tere kashf o karamaat ki duniya qaa'il
tum se ae dil n magar kaam hamaara nikla

है तिरे कश्फ़ ओ करामात की दुनिया क़ाइल
तुझ से ऐ दिल न मगर काम हमारा निकला

The world accepts
the power of your revelation
and miracle.
But, dear heart,
your help was inadequate
to get the job done.

◆

ibrat-angez hai kya us ki javaan-margi bhi
haaye vo dil jo hamaara n tumhaara nikla

इबरत-अंगेज़ है क्या उस की जवाँ-मर्गी भी
हाए वो दिल जो हमारा न तुम्हारा निकला

His demise at a young age
is quite a lesson.
Alas, that heart neither belonged to you
nor to me.

◆

i'shq ki lau se frishton ke bhi par jalte hain
rashk-e khurshiid-e qiyaamat ye sharaara nikla

इ'श्क़ की लौ से फ़रिश्तों के भी पर जलते हैं
रश्क-ए ख़ुर्शीद-ए क़यामत ये शरारा निकला

The flare of love burns even
the wings of angels.
On doomsday, this spark was the envy of the sun.

◆

rone vaale hue chup hijr ki duniya badli
sham'a be-nuur hui sub-h ka taara nikla

रोने वाले हुए चुप हिज्र की दुनिया बदली
शम्अ' बे-नूर हुई सुब्ह का तारा निकला

Those who lamented
became silent.
The world of separation changed.
The candle was extinguished,
and the morning star appeared.

◆

ungliyaan uthiin 'firaq'-e vatan-aavaara par
aaj jis samt se vo dard ka maara nikla

उँगलियाँ उट्ठीं 'फ़िराक़'-ए वतन-आवारा पर
आज जिस सम्त से वो दर्द का मारा निकला

People raised their fingers at Firaq,
land's most notorious vagrant,
in whichever direction
that tormented person moved.

Love's Dual Nature

aaii hai kuchh n puuchh qiyaamat kahaan kahaan

Firaq's poetry explores the often-tumultuous nature of love, describing how it can lead the lover to encounter an 'apocalypse' in various forms and places. Love is portrayed as a dual force that encompasses both union and separation, as well as joy and sorrow, life and death. The restiveness that accompanies both the beloved's presence and absence suggests that the experience of love forever alters the lover's existence. Firaq also explores the concept of the lover's surrender to the path of desire, which can lead to freedom and liberation, even if it entails significant risk and peril. The image of the wandering lover who has lefteven the companionship of his heart behind underscores the total abandonment and surrender that can accompany the journey of love. The metaphor of the 'beloved's silhouette and shadows' conveys how the lover's entire being is consumed by the presence of the beloved, even in their absence, with the lover's heart filled to the horizon with the beloved's shadows, suggesting the all-encompassing nature of the love experience. In the end, Firaq reflects on how love can be seen as a kind of 'playfulness' or 'mischief' on the part of the beloved, leading the lover to experience both the heights of ecstasy and the depths of despair, with the lover's mind jolted by the beloved's glance, highlighting how love can disrupt the foundations of the lover's being.

aaii hai kuchh n puuchh qiyaamat kahaan kahaan
uff le gaaii hai mujh ko muhabbat kahaan kahaan

आई है कुछ न पूछ क़यामत कहाँ कहाँ
उफ़ ले गई है मुझ को मोहब्बत कहाँ कहाँ

Please don't ask me about it—
I have encountered an apocalypse
in many places.
Such was my luck!
Yet I was driven by love
into even worse miseries.

◆

furqat ho ya visaal vohi iztiraab hai
tera asar hai ae gham-e furqat kahaan kahaan

फ़ुर्क़त हो या विसाल वही इज़्तिराब है
तेरा असर है ऐ ग़म-ए फ़ुर्क़त कहाँ कहाँ

Whether it is separation or union,
the restiveness remains same.
Oh, the torment of my solitariness!
You have made my life miserable.

◆

raah-e talab mein chhor diya dil ka saath bhi
phirte liye hue ye musiibat kahaan kahaan

राह-ए तलब में छोड़ दिया दिल का साथ भी
फिरते लिए हुए ये मुसीबत कहाँ कहाँ

On the path of desire,
I set my heart free.
As I wander about,
what a trouble it might be
to carry it around.

◆

dil ke ufaq tak ab to hain parchhaa-iyaan teri
le jaaye ab to dekh ye vahshat kahaan kahaan

दिल के उफ़क़ तक अब तो हैं परछाइयाँ तिरी
ले जाए अब तो देख ये वहशत कहाँ कहाँ

To the limits of the horizon of heart,
I observe the prolixity of your silhouette.
This madness, I'm not sure,
where it could take me.

◆

nairang-e i'shq ki hai koi intiha k ye
ye gham kahaan kahaan ye musarrat kahaan kahaan

नैरंग-ए इश्क़ की है कोई इंतिहा कि ये
ये ग़म कहाँ कहाँ ये मसर्रत कहाँ कहाँ

It is the utmost limit
of the miracle of love:
Sorrow all around,
joy abound.

◆

har gaam par tariiq-e mohabbat mein maut thi
is raah mein khule dar-e rahmat kahaan kahaan

हर गाम पर तरीक़-ए मोहब्बत में मौत थी
इस राह में खुले दर-ए रहमत कहाँ कहाँ

Love saw the mystery of death
on every path of the journey.
It's also true that the doors of grace
opened as I travelled on.

◆

hosh o junuun bhi ab to bas ik baat hai 'firaq'
hoti hai us nazar ki sharaarat kahaan kahaan

होश ओ जुनूँ भी अब तो बस इक बात हैं 'फ़िराक़'
होती है उस नज़र की शरारत कहाँ कहाँ

Staying in one's senses
or losing one's ability to think straight
are states of mind, says Firaq.
It is the playfulness of her eyes,
that jolts everything.

This Life Is Worth Living

ranj o raahat vasl o furqat hosh o vahshat kya nahien

This ghazal conveys profound insights into the human condition, love, pain, and the nature of existence itself. Life combines joy and sorrow, union and separation, clarity and confusion. These contrasting states are inherent parts of the human experience. Despite the struggles and pain, the poet argues that this world and life are still immensely valuable and 'worth living'. Love and beauty bring both desire and arrogance. Their actual depth cannot be fathomed by mere pleading or pride. Love could not find a lasting abode in this world under any circumstances. The pains of this world are no longer what they once were. The warmth and vibrancy of life's gatherings, which once drew from love's flames, can no longer be found even as embers in the heart's ashes. The poet exists in a state of 'nothingness,' and yet in this void exist multitudes of worlds. To say that the poet lives only in one world is thus inaccurate.

ranj o raahat vasl o furqat hosh o vahshat kya nahien
kaun kahta hai k rahne ki jagah duniya nahien

रंज ओ राहत वस्ल ओ फुरक़त होश ओ वहशत क्या नहीं
कौन कहता है क रहने की जगाह दुनिया नहीं

Grief and repose, union and separation,
consciousness and madness.
Who says they are worth nothing?
Who says that this world
is not an abode worth living in?

◆

husn sar-ta-pa tamanna i'shq sar-ta-sar gharuur
is ka andaaza niyaaz o naaz se hota nahien

हुस्न सर-ता-पा तमन्ना इ'श्क़ सर-ता-सर ग़ुरूर
इस का अंदाज़ा नियाज़ ओ नाज़ से होता नहीं

Beauty from head to toe
is nothing but desire.
Love from head to toe
is vainglory.
You can't assess this
through supplication.

◆

ek haalat par zamaane mein n guzri i'shq ki
dard ki duniya bhi ab to dard ki duniya nahien

एक हालत पर ज़माने में न गुज़री इ'श्क़ की
दर्द की दुनिया भी अब वो दर्द की दुनिया नहीं

Love couldn't survive in this world
under any circumstances.
The world of pain is no more
what it once was.

◆

jis ke sho'lon se thi kal tak garmi-e bazm-e hayaat
aaj is khaakistar-e dil se dhuaan uth-ta nahien

जिस के शो'लों से थी कल तक गर्मी-ए बज़्म-ए हयात
आज इस ख़ाकिस्तर-ए दिल से धुआँ उठता नहीं

From whose flames
the gathering of life
drew its warmth.
Today, no smoke rises from the ashes of this heart.

◆

main adam andar adam main huun jahaan andar jahaan
ek hi duniya ho meri ae 'firaq' aisa nahien

मैं अदम अंदर अदम मैं हूँ जहाँ अंदर जहाँ
एक ही दुनिया हो मेरी ऐ 'फ़िराक़' ऐसा नहीं

I'm inside nothingness,
and within that void,
I exist in the world.
To say that I only live in one world,
O Firaq, is not accurate.

Crazy and Paradoxical

haath aaye to vohi daaman-e jaanaan ho jaaye

Firaq captures the paradoxical nature of love, describing the push-and-pull longing for the beloved's presence, which is often challenging to attain or maintain. Love plays a mysterious game of hide-and-seek, but true beauty inevitably shines through, despite attempts at to conceal it. The poet explores the anguish of dwelling in one's misery and pain, wishing for an existence resembling the beloved's half-forgotten promise. The eye is only truly seeing when it beholds the beloved's splendour, and the heart is only authentic when filled with longing for the beloved. The paradox that love becomes more complicated when it appears to be simple is explored, suggesting that leaning into the difficulty could make it easier to handle. Love remains constant, whether in blissful union or heartbreaking separation—the forms changing but the core experience remaining the same. The poet wishes that the beloved's past indifference would transform into remorseful tenderness, soothing the deep wounds of love. The idea that disillusionment in love is inevitable, but that there is no valid reason to lose hope, defies logic.

haath aaye to vohi daaman-e jaanaan ho jaaye
chuut jaaye to vohi apna garebaan ho jaaye

हाथ आए तो वही दामन-ए जानाँ हो जाए
छूट जाए तो वही अपना गरेबाँ हो जाए

If I catch it,
it is the hem of the beloved.

Should it slip from my hands,
it is the hem of my garb.

◆

i'shq ab bhi hai vo mahram-e be-gaana-numa
husn yuun laakh chhupe laakh numaayaan ho jaaye

इ'श्क़ अब भी है वो महरम-ए बे-गाना-नुमा
हुस्न यूँ लाख छुपे लाख नुमायाँ हो जाए

Love hides and moves
like a stranger.
Beauty can try to hide a million times,
but its spectacle is unstoppable.

◆

yaad aati hai jab apni to tarap jaata huun
meri hasti tera bhuula hua paimaan ho jaaye

याद आती है जब अपनी तो तड़प जाता हूँ
मेरी हस्ती तिरा भूला हुआ पैमाँ हो जाए

When I think of my misery,
it hurts deeply.
How much I wish
my life to become
your forgotten promise!

◆

aankh vo hai jo teri jalva gah-e naaz bane
dil vohi hai jo saraapa tera armaan ho jaaye

आँख वो है जो तिरी जल्वा गह-ए नाज़ बने
दिल वही है जो सरापा तिरा अरमाँ हो जाए

The eye is real
when it can
see your beauty in full bloom.
The heart is true
when it is nothing
but filled
with your longing.

◆

sahl ho kar hui dushvaar mohabbat teri
use mushkil jo bana lein to kuchh aasaan ho jaaye

सहल हो कर हुइ दुश्वार मोहब्बत तेरी
उसे मुश्किल जो बना लें तो कुछ आसाँ हो जाए

When love became accessible,
it became more difficult.
If I make it difficult,
then it will become manageable.

◆

i'shq phir i'shq hai jis ruup mein jis bhes mein ho
i'shrat-e vasl bane ya gham-e hijraan ho jaaye

इ'श्क़ फिर इ'श्क़ है जिस रूप में जिस भेस में हो
इ'शरत-ए वस्ल बने या ग़म-ए हिज्राँ हो जाए

Love is love
in all its forms and shapes.
Be it the pleasure of union
or the misery of separation.

◆

kuchh mudaava bhi ho majruuh dilon ka ae dost
marham-e zakhm tera jaur-pashemaan ho jaaye

कुछ मुदावा भी हो मजरूह दिलों का ऐ दोस्त
मरहम-ए ज़ख़्म तिरा जौर-पशेमाँ हो जाए

O friend! There ought to be a cure
for the wounded hearts.
May your ointment
for wounds turn into a source of regret.

◆

ye bhi sach hai koi ulfat mein pareshaan kyuun ho
ye bhi sach hai koi kionkar n pareshaan ho jaaye

ये भी सच है कोई उल्फ़त में परेशाँ क्यूँ हो
ये भी सच है कोई क्यूँकर न परेशाँ हो जाए

No one should indeed get disillusioned
by love.
It is also true
that there is no reason
for one to not feel disheartened
by love.

◆

jhilmalaati hai sar-e bazm-e jahaan shama'e khudi
ye jo bujh jaaye charaagh-e rah-e irfaan ho jaaye

झिलमिलाती है सर-ए बज़्म-ए जहाँ शम'-ए ख़ुदी
जो ये बुझ जाए चराग़-ए रह-ए इरफाँ हो जाए

Thc lamp of self-esteem flickers
in the assembly of people.
If it is extinguished,
it becomes the light
illuminating the path to enlightenment.

◆

sar-e shoriida diya dasht o bayabaan bhi diye
ye meri khuubi-e qismat k vo zindaan ho jaaye

सर-ए शोरीदा दिया दश्त ओ बयाबाँ भी दिए
ये मिरी ख़ूबी-ए क़िस्मत कि वो ज़िंदाँ हो जाए

A frenzied mind was given.
Desert and wilderness were also offered.
It is my good fortune that these places
have become my prison.

◆

u'qda-e i'shq a'jab u'qda-e mohmal hai 'firaq'
kabhi la-hal kabhi mushkil kabhi aasaan ho jaaye

उक़्दा-ए-इ'श्क़ अजब उक़्दा-ए-मोहमल है 'फ़िराक़'
कभी ला-हल कभी मुश्किल कभी आसाँ हो जाए

The mystery of love
is a strange riddle, Firaq.
Sometimes, it muddles meaning,
sometimes, it is rigid,
and sometimes,
it is uncomplicated.

Three

GANDHARA (GA)

Firaq's poetry is the best example of realistic poetry. My life is coming to an end, but I wish to leave Ghazal in Firaq's care as I pass away from this world.

Yagana Changezi
(1883–1956)

THE FLAME IN THE PATH OF THE WIND

The 1940s started on a sombre note for Firaq's family. The loss of Prabha and Govind made the already-strained husband-wife relationship even more challenging. Finding a suitable match for Prema, the girl of average looks and intellect, proved difficult. Finally, in May 1943, she was married to Raj Nandan Prasad from Gaya. The couple received many gifts for the wedding, but the most significant came from Jawaharlal Nehru, who sent five thousand rupees—a substantial amount in those days. Pushpa was now the only child left in the care of her parents.

Before Prabha's untimely death in her mid-30s, Firaq led a very active social life. He participated in outside activities and hosted a poetry symposium once a month at his residence, which attracted Hindi and Urdu poets.

However, after Prabha and Govind, he severed most of his social ties and became more reclusive in his outlook. He also sold his car. In the early 1940s, the old enthusiasm for social activities returned, and Firaq started attending mushairas at various places in the country.

Pushpa's marriage to a cousin of Prema's husband was arranged in May 1954. Compared to Prema's wedding, it was a more straightforward affair. Although the nest was empty, Firaq's attachment to his daughters and their children didn't diminish one bit. He invited his grandchildren to spend time with him during the summer vacation.

Firaq was always fond of drinking, but over time, it became a habit that often caused him social embarrassment. He would get drunk in a mushaira and then use language that many people found abusive and offensive. At a university-sponsored event, he abused Amar Nath, the vice-chancellor. The latter issued a notice that Firaq should not be invited to any event after sunset. Another unpleasant incident occurred with the poet Ali Sardar Jafri, who was asked to come to Allahabad around 1950 to preside over a mushaira.

Ajay Mansingh, Firaq's nephew and his biographer, described the last phase of his life, that is, the period from 1955, and to his death, as 'the darkest era'.[9] Ramesh Chandra Dwivedi, whose background was unknown, entered Firaq's life and changed everything in an instant. Given the tensions in Firaq's married life, this event was the proverbial straw that broke the camel's back. Immediately after Pushpa's wedding, Ramesh moved into Firaq's home and took charge of everything—from daily chores to

[9]Mansingh, Ajai, *Firaq Gorakhpuri: The Poet of Pain and Ecstasy* Roli Books, New Delhi, 2015.

managing Firaq's finances. By this time, Kishori's health was also deteriorating. In 1955, Kishori was asked to move in with her brothers. Firaq clarified that his wife's banishment was not a temporary affair. He didn't want her to return. This news caused quite a stir among the relatives, but more importantly, in the university and in the local community. Firaq's private life became the talk of the town.

Firaq retired from his position at the University in 1958. He received many awards, including the prestigious Jnanpith Award, the first Urdu writer to receive this honor, and it carried a financial endowment of one hundred thousand rupees.

The Magic of the Eye

'Firaq' ik naii suurat nikal to sakti hai

The beloved's eyes can transform the world into something new and different. Firaq fears the magical spell that could be cast if her gaze falls on him. Even a blunt knife can inflict wounds when thrashed about forcefully. Her gaze can instantly relieve the grief of those in misery and fulfill their deepest desires for joy if she wishes. For those stuck in the alleys of grief, a mere breeze of the beloved's alley can open new paths. Even if there is no shade on love's arduous journey, the intensity of her sun-like gaze can make the sunshine seem pale and dim in comparison. A fleeting glimpse of her beautiful face can instantly make all hesitation vanish. If their eyes were to meet, what is written in the poet's destiny can completely transform. While the world may be tottering, her supportive gaze can bring it back into perfect balance. Her velvet-soft footsteps as the goddess of love can trample and crush the world.

The imagery of the beloved's powerful, soul-altering gaze and mere presence is evoked with stunning effect. It turns the eyes into vessels of spiritual transcendence. The poet is utterly overawed and humbled by this force.

'Firaq' ik naii suurat nikal to sakti hai
ba-qol us aankh ke duniya badal to sakti hai

'फ़िराक़' इक नई सूरत निकल तो सकती है
ब-क़ौल उस आँख के दुनिया बदल तो सकती है

Firaq, things can transform
in many surprising ways.
As the saying goes,
her eyes can transform the world.

◆

tere khayal ko kuchh chup si lag gaaii varna
kahaaniyon se shab-e gham bahal to sakti hai

तिरे ख़याल को कुछ चुप सी लग गई वर्ना
कहानियों से शब-ए ग़म बहल तो सकती है

You decided not to speak.
Stories would have added relief
to this sad night of grief.

◆

urus-e dahar chale kha ke thokrein lekin
qadam qadam pe javaani ubal to sakti hai

उरूस-ए दहर चले खा के ठोकरें लेकिन
क़दम क़दम पे जवानी उबल तो सकती है

I stumbled
but I continued to walk

towards my goal.
My youth can seethe
every step of the way.

◆

palat pare n kahien us nigaah ka jaadu
k duub kar ye chhuri kuchh uchhal to sakti hai

पलट पड़े न कहीं उस निगाह का जादू
कि डूब कर ये छुरी कुछ उछल तो सकती है

I'm afraid of the return
of the magic of her eyes.
An unsharp blade
can still gash.

◆

bujhe hue nahien itne bujhe hue dil bhi
fasurdagi mein tabii'yat machal to sakti hai

बुझे हुए नहीं इतने बुझे हुए दिल भी
फ़सुर्दगी में तबीअ'त मचल तो सकती है

Burnt-out hearts
still possess a spark of life.
In moments of grief,
they can find some solace.

◆

agar tu chaahe to gham vaale shaadmaan ho jaayein
nigaah-e yaar ye hasrat nikal to sakti hai

अगर तू चाहे तो ग़म वाले शादमाँ हो जाएँ
निगाह-ए यार ये हसरत निकल तो सकती है

If she wishes,
the miserable can find some joy.
The beloved's gaze
can certainly fulfill this desire.

◆

ab itni band nahien gham-qadon ki bhi raahein
havaa-e kuucha-e mahbuub chal to sakti hai

अब इतनी बंद नहीं ग़म-कदों की भी राहें
हवा-ए कूचा-ए महबूब चल तो सकती है

Avenues available to the aggrieved
are not limited.
They can get a whiff of fresh air
from the alley of the beloved.

◆

kare hain kos bahut manzil-e mohabbat ke
mile n chhanv magar dhuup dhal to sakti hai

कड़े हैं कोस बहुत मंज़िल-ए मोहब्बत के
मिले न छाँव मगर धूप ढल तो सकती है

The journey of love
is tough and unbreakable.
We may not find shade,
but the sun can set.

◆

hayaat lau tah-e daamaan-e marg de uthi
hava ki raah mein ye sham'a jal to sakti hai

हयात लौ तह-ए दामान-ए मर्ग दे उट्ठी
हवा की राह में ये शम्अ जल तो सकती है

Life showed the desire for death
in a roundabout way.
This flame can survive
in the path of the wind.

◆

azal se soii hai taqdiir-e i'shq maut ki niind
agar jagaaiye karvat badal to sakti hai

अज़ल से सोई है तक़दीर-ए इ'श्क़ मौत की नींद
अगर जगाइए करवट बदल तो सकती है

The fate of love
has been in deep slumber
since the beginning of existence.
If someone tries to awaken it,
it can turn a flank.

◆

gham-e zamaana o soz-e jahaan ki aanch to de
agar n tuute ye zanjiir gal to sakti hai

ग़म-ए ज़माना ओ सोज़-ए निहाँ की आँच तो दे
अगर न टूटे ये ज़ंजीर गल तो सकती है

Give me the sorrows of the world
and the hidden pain's heat,
If this chain does not break,
it can still melt.

◆

shariik-e sharm o hayaa kuchh hai bad-gumaani-e husn
nazar uttha ye jihjik si nikal to sakti hai

शरीक-ए शर्म ओ हया कुछ है बद-गुमानी-ए हुस्न
नज़र उठा ये झिजक सी निकल तो सकती है

The friend who is my partner
is coquettish and whimsical.
Yet, with just a fleeting glimpse of her face,
this hesitation can vanish.

◆

kabhi vo mil n sake gi main ye nahien kahta
vo aankh aankh mein par kar badal to sakti hai

कभी वो मिल न सकेगी मैं ये नहीं कहता
वो आँख आँख में पड़ कर बदल तो सकती है

I don't claim that I can't have her.
If our eyes meet,
the fate written in my stars
can change.

◆

teri nigaah sahaara n de to baat hai aur
k girte girte bhi duniya sambhal to sakti hai

तिरी निगाह सहारा न दे तो बात है और
कि गिरते गिरते भी दुनिया सँभल तो सकती है

That your eyes can't support it,
is another matter.
Even while falling apart,
this world can regain its balance.

◆

suna hai barf ke tukre hain dil hasiinon ke
kuchh aanch pa ke ye chaandi pighal to sakti hai

सुना है बर्फ़ के टुकड़े हैं दिल हसीनों के
कुछ आँच पा के ये चाँदी पिघल तो सकती है

There are rumours that
damsels have cold hearts.
They too can melt
with a little passion.

◆

guzar rahi hai dabe paaon i'shq ki devi
subuk-ravi se jahaan ko masal to sakti hai

गुज़र रही है दबे पाँव इ'श्क़ की देवी
सुबुक-रवी से जहाँ को मसल तो सकती है

The goddess of love
passes by by softly.
With the touch of her velvety, silken feet,
she can crush this world.

◆

n bhuulna ye hai taakhiir husn ki taakhiir
'Firaq' aaii hui maut tal to sakti hai

न भूलना ये है ताख़ीर हुस्न की ताख़ीर
'फ़िराक़' आई हुई मौत टल तो सकती है

Remember that this is
the delay of beauty.
'Firaq,' the impending death,
can be delayed.

Immersed in Its Own Essence

ras mein duuba hua lahraata badan kya kehna

Firaq draws on the poetic Sanskrit concept of *rasa,* in which a thing is reduced to its essence in order to reveal its purest truth and beauty. The first line paints the picture of the beloved's body immersed in its essence, rising like a wave that leaves the poet in awe, asking, 'What can I say?' The second line evokes the morning in a garden with all its visual and aromatic splendour, manifesting itself in swirling movements and again leaving the poet speechless. The intoxicating gaze of love late at night is likened to a moonbeam sinking into slumber. There is a reference to the enchanting scent of the beloved's body after the rain in paradise. The softness of the beloved's waist is likened to the movements of a flickering spark. The colours and the sight of the beloved are like a partially unveiled bride. The beloved's gaze has settled gently in the poet's heart like a stream of water. The swaying grace of the beloved's height, youth and locks like the fragrant nights of a forest. The beloved is the star of love, her youth the union of the wedding night, her beauty fiery rubies. The glittering, night-dark tresses, the silver figure like lamps on the sacred rivers. Line by line, Firaq conjures up extraordinarily lush imagery of sight, sound, movement and scent to capture the essence of the beloved. Words do not do justice to this multi-sensory experience of divine beauty. It leaves the poet, and probably the reader, utterly spellbound in awe and wonder.

ras mein duuba hua lahraata badan kya kehna
karvatein leti hui sub-h-e chaman kya kehna

रस में डूबा हुआ लहराता बदन क्या कहना
करवटें लेती हुई सुब्ह-ए चमन क्या कहना

The body emerging like a wave
drenched in its essence
What shall I say?
The morning of the garden,

turning over.
What shall I say?

◆

nigaah-e naaz mein ye pichhle pehar rang-e khumaar
niind mein duubi hui chandar-kiran kya kehna

निगह-ए नाज़ में ये पिछले पहर रंग-ए ख़ुमार
नींद में डूबी हुई चंद्र-किरन क्या कहना

The colour of intoxication
in the glance of love
late at night,
as if the moonbeam
drowned in sleep.
What shall I say?

◆

baagh-e jannat pe ghata jaise baras ke khul jaaye
ye suhaani teri khushbu-e badan kya kehna

बाग़-ए जन्नत पे घटा जैसे बरस के खुल जाए
ये सुहानी तिरी ख़ुशबू-ए बदन क्या कहना

As the clouds open after a shower of rain
in the garden of paradise,
how enchanting is the scent
of your body?
What shall I say?

◆

ruup sangiit ne dhaara hai badan ka ye rachaav
tujh pe lah-luut hai be-saakhta-pan kya kehna

रूप संगीत ने धारा है बदन का ये रचाव
तुझ पे लहलूट है बे-साख़्ता-पन क्या कहना

The beauty of music has moulded your body.
Infatuation with you
is instantaneous.
What shall I say?

◆

jaise lahraaye koi sho'la-kamar ki ye lachak
sar-b-sar aatish-s sayyaal badan kaya kena

जैसे लहराए कोई शो'ला-कमर की ये लचक
सर-ब-सर आतिश-ए सय्याल बदन क्या कहना

Like a flame,
your waist sways.
Your body is liquid fire.
What shall I say?

◆

jalva o parde ka ye rang dam-e nazzaarra
jis tarah adh-khile ghuunghat mein dulhan kya kehna

जल्वा ओ पर्दे का ये रंग दम-ए नज़्ज़ारा
जिस तरह अध-खुले घुँघट में दुल्हन क्या कहना

The colour of the display and the veil
at the time of your spectacle
is like the bride in half-open veil
What shall I say?

◆

dil ke aaiine mein is tarah utarti hai nigaah
jaise paani mein lachak jaaye kiran kya kehna

दिल के आईने में इस तरह उतरती है निगाह
जैसे पानी में लचक जाए किरन क्या कहना

The beloved's gaze settles in mirror of the heart
just like sunlight disperses on water.
What can I say?

◆

lahlahaata hua ye qad ye lahakta joban
zulf sau mahki hui raaton ka ban kya kehna

लहलहाता हुआ ये क़द ये लहकता जोबन
ज़ुल्फ़ सौ महकी हुई रातों का बन क्या कहना

Your swaying stature,
your vibrant youth.
Your locks are like a hundred fragrant nights
of a forest.
What shall I say?

◆

tu mohabbat ka sitaara tu javaani ka suhaag
husn lau deta hai laal-e yaman kya kehna

तू मोहब्बत का सितारा तू जवानी का सुहाग
हुस्न लौ देता है लाल-ए यमन क्या कहना

You're the star of love;
your youth symbolizes
a wedding night's union.
Your beauty is a candle's flame and
reminds one of the rubies of Yemen.
What shall I say?

◆

zulf-e shab-guun ki chamak paikar-e siimiin ki damak
dip-maala hai sar-e gang o jaman kya kehna

ज़ुल्फ़-ए शब-गूँ की चमक पैकर-ए सीमीं की दमक
दीप-माला है सर-ए गंग ओ जमन क्या कहन

The glitter of the tresses of the night and
the flush of a silvery-white figure.
There is a row of lamps
on top of Ganga and Yamuna.
What can I say?

◆

niil-guun shabnami kapron mein badan ki ye jot
jaise chhanti ho sitaaron ki kiran kya kehna

नीलगूँ शबनमी कपड़ों में बदन की ये जोत
जैसे छनती हो सितारों की किरन क्या कहना

The body's flame, cloaked in deep blue,
acts like a sieve, filtering the light of the stars.
What can I say?

Stars on a Night of Separation

sitaaron se ulajhata ja raha huun

This ghazal encapsulates the tumultuous emotions and experiences of love, as well as the eternal quest for meaning. The opening lines describe the feeling of being lost and unsettled amid the stars on a night of separation from the beloved. The pain over the deceptive 'innocent eyes' of the beloved, which has caused lasting hurt, continues. The paradoxical feeling of getting farther from the beloved, even when physically close, suggests emotional distance. An allusion to Adam's ancient riddle or the knot that the poet is still trying to untangle today evokes the eternal human struggle. Love changes from pure affection to something more profound, even if the memory of the beloved slowly fades. The poet sings melodies of life so powerful that even death is touched when it hears them—a reference to the transcendent capacity of art. In the silence, the poet finds an 'echo' of his footsteps, an inkling of his path, and a journey of self-discovery.

sitaaron se ulajhata ja raha huun
shab-e furqat bahut ghabra raha huun

सितारों से उलझता जा रहा हूँ
शब-ए-फ़ुर्क़त बहुत घबरा रहा हूँ

Intertwined with the stars,
I lose my tranquility
in this night of separation.

◆

jo un maa'suum aankhon ne diye the
vo dhoke aaj tak main kha raha huun

जो उन मा'सूम आँखों ने दिए थे
वो धोके आज तक मैं खा रहा हूँ

The deceitfulness of these innocent eyes,
I'm a victim of their deceptions,
even today.

◆

tere pahlu mein kyon hota hai mahsuus
ke tujh se duur hota ja raha huun

तिरे पहलू में क्यूँ होता है महसूस
कि तुझ से दूर होता जा रहा हूँ

Why do I have this feeling

when I get close to you?
That I am moving away from you.

◆

jo uljhi thi kabhi aadam ke haathon
vo gutthi aaj tak suljha raha huun

जो उलझी थी कभी आदम के हाथों
वो गुत्थी आज तक सुलझा रहा हूँ

Adam's entanglement?
I have been trying
to solve the same puzzle until today.

◆

mohabbat ab mohabbat ho chali hai
tujhe kuchh bhuulta sa ja raha huun

मोहब्बत अब मोहब्बत हो चली है
तुझे कुछ भूलता सा जा रहा हूँ

Affection turns
into an enduring love.
Little by little, I forget you.

◆

ajal bhi jin ko sun kar jhuumti hai
vo naghme zindagi ke ga raha huun

अजल भी जिन को सुन कर झूमती है
वो नग़मे ज़िंदगी के गा रहा हूँ

Even death dances to them
I sing those
melodies of life.

◆

ye sannaata hai mere paaon ki chaap
'Firaq' apni kuchh aahat paa raha huun

ये सन्नाटा है मेरे पाँव की चाप
'फ़िराक़' अपनी कुछ आहट पा रहा हूँ

This silence is the sound
of my footsteps.
Firaq finds
an inkling of his stride.

Four

MADHAYAMA (MA)

The feeling of unity and separation gives birth to the melodies of poetry. Poetry is the art of falling in love with the universe, which produces boundless joys and woes. The consciousness of separation, along with the consciousness of being one with reality, lies at the root of the weals and woes of existence.[10]

—Firaq

ALLAHABAD WITHOUT FIRAQ

In January 1981, Firaq met Prime Minister Indira Gandhi when he came to Delhi to receive the Ghalib Award from the Ghalib Academy. When he mentioned to the prime minister that he had a problem with his eyes and needed cataract surgery to correct the problem, the prime minister referred him to the All-India Institute of Medical Sciences (AIIMS). He was scheduled for surgery in early February, but the surgery was delayed because his blood sugar levels were too high. During his time in the hospital, Mrs Gandhi visited him three times, and on each visit she showed her love for the poet by providing generous financial assistance. On each of the first two visits, she offered five thousand rupees, and on her third visit, a handsome sum of fifty

[10]Shuaq, Sumant Prakash, *Thus Spoke Firaq: A Collection of Interviews* Suneel Sachdev, New Delhi, 1992.

thousand rupees, which was a gift from Parliament. When his health stabilized somewhat, Firaq was moved to the residence of one of his students, R. K. Garg, a professional lawyer. On 21 February, Firaq received news of the death of his long-time friend Josh Malihabadi, who had migrated to Pakistan, which saddened him greatly. The relationship between the two friends had seen several ups and downs, and it had suffered considerably when Josh decided to emigrate to Pakistan single-mindedly. Yet the deep emotional affinity between the two had sustained, and Firaq saw this death as a message of his own mortality. He was heard repeating one of his couplets:

jin jin ko tha ye i'shq ka aazaar mar gaye
aakhir haamare saath ke biimaar mar gaye

जिन जिन को था ये इ'श्क़ का आज़ार मर गए
आख़िर हमारे साथ के बीमार मर गए

Those who suffered from the malady of love died.
Those who were sick with love, like me, died.

Firaq breathed his last precisely on the tenth day of Josh's demise on 3 March 1982, without a relative by his side. The news was broadcast on the radio and television, and the press was quick to report. Mrs Gandhi was out of the country at the time. There were conflicting reports about whether the funeral would be held in Delhi or Lucknow, but the family chose Allahabad. The body was taken by train from Delhi to Allahabad. Kishori Devi, who had not seen her husband for a quarter of a century, reached Allahabad with her daughters. As expected, the funeral on the banks of the Ganga became one of the biggest in the city's history. A contingent of state police arrived as the funeral pyre was lit. The poet had already imagined the day of his departure in one of his couplets.

aaj Allahabad hai suuna shaa'yir ke uth jaane se
sadiyon sadiyon dhuundo ge lekin kahaan Firaq ko paao ge

आज अल्लाहाबाद है सूना शा'इर के उठ जाने से
सदियों सदियों ढूँढों गे लेकिन कहाँ फ़िराक़ को पाओ गे

Today, Allahabad is forlorn and bereft
because of the poet's demise.
You will search for Firaq for centuries,
but you will not find him.

Something Unusual Is Happening

ye surmaaii fazaaaon ki kunmunahatein

Firaq's mastery of the Hindi-Urdu language and his ability to create evocative imagery with words like *kunmunahatein*, *sarsarahtein* and *tharthrahatein* is exceptional. The entire ghazal is a marvel of poetic craft and imagination. The opening lines create a sense of mysticism with the 'moaning of grey climes,' which allows the poet to hear the arrival of his beloved in the late hours of the night—an atmospheric, auditory portrayal. Then, in the 'universe of the desolate expanse of sorrow', the beloved's smile comes like a much-needed ray of light that dispels the gloom. The imagery changes again when the 'gentle breeze' inspired by her graceful walk carries the rustle of her hems. Even the sadness of the beauty is cheerful, the smile swims in the tears, and powerfully embodies the feelings. In the fear of separation's anguish, the poet strives to find closeness to himself, seeking his own rhythm and voice. Finally, Firaq invites us to consider the vibrations of thinking of the beloved in the evening as the very soul of his poetic composition. The metaphors evoke many senses—sights, sounds, colours, emotions—all woven around themes of love, longing, sorrow and poetic inspiration. It is a true linguistic and imaginative tour de force.

ye surmaaii fazaaaon ki kunmunahatein
milti hain mujh ko pichhle pahar teri aahatein

ये सुरमई फ़ज़ाओं की कुन्मुनाहटें
मिलती हैं मुझ को पिछले पहर तेरी आहटें

Oh, this moaning of greyish climes!
I hear
the sound of your arrival late at night.

◆

is kaaenaat-e gham ki fasurda fazaaon mein
bikhra gaye hain aa ke vo kuchh muskarahtein

इस काएनात-ए ग़म की फ़सुर्दा फ़ज़ाओं में
बिखरा गए हैं आ के वो कुछ मुस्कुराहटें

In the desolate climes
of this universe of sorrow,
they have come to spread
some smiles.

◆

chalti hai jab nasiim-e khayal-e khiraam-e naaz
sunta huun daamnon ki tere sarsarahtein

चलती है जब नसीम-ए ख़याल-ए ख़िराम-ए नाज़
सुनता हूँ दामनों की तिरे सरसराहटें

As the gentle breeze begins to blow,
reminding me of my beloved's graceful stride,
I hear the rustling
of the hems of her garments.

◆

kis des ko sidhaar gaaien ae jamaal-e yaar
rangiin labon pe khel ke kuchh muskarahatein

किस देस को सिधार गईं ऐ जमाल-ए यार
रंगीं लबों पे खेल के कुछ मुस्कुराहटें

O the grandeur
of my beautiful friend!
Where have they gone?
That smile playing
on those colourful lips.

◆

aazurdagi-e husn bhi kis darja shokh hai
ashkon mein tairti hui kuchh muskarahatein

आज़ुर्दगी-ए-हुस्न भी किस दर्जा शोख़ है
अश्कों में तैरती हुई कुछ मुस्कुराहटें

Even the sadness of beauty
is remarkably cheerful.
The smiles
that swim in tears.

◆

hone laga huun khud se qariin ae shab-e alam
main pa raha huun hijr mein apni aahatein

होने लगा हूँ ख़ुद से क़रीं ऐ शब-ए-अलम
मैं पा रहा हूँ हिज्र में कुछ अपनी आहटें

On the tragic evening,
I try to be close to myself.
I try to find my movement
amid separation.

◆

meri ghazal ki jaan samajhana unhein 'Firaq'
sham-e khayal-e yaar ki ye tharthrahatein

मेरी ग़ज़ल की जान समझना उन्हें 'फ़िराक़'
शम'-ए ख़याल-ए यार की ये थरथराहटें

Consider these
as the soul of my ghazal, Firaq!
Those evenings when I receive
the quivers of the fire
ignited by the beloved's memory.

Self-Awareness, Empathy, Balance and Wisdom

tez ehsaas-e khudi darkaar hai

Firaq emphasizes the need for self-awareness and wisdom in life's journey. An intense sense of self-knowledge is as essential as sustenance of life. While deities may commune with the divine, humans fundamentally need to connect. Poetry is a means of cultivating the heart and emotions, but requires the gentle structuring of grief. More than artistic words, poetry requires a magical, imaginative mind. Although the intellect is entirely rational, it needs a touch of 'madness' or transcendence to flourish. Reason alone is insufficient—love needs an inner illumination to guide it. While the poet's verses contain the truths of life, the audience often merely seeks entertainment. Intellect itself recognizes that it needs the essence of a fulfilled human life. The rapidly progressing modern world order requires slowing down and learning to relax gently. Through these nuanced metaphors, Firaq underscores key lessons—striving for self-understanding, nurturing human bonds, balancing heart and head, as well as imagination and reason, love and wisdom.

tez ehsaas-e khudi darkaar hai
zindagi ko zindagi darkaar hai

तेज़ एहसास-ए ख़ुदी दरकार है
ज़िंदगी को ज़िंदगी दरकार है

An intense sense of
self-awareness is required.
Just as life needs life.

◆

devtaaon ka khuda se hoga kaam
aadmi ko aadmi darkaar hai

देवताओं का ख़ुदा से होगा काम
आदमी को आदमी दरकार है

Deities may have
something to do with God
but humans need
one another.

◆

shaayi'ri hai sar-basar tahziib-e qalb
us ko gham shaaistigi darkaar hai

शा'एरी है सर-बसर तहज़ीब-ए क़ल्ब
उस को ग़म शाइस्तगी दरकार है

Poetry is knowing the heart in
its purest form.
But it asks for a sophisticated
melancholy.

◆

khuubi-e lafz o biyaan se kuchh siva
shaa'yiri ko saahiri darkaar hai

ख़ूबी-ए लफ़्ज़ ओ बयाँ से कुछ सिवा
शा'एरी को साहिरी दरकार है

More than words,
beautifully arranged,
poetry requires
a magical imagination.

◆

a'ql mein yuun to nahien koi kami
ik zara divaangi darkaar hai

अ'क़्ल में यूँ तो नहीं कोई कमी
इक ज़रा दीवानगी दरकार है

There is an abundance of intellect.
What is required is just a touch of insanity.

◆

dosto kaafi nahien chashm-e khirad
i'shq ko bhi raushni darkaar hai

दोस्तो काफ़ी नहीं चश्म-ए ख़िरद
इ'श्क़ को भी रौशनी दरकार है

Friends, the eye of reason
is not enough.

Love requires
inner illumination.

◆

meri ghazlon mein haqaaiq hain faqat
aap ko to shaayi'ri darkaar hai

मेरी ग़ज़लों में हक़ाएक़ हैं फ़क़त
आप को तो शा'ईरी दरकार है

My ghazals contain
truths of real life.
What you demand is
entertaining verse.

◆

a'ql ne kal mere kaanon mein kaha
mujh ko teri zindagi darkaar hai

अ'क़्ल ने कल मेरे कानों में कहा
मुझ को तेरी ज़िंदगी दरकार है

Yesterday, intellect whispered
into my ears.
I need your life and
your essence.

◆

tez rau tahziib-e aa'lam ko 'Firaq'
ik zara aahistigi darkaar hai

तेज़-रौ तहज़ीब-ए आ'लम को 'फ़िराक़'
इक ज़रा आहिस्तगी दरकार है

This fast-paced
world order, Firaq,

must slow down, and
learn to relax.

Life Is This and More

zindagi dard ki kahaani hai

Firaq explores the profound depths of life and the human condition, with each couplet revealing a different facet of his reflections. The verses depict life as a tale of sorrow, where even the stars shed tears in silent sympathy. The beloved is likened to a delicate rose that blooms in the darkest hours, embodying innocence and perceptiveness. The poet reveals that each story reflects his own life, mirrored in the experiences of others, with the heart beating for the one who rules the earthly and heavenly domains. Love stories, timeless and eternal, echo through the ages, their essence remaining unchanged despite the passage of time. The paradoxical nature of the heart is explored, a spark of passion when it is tamed, and a pool of tears when emotions overflow. Secrets and silences, the unspoken language of love, permeate the verses, hinting at the depth of feelings that words cannot express. Life reveals itself as a story of separation from the beloved, as a longing that knows no end. At the same time, the boundless nature of existence is contemplated, in which even a single drop of water harbours the vastness of the ocean of life. Bound by a divine decree, the lovers turn to dust and surrender to the eternal cycle of creation and decay. The poet's newfound understanding of life appears like a revelation, shedding new light on the mysteries of existence, in which youth, night and sleep are interwoven in an untold story to be unravelled. The couplets are embellished with rich imagery inspired by nature, cosmology and philosophy, while acknowledging the duality of the earthly and the heavenly, the temporal and the eternal, linked by the decrees of the divine.

zindagi dard ki kahaani hai
chashm-e anjum mein bhi to paani hai

ज़िंदगी दर्द की कहानी है
चश्म-ए-अंजुम में भी तो पानी है

Life is a tale of sorrow and melancholy.
The gaze of the star
is nothing but tears.

◆

vo kabhi rang vo kabhi khushbu
gaah gul gaah raat-rani hai

वो कभी रंग वो कभी ख़ुशबू
गाह गुल गाह रात-रानी है

She is a splash of colour
and a whiff of fragrance.
Sometimes, she is a rose.
Sometimes, she is a fragrant flower
that blooms at night.

◆

ban ke maa'suum sab ko taar gaaii
aankh us ki bari siyaani hai

बन के मासूम सब को ताड़ गई
आँख उस की बड़ी सियानी है

Posing her innocence,
she understood it all.
She has an eye
that sees through the chaos.

◆

aap-biiti kaho ke jag-biiti
har kahaani meri kahaani hai

आप-बीती कहो कि जग-बीती
हर कहानी मिरी कहानी है

You can call it a personal story
or a story of everyone else.
Each narrative is my chronicle.

◆

dono aa'lam hai jis ke zer-e nagiin
dil usi gham ki raajdhaani hai

दोनों आलम हैं जिस के ज़ेर-ए नगीं
दिल उसी ग़म की राजधानी है

For the one who controls
this world and the next,
the heart is an epicentre
of sadness.

◆

aaj bhi sun rahe hain qissa-e i'shq
go kahaani bahut puraani hai

आज भी सुन रहे हैं क़िस्सा-ए इ'श्क़
गो कहानी बहुत पुरानी है

We still hear
the tale of love,
although this legend
is as old as the day of creation.

◆

zabt kiije to dil hai angaara
aur agar roiye to paani hai

ज़ब्त कीजे तो दिल है अँगारा
और अगर रोइए तो पानी है

If we can rein it,
the heart is like a glowing spark.
But if we shed tears,
it is nothing but water.

◆

ae lab-e naaz kya hai vo asraar
khaamushi jin ki tarjumaani hai

ऐ लब-ए नाज़ क्या हैं वो असरार
ख़ामुशी जिन की तर्जुमानी है

The one with enticing lips,
I have a question for you.
What is the name of the secret
that silence reveals?

◆

mujh se kahta tha kal farishta-e i'shq
zindagi hijr ki kahaani hai

मुझ से कहता था कल फ़रिश्ता-ए इ'श्क़
ज़िंदगी हिज्र की कहानी है

The angel of love
whispered to me yesterday—
life is the story of separation
from the one you love.

◆

bahr-e hasti bhi jis mein kho jaaye
buund mein bhi vo be-karaani hai

बहर-ए हस्ती भी जिस में खो जाए
बूँद में भी वो बे-करानी है

The ocean of life
can drown itself—
a single droplet
holds infinite vastness.

◆

mil gaye khaak mein tere u'shshaaq
ye bhi ik amr-e aasmaani hai

मिल गए ख़ाक में तिरे उ'श्शाक़
ये भी इक अमर-ए आसमानी है

Your lovers were reduced
to dust and ashes.
It looks like the fulfillment
of a divine calling.

◆

zindagi intizaar hai tera
ham ne ik baat aaj jaani hai

ज़िंदगी इंतिज़ार है तेरा
हम ने इक बात आज जानी है

Life, I'm still waiting for you!
Today, I had a revelation
that I wish to share with you.

◆

kuchh n puuchho 'Firaq' ahd-e shabaab
raat hai niind hai kahaani hai

कुछ न पूछो 'फ़िराक़' अहद-ए शबाब
रात है नींद है कहानी है

Don't ask me, Firaq,
about the time of youth.
It's night, it's sleep,
and it's a story.

Five

PANCHAMA (PA)

Realistic poetry, whether written as a ghazal or something else, requires ghazliat (the essence of ghazal-writing) as an essential ingredient of any poetry. Ghazal is a subgenre, but ghazliat is the pearl of poetry. You can write couplets and poems on selected topics, and they have been written. But life and nature are poetry's real subject matter. The complexities of sexual and romantic relationships are significant ghazal aspects, and ghazal helps the poet capture the complexities of romantic feelings. Romance is not accidental or mechanical. Without it, our life will become empty, and we will lose its meaning. Action is not part of all our efforts and thinking, but love demands action on our part. Our political life reflects our personal life. Ghazal's poetry reveals the beauty and elegance of our lives, drawing us closer to the underlying meaning.[11]

—Firaq

Themes and Vibrations

Firaq was a good conversationalist. He conducted numerous interviews and wrote lengthy letters to his friends, covering a wide range of topics. Most of this material is scattered over several books and old magazine issues that are not

[11] *Firaq Gorakhpuri: Shakhsiyat, Shairi aur Shanakhat*, Aziz Nabeel (eds), Majlis-e-Fakhr-e-Bahrain, 2014, p. 107.

easily accessible. We decided to gather some of his ideas and beliefs in one place, categorize them for easy understanding, and make them available to the reader. There are questions for which answers are required. How did Firaq transition from a highly religious environment at home during his childhood to become a leading Urdu poet? Why did he leave his position with the Indian Civil Service, a dream job for educated Indians at the time? Was he part of the progressive writers' movement? What kind of poet did he end up becoming? How did he change the tenor of Urdu's romantic poetry? What was his concept of love? The answers to these questions have been assembled from various sources. The reader should treat these pieces as summaries of statements rather than the precise spoken or written words.

About Childhood

During his childhood, Firaq was exposed to Hindu religious scriptures, particularly Tulsidasa's *Ramayana* and Surdasa's *dohas,* which had a profound impact on his psyche. Although his father was a lawyer and an Urdu poet, the home atmosphere was not conducive to writing poetry. Because his mother conversed only in Bhojpuri, that was the language of all domestic communication and thc language in which everybody spoke. When Firaq moved to Allahabad, first as a student and then as a lecturer in English, that was a significant break from the constraints of his early years. The Urdu spoken in Allahabad was closer to what he had heard at Gorakhpur. He was happy that he hadn't settled down in Delhi or Lucknow because both places had different traditions regarding the use of Urdu in writing and daily conversations.

Every poet evolves his or her style. Firaq developed

a habit of reflecting deeply on complex philosophical questions, such as the nature of the universe and its relationship with its Creator. The physical beauty of forests, rivers, and oceans, and what sustains it. How do societies and cultures evolve? How do human beings relate to one another? When he got clarity on something, Firaq picked up his pen and wrote a couplet, a ruba'i, or a short poem. He was unhappy with Urdu poetry, which most poets wrote. There was an excessive amount of Persian and Arabic flavor, but minimal of what one might consider Indian-ness. This kind of poetry lacked the softness that Firaq cherished in his study of Sanskrit poetics. Although he had no hesitation in choosing Urdu as the language of his poetic expression, he endeavored to create a distinctive flavor. He got some help from Mir Taqi Mir, who mostly wrote his ghazals in the language spoken in Agra and Delhi.

About the Indian Civil Service

Firaq left his job as a deputy collector because of his domestic circumstances. After his father passed away, the responsibility of supporting the whole family fell on his shoulders. There was a lot of struggle and unhappiness, but no love. His wife was a functionally illiterate woman. She would have been an embarrassment in his official circles. Wives of civil servants were generally well-educated; they were fluent in English and wore modern dresses. His wife had none of those attributes, and she was a poor learner. These considerations weighed on him to quit the civil service position. He was hungry for love; his body wanted love, but he found nothing that fulfilled that need. He saw constraints, one bigger than the other. What could he do? He had to start his life as a commoner, devoted to confronting the challenges of daily life, rather than the life of a bureaucrat who served the interests of a foreign power.

About the Progressive Writers' Movement

Firaq was against capitalism because it was based on greed and exploitation, but he didn't want to replace it with communism. His commitment to a democratic form of government was total. People should have the right to choose the government they prefer. The Progressive Writers' Movement was a façade to promote the communist ideology. These writers, he felt, were using literature to weaponize the communist agenda. Firaq had close friends who were active players in the movement. He read and commented on their writings, but he couldn't find one poem or piece of writing that provided a complete picture of the society these writers envisioned for their fellow human beings. On the contrary, they had created an environment in which new writers felt insecure.

Most literary journals entertained works that were supportive of the movement. Non-believers were labeled 'reactionaries' and friends of the colonial regime. Firaq firmly believed that the system itself could not produce productive and innovative human beings. On the contrary, human beings create a system that allows them to express themselves most effectively. The system alone could not have produced great artists like Tansen and Beethoven. These people were highly gifted, creating a pathway for their progress. Firaq also believed that progressive ideology contradicted what was best in the Indian culture. The greatness of India rested on the fact that it was an open society. There were no compulsions. There were ways to escape the attention of autocratic rulers and oppressive institutions. However, the communist model closed all options by taking away personal freedoms. Cultural liberalism, the true force behind the Indian way of life, was the best option for an independent India. Firaq also bemoaned the narrow-mindedness of both Muslim and British rulers, as they had not made any serious effort to understand the Hindu religion. They had not paid attention to the works of Hindu thought leaders, and this attitude created a barrier to national integration. The British policy of divide and rule worsened the preexisting religious hatred and fanaticism.

About the Poetic Style

Firaq liked simplicity. He emphasized small things that improved the quality of life. He wanted people to get closer to one another to create what the English poet Matthew Arnold (1822-1888) had called 'a sense of intimacy.' When Firaq went into deep reflection, he would often become emotional. He used to say, 'When I think, even the eyes of my imagination get wet.' It was a metaphor, but this idea underlined that he approached everything with great humility. He never wished to impose himself on others. He never used themes to impress others. He wanted his ideas to speak for themselves. When he wrote poetry, he downplayed his role as a poet. More than presenting himself as a poet, he wanted people to pay attention to his humanity. He read what he had written several times. He even recited his ghazals alone to find their underlying musicality. He wrote ghazals that were voluminous. Each ghazal is expected to contain seven or eight couplets, but Firaq wrote ghazals with upwards of two dozen couplets. People failed to understand what was behind it. A ghazal for Firaq was the product of a certain mood, an aggregation of feelings and emotions. It was the mood that drove the length. When Firaq wrote, his writing became a stream filling itself with water. He worked on each ghazal for days, until all his energy was exhausted. Writing a ghazal was not a task for him. Poetry, he felt, was not our breath but our soul's breath. It was true meditation. There was a close connection between the rhythm of our breathing and the lyricism that we brought into our poetic work. If you have complaints about life, he used to say, don't inject them into your poetry. However, if you experience sadness, loneliness, or other forms of suffering, allow them to flow into your work naturally.

About Romance in Urdu Poetry

Firaq admired both Mir and Ghalib, who were great romantic poets. Their verse is filled with longing, primarily sensual feelings of the lover for the beloved. Other poets also explored the same themes, but the way they navigated this path, things gradually went downhill. Firaq entered the scene with a determination to change the course. While other poets started with the woman as a subject in Urdu poetry, which was a source of pleasure, Firaq made her a source of light. In his romantic verse, he introduces innocence, simplicity, sincerity, purity, and spirituality. These qualities were not new; they were found in ancient Sanskrit poetry. Firaq tried to revive these themes in his ghazals.

Indian culture is complex. On the one hand, it gives the impression of being very religious, but on the other hand, it is also very liberal, open-minded, progressive, and secular. In matters of sexuality, it was open. Sexual relations between men and women were depicted in the art more explicitly than in any other culture. But Islamic rule changed this free and easy-going trend. Even Hindu women were compelled to veil themselves for personal security.

Given these developments, Urdu poets didn't take advantage of the possibilities that were open to them because they respected Islamic cultural norms. They were very conservative in depicting romance in their verse, with few exceptions. As a result, Urdu poetry explored a wide range of themes, but it lacked depth.

Firaq emphasized the role of feelings and emotions in a romantic relationship. In traditional Urdu poetry, union and separation were depicted as opposite poles; while the former provided unlimited joy, the latter offered much suffering. For Firaq, union with the beloved didn't bring all hell to an end. Separation had some redeeming features that could not be ignored. The beloved in Firaq's poetry is not the work of her lover's imagination. She lives in her place, and she possesses thoughts and feelings with unique complexities. Union is not a moment of liberation for her or the lover; it is a precursor to loneliness. It has shadows of detachment and severance. The poet lives in the real world, and he can't hide the pain and suffering of his own life. Romance, therefore, embraces both intimacy and philosophical distancing. The following couplets are good examples.

tujhe to haath lagaaya hai baar-ha lekin
tere khayal ko chhute hue bhi darta huun

तुझे तो हाथ लगाया है बार-हा लेकिन
तेरे ख़याल को छूते हुए भी डरता हूँ

I've touched you many a time,
but the mere thought of you makes me wary.

◆

tera visaal bari chiiz hai magar dost
visaal ko meri duniy-e aarzu n bana

तेरा विसाल बड़ी चीज़ है मगर दोस्त
विसाल को मेरी दुनिया-ए आरज़ू न बना

A union with you is my prized possession,
but my friend, please don't make it
the world of my desires.

◆

faza tabassum-e sub-h-e bahaar thi lekin
pahunch ke manzil-e jaanaan pe aankh bhar aaii

फ़ज़ा तबस्सम-ए सुबह-ए बहार थी लेकिन
पहुँच के मंज़िल-ए जानां पे आँख भर आई

It was like the smile of a spring morning.
But when I reached my beloved's abode,
tears filled my eyes.

About the Concept of Love

Love is an intense feeling. It has its roots in the sensual needs of humans. Love arises from great depths, and it overpowers the person in love from all sides. Life can turn into a living hell if it meets resistance or failure. Love doesn't respect traditional gender boundaries. That is why there is love between people of the same gender. There was nothing evil about it. Firaq believed that same-sex love was a kind of revolt against oppressive societal norms. Yet, it was not a replacement for a normal man-woman relationship. When Firaq tried to write about love in his poetry, he kept some distance from red lips, rosy cheeks, etc. He tried to delve deeply into the world of feelings and emotions. What were lovers thinking? What were they aspiring to get out of a loving relationship? Firaq started writing poetry under harrowing circumstances. He gained his voice over time. He didn't think that he was writing for a reader. His poetry was an elixir, a concoction to heal his failings because of much bitterness. He used his verse to gain peace and tranquility, which was life-giving. He wanted to capture the best life had to offer in his couplets. He drew heavily from English poets, such as Wordsworth, and the ancient Sanskrit poets. He had no hesitation in admitting that non-Urdu sources had played a significant role in the evolution of his poetry. If there were things in his poetry that others considered sublime, they were gifts of his Indian-ness. Love poetry reveals the inner essence of people living in a culture. It reflects ideas or values they hold dear.

About the Hindi-Urdu Controversy

Firaq had a receptive ear for different languages. If anyone in his presence spoke Bengali or a South Indian language, he paid particular attention to the language's lyricism. Each language is born with distinctive qualities, but in some respects, no Indian language can do better than Urdu in sheer eloquence, rhetoric, fluency, and sound patterns. Both Hindi and Urdu stand on a common foundation of Khari Boli, but according to Firaq, Urdu did a better job of preserving the beauty of its foundation. It is seen in Prem Chand's writing. His Hindi is nowhere near as good as his Urdu. Layers of colourful expressions are available in Urdu that we can't find in Hindi. Firaq read works of Hindi writers who had won prizes and awards. He discovered their writings disappointing and felt that Hindi was losing its grip on Khari Boli and its magic. His Hindi friends told him it was just the beginning, just as

Mir was the beginning of Urdu poetry and Chaucer was the beginning of English. In Firaq's view, this beginning posed a long-term danger. It indicated that Hindi's evolution would stagnate, and its progress would not move forward. Also, Firaq noticed that Hindi writers were not trying to master the English language. These individuals could not have produced great literature without studying the works of Aristotle, Shakespeare, Schopenhauer, and others. A tiny brain can't make great literature. Unless modern Hindi writers bring home big ideas from world literature, their language will not gain a permanent place in people's hearts.

Once, there was a mushaira in Kolkata, Firaq recalled, when thousands of Bengalis who didn't understand Urdu spent much of the night listening to Urdu poetry. These people said in newspaper interviews that although they couldn't understand the language, they liked the poetry and how it sounded. The speech itself made an impression on the listeners. Hindi and Urdu, Firaq pleaded, should come closer. They should start borrowing from each other. Firaq wasn't saying that everything was well with Urdu. If changes were needed, they must be considered and implemented. We need a *sangam* (confluence) of Hindi and Urdu. Our history was keenly looking forward to the fulfillment of that dream.

Firaq was asked about some of the articles that he had published, which created the impression that he was anti-Hindi in his outlook. He said that what he had mentioned was not understood. He clarified that he loved both languages but was disappointed that Hindi writers were not trying to master Khari Boli. If Hindi writers used a language with Sanskrit and Persian words, the language would be easier to understand and find ready acceptance. But filling the language with Sanskrit words only will produce a speech that will neither find social acceptance nor a place in literature. While he lamented the excessive use of Sanskrit in Hindi, Firaq was unhappy that Urdu writers ignored Sanskrit and mindlessly used Persian and Arabic words, making Urdu appear like a foreign language. They need to pay attention to drawing more from Sanskrit, both in terms of vocabulary and expressions, because this language is the soul of India. A well-balanced and more appealing Urdu can emerge if words are drawn from different languages that lie buried in the collective consciousness, thereby avoiding an archaic or foreign feel.

Darkness Is Deep and Dense

sakuut-e shaam mitaao bahut andhera hai

Firaq delves into the depths of the soul's darkness, weaving a tapestry of haunting imagery and profound metaphors that expose the raw essence of the human condition. The central theme revolves around the transformative power of poetry, represented by the radiant candle of verse, which has the potential to illuminate even the darkest corners of our existence and provide solace amidst the suffocating darkness. The opening lines serve as a call, urging the reader to shatter the oppressive silence and ignite the candle of verse as a beacon of hope (*sakuut-e shaam mitaao / sukhan ki sham'a jalaao).* The poet acknowledges the limitations of ordinary light, suggesting that tears, born of profound emotion, may ultimately guide us toward proper illumination. As the ghazal progresses, the image of life vanishing into the embrace of the dark evening emerges, reminding readers of the loss and alienation that often accompany the soul's darkest hours. Yet, even in darkness, the poet offers a glimmer of hope, encouraging us to find solace in the memories of brighter days and reignite the extinguished lamps of our past. The final stanza compares life to a restless, fitful sleep, with the poet urging himself to remain in slumber, acknowledging the all-consuming nature of darkness. The refrain *bahut andhera hai* (darkness is deep and dense) underscores the inescapable and pervasive nature of the darkness that the poet seeks to illuminate through the power of his words.

sakuut-e shaam mitaao bahut andhera hai
sukhan ki sham'a jalaao bahut andhera hai

सकूते शाम मिटाओ बहुत अँधेरा है
सुख़न की शमा' जलाओ बहुत अँधेरा है

Break the hushed silence
of this evening.
Darkness is deep and dense.
Light the candle of verse.
Darkness is deep and dense.

◆

har ik charaagh se har tiirgi nahien mit-ti
charaagh-e ashk jalaao bahut andhera hai

हर इक चराग़ से हर तीरगी नहीं मिटती
चराग़े अश्क जलाओ बहुत अँधेरा है

Not every lamp succeeds in
entirely dispelling darkness.
Light the lamp of tears.
Darkness is deep and dense.

◆

shab-e siyaah mein gum ho gaai hai hayaat
qadam sambhal ke uthaao bahut udaas hai raat

शबे सियाह में गुम हो गई है हयात
क़दम संभल के उठाओ बहुत अँधेरा है

Life has vanished
and gone missing
amid this dark evening.
Beware how you move forward.
Darkness is deep and dense.

◆

guzashta a'hd ki yaadon ko phir karo taaza
bujhe charaagh jalaao bahut andhera hai

गुज़श्ता अ'हद की यादों को फिर करो ताज़ा
बुझे चराग़ जलाओ बहुत अँधेरा है

Freshen up memories
of the days past.
Rekindle lamps that were doused.
Darkness is deep and dense.

◆

thi ik uchat-ti hui niind zindagi ki
'firaq' ko n jagaao bahut andhera hai

थी इक उचटती हुई नींद ज़िन्दगी उस की
'फ़िराक़' को न जगाओ बहुत अँधेरा है

His life was like some fitful sleep.
Don't wake up, Firaq!
Darkness is deep and dense.

When I Remembered Her Locks

us zulf ki yaad jab aane lagi

This ghazal is a beautiful journey through love and how time shapes our lives. The whole thing is tied together by memories resurfacing and how they can emotionally affect you. From the beginning, Firaq captivates us with the image of his beloved's locks, akin to a 'nagin' in motion (*ik naagin si lahraane lagi*). This unique metaphor adds a sensual touch to the ghazal and alludes to the transformative power of love, as serpents often symbolize change in mythology. As the ghazal unfolds, the poet's unease and sadness become palpable, as if the resurfacing memories inflict a profound emotional toll. This portrayal of the poet's vulnerability draws us deeper into the narrative. Then, he takes a step back and looks at his whole life journey, thinking about all the different stages and moments that mattered. He realizes the importance of cherishing all the experiences and people he has encountered. In the next part, he uses vivid imagery of stars breaking and tears falling like pearls to show his intense feelings. The memories bring up this deep sense of loss and grief. Finally, he reveals that the ghazal was born quietly as the stars got sleepy. Firaq does a fantastic job of weaving together all these themes and creating a ghazal that feels both super personal and relatable to everyone.

us zulf ki yaad jab aane lagi
ik naagin si lahraane lagi

उस ज़ुल्फ़ की याद जब आने लगी
इक नागन सी लहराने लगी

Her locks began to sway
like a serpent,
when memories surfaced.

◆

ya-rabb ye chal gayi kaisi hava
kyon dil ki kali murjhaane lagi

या-रब्ब ये चल गई कैसी हवा
क्यों दिल की कली मुरझाने लगी

Oh God, what is happening?
The heart's bud
has started to get scorched.

◆

jab rah-e zindagi kaat chuke
har manzil ki yaad aane lagi

जब राह-ए ज़िन्दगी काट चुके
हर मंज़िल की याद आने लगी

At the end of my journey,
I remembered all the places
where I had stopped
and rested.

◆

taare tuute ya aankh koi
ashkon ke guhar barsaane lagi

तारे टूटे या आँख कोई
अश्कों के गुहर बरसाने लगी

Stars broke into pieces,
or was that an eye?
Pearls of tears started to rain.

◆

us vaqt 'Firaq' hui ye ghazal
jab taaron ko niind aane lagi

उस वक़्त 'फ़िराक़' हुई ये ग़ज़ल
जब तारों को नींद आने लगी

As stars started to feel sleepy,
Firaq, at that moment
this ghazal was born.

The Nine Wonders

nau-ras ghunche pankharion
ki naazuk girhein kholein hain

Firaq makes a veiled reference in this ghazal to a theory central to Indian aesthetics. Its best exposition is in *Natyashastra* (written between 200 BCE and AD 200). A combination of causes, consequences, and transitory states produces Rasa. *Natyashastra* recognized eight *rasas*; later, other authors added the meditative ninth. The two most essential *rasas* are *sringraha* (the first) and *santam* (the ninth). *Sringraha* is love and romance, while *santam* is peace and tranquility. Firaq uses the combined force of all nine *rasas* to describe the freshness of roses if we must fully describe the beauty of roses. In that case, we must use the vocabulary to narrate the nine *rasas* –love, joy, compassion, heroism, wonder, amazement, and soul-satisfying tranquility.

nau-ras ghunche pankharion ki naazuk girhein kholein hain
ya ur jaane ko rang o bu gulshan mein par tolein hain

नौरस गुंचे पंखडिओं की नाज़ुक गिरहें खोलें हैं
या उड़ जाने को रंगो-बू गुलशन में पर तोलें हैं

Are the fresh buds of roses
opening their delicate,
tangled branches?
Or colour and fragrance actually
spreading their wings to fly?

◆

ham hon ya qismat ho hamaari donon ko ik hi kaam mila
qismat ham ko ro leve hai ham qismat ko ro lein hain

हम हों या किस्मत हो हमारी दोनों को इक ही काम मिला
किस्मत हम को रो लेवे है हम किस्मत को रो लें हैं

It is either I or my luck –
both have only one task to do.
My bad destiny can shed tears about me,
or I can cry for my ill fate.

◆

jo mujh ko badnaam karein hain kaash ve itna soch sakein
mera parda kholein hain ya apna parda kholein hain

जो मुझ को बदनाम करें हैं काश वे इतना सोच सकें
मेरा परदा खोलें हैं या अपना परदा खोलें हैं

I wish those who say bad things about me
should stop and think.
Are they unveiling me, or are they
lifting their *purdah*?

◆

sadqe 'firaq' ijaaz-e sukhan ke kaise ura li ye aavaaz
in ghazlon ke pardon mein to 'mir' ki ghazlein bolein hain

सदक़े 'फ़िराक़' एजाज़े सुख़न के कैसे उड़ा ली ये आवाज़
इन ग़ज़लों के परदों में तो 'मीर' की ग़ज़लें बोले हैं

Praise the beautiful verse of Firaq
and the way he raised his voice!
Behind the veil of his ghazals,
there are echoes of Mir's ghazals.

If You Call Me a Poet

mujh ko shaa'yir kahne vaalo main
kya meri ghazlein kya

Firaq humbly reflects on his role as a poet and the significance of his work. He downplays his importance and the value of his ghazals (*main kya meri ghazlein kya)*, stating that his efforts are merely offerings of praise to the majesty of love (*sarkaar-e i'shq).* The poet emphasizes the importance of learning compassion from those who have experienced the world's suffering, as they have intimate knowledge of the pain and anguish that permeate existence. Firaq also explores the themes of displacement and alienation, highlighting the growing sense of homelessness and poverty within his homeland. Finally, he reflects on his journey from relative obscurity to widespread recognition, noting that while few knew of his struggles and losses in the past, his stories and experiences have now become a part of the world's collective narrative.

mujh ko shaa'yir kahne vaalo main kya meri ghazlein kya
main ne to bas sarkaar-e i'shq mein kuchh parche guzraane hain

मुझ को शाइ'र कहने वालो मैं क्या मेरी ग़ज़लें क्या
मैं ने तो बस सरकार-ए इ'श्क़ में कुछ पर्चे गुज़राने हैं

Those who call me a poet,
I want to let them know.
What's my worth,
and what's the value of my ghazals?
My effort was nothing
more than offering notes praising love's majesty.

◆

shaa'yir se hamdardi siikho duniya ke gham-khaane mein
jitney gham hain duniya bhar mein is ke maa'ne jaane hain

शाइ'र से हमदर्दी सीखो दुनिया के ग़म-ख़ाने में
जितने ग़म हैं दुनिया भर में इस के माने-जाने हैं

Learn compassion from the poet
because this world is an abode of suffering.
Anguish, pain, affliction –
he has known them all.

◆

aaj se pehle kab the vatan mein be-vatani ke ye lachhan
logon ko kehte suna hai ghar bhi ghurbat-khaane hain

आज से पहले कब थे वतन में बे-वतनी के ये लच्छन
लोगों को ये कहते सुना है घर भी ग़ुर्बत-ख़ाने हैं

Before today, who could find
such unwelcome symptoms
within this land?
I have heard people saying
that they live in impoverished homes.

◆

is gum-karda-e diida o dil ko kal tak kitne jaante the
ab to 'firaq'-e be-khud ke aa'lam aa'lam afsaane hain

इस गुम-कर्दा-ए दीदा ओ दिल को कल तक कितने जानते थे
अब तो 'फ़िराक़'-ए बे-ख़ुद के आ'लम आ'लम अफ़्साने हैं

How many people knew the one
who had lost the eye and the heart?
But now the whole world
has stories to tell
about this drunk named Firaq.

A Different Secret

raaz-e aa'lam se hai shaayad k mera raaz juda

Firaq explores the uniqueness of his own experiences and emotions, particularly those related to love and the passage of time. The central theme that unifies his work is the distinctiveness of his journey and perception, which sets him apart from his contemporaries. He distinguishes his profound emotions from universal sorrows, highlighting his special connection with his beloved through meeting her gaze. He questions the need to dwell on memories of his beloved when they are still so fresh, vividly describing her captivating features, such as her curly hair, colourful lips, and flirty glance. He also touches on the universal experience of marching towards death, yet he feels that his past lives call out to him in a distinct voice, making his journey stand out from the rest. He hints at the hidden delights and secrets behind his beloved's flirtatious nature, emphasizing how their unique communication and expression set their bond apart. The repeated use of the word *juda* (different or separate) throughout the ghazal underscores Firaq's perception of his experiences as distinct from those of others.

raaz-e aa'lam se hai shaayad k mera raaz juda
mujh se milne mein hai us aankh ka andaaz juda

राज़-ए आलम से है शायद कि मिरा राज़ जुदा
मुझ से मिलने में है उस आँख का अंदाज़ जुदा

My secret, I suppose, is different
from the mystery of sorrow.
When that eye meets me,
it shows a different form.

◆

yuun hi kya kam hai teri yaad k dil ko chherein
zulf-e pur-kham lab-e rangiin nigaah-e naaz juda

यूँ ही क्या कम है तिरी याद कि दिल को छेड़ें
ज़ुल्फ़-ए पुर-ख़म लब-ए रंगीं निगह-ए नाज़ जुदा

Why start with the heart
when her memory is still fresh?
Curly tresses, colourful lips,
philandering glance—
everything is different.

◆

barhte hi jaate hain sab ahl-e jahaan su-e a'dam
u'mr-e rafta bhi diye jaati hai aavaaz juda

बढ़ते भी जाते हैं सब अहल-ए जहाँ सू-ए-अदम
उम्र-ए रफ़्ता भी दिए जाती है आवाज़ जुदा

The people of the world
march

to the valley of death.
Past lives call
in a different voice.

◆

kuchh ishaare hain udhar shokhi-e pinhaan ke 'firaq'
hai sukuut-e nigaah-e naaz sukhan saaz juda

कुछ इशारे हैं उधर शोख़ी-ए पिन्हाँ के 'फ़िराक़'
है सुकूत-ए निगहा-ए नाज़ सुख़न-साज़ जुदा

There are indications
of the hidden delights, Firaq.
The stillness of the trifling eye
of someone fluent but insincere,
is different.

Yearning for Union

suna to hai k abhi be-niyaaz-e gham thi hayaat

Firaq explores the idea that our current reality is a fleeting shadow of our true essence. Our journey through the cycles of life and death is an endless odyssey until we attain ultimate union with the divine, reflecting a Vedantic viewpoint. The opening couplet sets a nostalgic tone, hinting at a time of blissful unawareness of sorrow, now stirred by the beloved's eyes. The poet describes moments that stretch into infinity and eternity, suggesting that these are dreams within the larger illusion of life, inviting readers to question their perceived reality and ponder existence beyond their limited understanding. Firaq also highlights the ambiguous nature of life for those trapped in hell, emphasizing the uncertainty of suffering and the hope of deliverance. Amidst the darkness, he speaks of a divine secret permeating the world, where time loses its hold, and the beloved's glances bring forth both dawn and dusk, alluding to the transformative power of true love. The intoxicating wisdom of old wine, a metaphor for insights gained through a well-lived life, is celebrated as the source of life's miracles. The poet emphasizes the importance of silence becoming a fable and the power of love to sustain the soul's eternal conversation. Drawing upon Vedantic teachings, he asserts that the world and non-existence are mere reflections of a higher reality, with the endless cycle of life and death likened to a maze of mirrors (*aaiina-dar-aaiina hayaat o mamaat)*. The ghazal's penultimate couplet depicts the weariness and fatigue of separation, while the final couplet offers hope through the transformative power of poetry, breathing new life into the soul.

suna to hai k abhi be-niyaaz-e gham thi hayaat
dilaaii yaad nigaahon ne teri kab ki baat

सुना तो है कि कभी बे-नियाज़-ए ग़म थी हयात
दिलाई याद निगाहों ने तेरी कब की बात

I have heard that life was oblivious
of sorrow once.
Your eyes reminded meof this
old story.

◆

hayaat ban gaaii thi jin mein ek khwaab-e hayaat
ar-re davaam o abad the vohi to kuchh lamhaat

हयात बन गई थी जिन में एक ख़्वाब-ए हयात
अरे दवाम ओ अबद थे वही तो कुछ लम्हात

Life became a dream
in which life was a dream.
Oh, time and eternity
were just moments.

◆

hayaat-e dozkhiaan bhi tamaam mub-ham hai
azaab bhi n mayussar hua kahaan ki najaat

हयात-ए दोज़ख़ियाँ भी तमाम मुबहम है
अज़ाब भी न मयस्सर हुआ कहाँ की नजात

The life of those living in hell
is ambiguous.
Don't talk of deliverance.
These folks were denied
even grief.

◆

teri nigaah ki sub-hien nigaah ki shaamein
hariim-e raaz ye duniya jahaan n din hain n raat

तिरी निगाह की सुब्हें निगाह की शामें
हरीम-ए राज़ ये दुनिया जहाँ न दिन हैं न रात

Ah, the dawns and evenings
of your glances!
The world is a divine secret
where there are no days
and no nights.

◆

bas ik sharaab-e kuhan ke karishme hain saqi
naye zamaane nai mastiyaan nai barsaat

बस इक शराब-ए कुहन के करिश्मे हैं साक़ी
नए ज़माने नई मस्तियाँ नई बरसात

Saqi, these are all miracles
of the old wine!
New times, new intoxications,
and the new rainy season!

◆

sakuut-e raaz vohi hai jo daastaan ban jaaye
nigaah-e naaz vohi jo nikaale baat mein baat

सुकूत-ए राज़ वही है जो दास्ताँ बन जाए
निगाह-ए नाज़ वही जो निकाले बात में बात

The silence of the secret—
it should become a fable.
The look of love is one
that keeps the conversation flowing.

◆

tamaam aks hai duniya tamaam aks adam
kahaan tak aaiina-dar-aaiina hayaat o mamaat

तमाम अक्स है दुनिया तमाम अक्स अदम
कहाँ तक आइना-दर-आइना हयात ओ ममात

All this world
and all this non-existence
are nothing but a reflection
of something else.
Mirror after mirror,
life after death is nothing
but a never-ending cavalcade.

◆

faza mein mahki hui chaandni k naghma-e raaz
k utre siina-e shaa'yir mein jis tarah naghmaat

फ़ज़ा में महकी हुई चाँदनी कि नग़मा-ए राज़
कि उतरें सीना-ए शाइ'र में जिस तरह नग़मात

The ambiance is fragrant,
like moonlight,
or is it a secret melody?
Is it the same as verses calmly
enter a poet's heart?

◆

chamakte dard khile chehre muskaraate ashk
sajaaii jaye gi ab tarz-e nau se bazm-e hayaat

चमकते दर्द खिले चेहरे मुस्कुराते अश्क
सजाई जाएगी अब तर्ज़-ए नौ से बज़्म-ए हयात

Pain that glitters,
blooming faces,
and smiling tears.
The congregation of life
will now be embellished
in a new manner.

◆

jise sab ahl-e jahaan zindagi samajhte hain
kabhi kabhi to mile aisi zindagi se najaat

जिसे सब अहल-ए जहाँ ज़िंदगी समझते हैं
कभी कभी तो मिले ऐसी ज़िंदगी से नजात

What people of the world call life,
we should sometimes

get deliverance
from such a life.

◆

agar khuda bhi mile to n le k o nadaan
hai tu hi kaa'ba-e diin tu hi qibla-e hajaat

अगर ख़ुदा भी मिले तो न ले कि ओ नादाँ
है तू ही काबा-ए दीं तू ही क़िबला-ए हाजात

O ignorant being,
never choose God
if you get an offer,
because you are the Ka'ba
of faith and a fountain
of compassion for others.

◆

tamaam khastagi o maandgi hai aa'lam-e hijr
thake thake se ye taare thaki thaki si ye raat

तमाम ख़स्तगी ओ माँदगी है आ'लम-ए हिज्र
थके थके से ये तारे थकी थकी सी ये रात

All this fragility
and fatigue are symptomatic
of the state of separation.
The stars are tired,
and the night, too,
is worn out.

◆

teri ghazal to nai ruuh phuunk deti hai
'firaq' der se chhuuti hui hai nabz-e hayaat

तिरी ग़ज़ल तो नई रूह फूँक देती है
'फ़िराक़' देर से छूटी हुई है नब्ज़-ए हयात

A new ghazal by you brings
a new vigor to one's soul.
O Firaq, for a long time,
the pulse of life
is struggling to stay afloat.

Never-Ending Cycle of Union and Separation

jise log kahte hain tiirgi vohi shab hijab-e sahar bhi hai

Firaq explores the eternal cycle of love, where the anguish of parting often follows union. The verses suggest that even in the darkest times, a new beginning is always waiting, and those who have let go of their fear of death truly understand the essence of living. He weaves a net of love's contradictions, blurring the lines between togetherness and separation. He portrays love as a mysterious force that inflicts heartache and soul wounds, even in the face of conquest. The pain and joy of love are intertwined, and the lover must endure the endless twists and turns of fate, stuck on a rollercoaster of hope and heartbreak. He flips the script on life and death, revealing how the darkness of death conceals the brilliance of life within, using vivid imagery of sparks and dancing flames to symbolize hope and energy burning brightly, even in the darkest places. Firaq explores the dual nature of love, calling it both a pain and a cure, bringing life and death simultaneously (*unhi zulmaton ke hijaab mein ye chamak ye raqs-e sharar bhi hai)*. Love is compared to arrows shot by the beloved, but it also serves as a shield to guard the heart.

jise log kahte hain tiirgi vohi shab hijab-e sahar bhi hai
jinhein be-khudi-e fana mili unhein zindagi ki khabar bhi hai

जिसे लोग कहते हैं तीरगी वही शब हिजाब-ए सहर भी है
जिन्हें बे-ख़ुदी-ए फ़ना मिली उन्हें ज़िंदगी की ख़बर भी है

What people call darkness
is a veil of the coming dawn.
Those who freed themselves
from the fear of death,
know the meaning of life.

◆

ye nasiib-e i'shq ki gardishein k zaman makaan se guzar ke bhi
vohi aasmaan vohi shaam-e gham vohi i'shq siina-sipar bhi hai

ये नसीब-ए इ'श्क़ की गर्दिशें कि ज़माँ मकाँ से गुज़र के भी
वही आसमाँ वही शाम-ए ग़म वही शाम-ए ग़म की सहर भी है

Oh, these ups and downs of being in love.
Even after I travelled across time,
I still have the same sky,
the same evening of gloom,
and its inevitable dawn.

◆

ye visaal o hijr ki bahas kya k u'jiib chiiz hai i'shq bhi
tujhe pa ke hai vohi dard-e dil vohi rang-e zakhm-e jigar bhi hai

ये विसाल ओ हिज्र की बहस क्या कि अजीब चीज़ है इ'श्क़ भी
तुझे पा के है वही दर्द-ए दिल वही रंग-ए ज़ख़्म-ए जिगर भी है

What is this argument
about the union and the separation?
Love is a strange phenomenon.
Even after winning your heart,
the pain persists,
and the wounds remain unhealed.

◆

usi shaam-e marg ki tiirgi mein hai jalva-ha-e hayaat bhi
unhi zulmaton ke hijaab mein ye chamak ye raqs-e sharar bhi hai

उसी शाम-ए मर्ग की तीरगी में हैं जल्वा-हा-ए हयात भी
उन्हीं ज़ुल्मतों के हिजाब में ये चमक ये रक़्स-ए शरर भी है

The darkness of the evening of death
is hidden in the manifestation of life.
In the veils of those dark places,
there is light and the dance of sparks.

◆

vohi dard bhi hai dava bhi hai vohi maut bhi hai hayaat bhi
vohi i'shq naavak-e naaz hai vohi zindagi siina-sapar bhi hai

वही दर्द भी है दवा भी है वही मौत भी है हयात भी
वही इ'श्क़ नावक-ए नाज़ है वही इ'श्क़ सीना-सिपर भी है

It's a pain and a remedy for pain.
It's life as well as death.
Love is the arrow and
also the shield.

◆

dam-e hashr azal ki bhi yaad kar ye zabaan kya ye nigaah kya
jo kisi se aaj n ho saka vo savaal baar-e digar bhi hai

दम-ए हश्र अज़ल की भी याद कर ये ज़बान क्या ये निगाह क्या
जो किसी से आज न हो सका वो सवाल बार-ए दिगर भी है

Keep in mind the doomsday
and the start of eternity.
What is the meaning of this power
of speech and a glance?
Something that no one could answer
that question is a burden
on everyone's shoulders.

♦

tere gham ki u'mr-e daraaz mein kaii inqilaab hue magar
vohi tuul-e shaam-e 'Firaq' hai vohi intezaar-e sahar bhi hai

तिरे ग़म की उम्र-ए दराज़ में कई इंक़लाब हुए मगर
वही तूल-ए शाम-ए 'फ़िराक़' है वही इंतिज़ार-ए सहर भी है

In a long time of grief
during separation from you,
many revolutions occurred.
Firaq's evening is still stretched out
and he is still waiting for the dawn.

♦

ye shab-e daraaz bhi kat gai vo sitaare duube vo po phati
sar-e raah ghaflat-e khwaab se ab utho k vaqt-e sahar bhi hai

ये शब-ए दराज़ भी कट गई वो सितारे डूबे वो पौ फटी
सर-ए राह ग़फ़लत-ए ख़्वाब से अब उठो कि वक़्त-ए सहर भी है

The long night has passed.
Stars have disappeared,
and lo, the dawn is here!
Rise from the deceptive, dreamy state
because it's time
to celebrate the morning.

Nothing Clear, Nothing Hidden

kuchh bhi ayaan nihaan n
tha koi zamaan makaan n tha

Firaq explores the power of love and its profound impact on life. The first couplet sets the stage by describing a situation where clarity and obscurity blend, and the concepts of time and place seem to disappear. In this state, the only thing that matters is waiting for that special someone's glance, which can transform the world. Love is portrayed as a force that transcends the boundaries of the physical world, making one question the nature of reality. Firaq emphasizes the omnipresence of love, using colourful imagery to depict music in every drop of water and passion in every tiny particle of the universe. He highlights how everyone is consumed by thoughts of their beloved and the pain of separation, suggesting that love is an inherent and inescapable part of the human condition. The poet employs metaphors to convey the disorienting and vulnerable nature of love, such as having no ground under one's feet and no sky above one's head (*paanv tale zamiin n thi sar pe ye aasmaan n tha).* Love is portrayed as a force that requires courage and resilience to face uncertainty and hardship.

Firaq also explores the idea of love being left alone in the sanctuary of the beloved's beauty, describing a state where patience and awareness have abandoned the lover, leaving him entirely at the mercy of his emotions.

kuchh bhi ayaan nihaan n tha koi zamaan makaan n tha
der thi ik nigaah ki phir ye jahaan jahaan n tha

कुछ भी अयाँ निहाँ न था कोई ज़माँ मकाँ न था
देर थी इक निगाह की फिर ये जहाँ जहाँ न था

Nothing was clear,
and nothing was hidden.
There was no sense of time and place.
Only her glance was awaited.
Then, this world was not the same place.

◆

saaz vo qatre qatre mein soz vo zarre zarre mein
yaad teri kise n thi dard tera kahaan n tha

साज़ वो क़तरे क़तरे में सोज़ वो ज़र्रे ज़र्रे में
याद तिरी किसे न थी दर्द तिरा कहाँ न था

There was music in each drop
and passion in each particle.
Who wasn't lost in your thoughts?
Who wasn't suffering
from the grief of your separation?

◆

i'shq ki aazmaaeshein aur fazaaon mein huin
paanv tale zamiin n thi sar pe ye aasmaan n tha

इ'श्क़ की आज़माइशें और फ़ज़ाओं में हुईं
पाँव तले ज़मीं न थी सर पे ये आसमाँ न था

Love was tested
under different circumstances.
There was no ground under one's feet,
and there was no sky over one's head.

◆

i'shq hariim-e husn mein apne sahaare rah gaya
sabr ka bhi pata n tha hosh ka bhi nishaan n tha

इ'श्क़ हरीम-ए-हुस्न में अपने सहारे रह गया
सब्र का भी पता न था होश का भी निशाँ न था

Love was left alone
in the sanctuary of your beauty.
Patience was not to be found,
and consciousness had not left any trace.

◆

ek ko ek ki khabar manzil-e i'shq mein n thi
koi bhi ahl-e kaarvaan shaamil-e kaarvaan n tha

एक को एक की ख़बर मंज़िल-ए-इश्क़ में न थी
कोई भी अहल-ए कारवाँ शामिल-ए-कारवाँ न था

When love reached its destination,
no one took care of one another.
No one was found in the caravan,
and no one had joined the march.

◆

i'shq ne apni jaan ko rog kaii laga liye
hijr o visaal ummid o biim kaun bala-e jaan n tha

इ'श्क़ ने अपनी जान को रोग कई लगा लिए
हिज्र ओ विसाल उमीद ओ बीम कौन बला-ए जाँ न था

Love exposed itself to many ailments.
Separation and union, hope and despair,
each one of them was a calamity.

A Deep Yearning for Connection

be-thikaane hai dil-e gham-giin thikaane ki kaho

Firaq discusses the emotions of a heart burdened with sorrow and longing, evoking a profound yearning for connection and understanding. The poet's plea, 'Let's talk about finding a place to call home' (*thikaane ki kaho*), suggests a state of separation and a desire for hopeful reassurance from friends regarding the possibility of his beloved's return. He conveys a sense of feeling trapped, like a prisoner in a cage, longing for the comfort and security of a nest that friends, free to roam in the gardens, might be able to describe. Firaq tells the tale of a heart that poured out its story before surrendering, requesting a recount of how the candle of life's gathering flickered and shimmered. This poignant reminder to celebrate and cherish the beauty and vibrancy of life, even in the face of loss, is powerful. He calls upon the wise to share stories about a heart that has passed away, remembering someone who had a profound impact and brought life to deserted places, keeping their memory alive. The poet marvels at the captivating narrative of life, beckoning us to delve deep into the tale that began with the very inception of existence (*jo azal se chhir gaya hai us fasaane ki kaho*). He invites a personal and reflective conversation, as people have been waiting for the poetry recitation since the evening began, asking Firaq to share something about himself and the times they're living in.

be-thikaane hai dil-e gham-giin thikaane ki kaho
shaam-e hijraan dosto kuchh is ke aane ki kaho

बे-ठिकाने है दिल-ए ग़म-गीं ठिकाने की कहो
शाम-ए हिज्राँ दोस्तो कुछ इस के आने की कहो

The heart is filled with grief
and it has lost its abode.
Let's talk about places to live.
It is an evening of separation.
Friends talk about
the possibility of her arrival.

◆

haan n puuchh ik giraftaar-e qafas ki zindagi
ham-safiraan-e chaman kuchh aashiaane ki kaho

हाँ न पूछ इक गिरफ़्तार-ए क़फ़स की ज़िंदगी
हम-सफ़ीरान-ए चमन कुछ आशियाने की कहो

Could you not ask me about
my life as a prisoner in a refuge?
Tell me something about your home,
Fellow travellers of the garden.

◆

baat itni aur baaton se nazar aati nahien
is nigaah-e naaz ki baatein banaane ki kaho

बात बनती और बातों से नज़र आती नहीं
इस निगाह-ए नाज़ की बातें बनाने की कहो

Our conversation
is getting somewhere,
but it is not transparent.
Describe briefly

why that glance of love
is so enchanting.

◆

daastaan vo thi jise dil bujhate bujhate kah gaya
sham-e bazm-e zindagi ke jhilmilaane ki kaho

दास्ताँ वो थी जिसे दिल बुझते बुझते कह गया
शम'-ए बज़्म-ए ज़िंदगी के झिलमिलाने की कहो

This story, the
heart narrated before giving up.
Let us recount how the candle
of the gathering of life
flickered and shimmered.

◆

kuchh dil-e marhuum ki baatein karo ae ahl-e i'lm
jis se viiraane the aabaad us diivaane ki kaho

कुछ दिल-ए मरहूम की बातें करो ऐ अहल-ए इल्म
जिस से वीराने थे आबाद उस दिवाने की कहो

O sages! Talk of the deprived heart.
Talk of the fiend who turned
the barren into the prosperous.

◆

daastaan-e zindagi bhi kis qadar dilchasp hai
jo azal se chhir gaya hai us fasaane ki kaho

दास्तान-ए ज़िंदगी भी किस क़दर दिलचस्प है
जो अज़ल से छिड़ गया है उस फ़साने की कहो

The chronicle of life
is filled with amazement.

Something that started
with the advent of life,
let us talk about that story.

◆

ye fasuun-e niim shab ye khwaab-saamaan khaamushi
saamari fan aankh ke jaadu jagaane ki kaho

ये फ़ुसून-ए नीम-ए शब ये ख़्वाब-सामाँ ख़ामुशी
सामरी फ़न आँख के जादू जगाने की कहो

This enchantment of midnight and this dream-inducing silence.
Let us talk of the beauty of the glance that brings great magic into play.

◆

shaam hi se gosh-bar-aavaaz hai bazm-e sukhan
kuchh 'firaq' apni sunaao kuchh zamaane ki kaho

शाम ही से गोश-बर-आवाज़ है बज़्म-ए सुख़न
कुछ 'फ़िराक़' अपनी सुनाओ कुछ ज़माने की कहो

We have waited for the poetry recitation since the start of the evening.
Say something, Firaq, about yourself, and these trying times.

What You Expect Is Not What You Get

lutf-saamaan itaab-e yaar bhi hai

Firaq captures the emotional turmoil of the lover who finds delight even in the beloved's ill temper, extending pleasure to all aspects of the beloved, including the challenging ones. However, the confidant of love, privy to the lover's secrets, experiences regret or shame, portraying the complexities of love and evoking empathy and connection. The poet describes the beloved's slow promise-keeping and carefree attitude, yet her beauty remains a picture of patience, with the lover willing to wait and endure because the beloved's beauty is worth it. Firaq questions what the glance of love can do when it is simultaneously happy and grieving, depicting love as a complex mix of emotions that cannot be easily untangled or understood. Through a beautiful metaphor, the poet identifies himself as the garden of love, where his autumn is the reason for the colourfulness of spring (*gulshan-e i'shq huun khizaan meri / vajah-e rangiini-e bahaar bhi hai*). The pain and decay of love, symbolized by the falling leaves of autumn, make the renewal and vibrancy of spring possible, suggesting that the hardships of love are integral to its beauty. The final verse is a poignant reflection, with Firaq contemplating his role in the pain of separation from the beloved. He ponders if this separation and anguish are his choices on some level, inviting the reader to reflect on the interplay of free will and destiny in love.

lutf-saamaan itaab-e yaar bhi hai
marham-e i'shq sharam-saar bhi hai

लुत्फ़-सामाँ इताब-ए यार भी है
महरम-ए इ'श्क़ शर्मसार भी है

The ill temper of the beloved
is a thing of joy.
The confidant of love
is regretful, too.

◆

sust-paimaan o be-niyaaz sahi
husn tasviir-e intezaar bhi hai

सुस्त-पैमान ओ बे-नियाज़ सही
हुस्न तस्वीर-ए इंतिज़ार भी है

Late in fulfilling promises
and of a carefree nature.
But the beauty is a portrait
of patience as well.

◆

kaya kare vo nigaah-e lutf k i'shq
shaadmaan bhi hai sogvaar bhi hai

क्या करे वो निगाह-ए लुत्फ़ कि इ'श्क़
शादमाँ भी है सोगवार भी है

What can the glance of love do
when love is happy
and grieved at the same time.

◆

gulshan-e i'shq huun khizaan meri
vajah-e rangiini-e bahaar bhi hai

गुलशन-ए इ'श्क़ हूँ ख़िज़ाँ मेरी
वज्ह-ए रंगीनी-ए बहार भी है

I am the garden of love,
Autumn, the reason for
the colours of my spring.

◆

raaz us aankh ka nahien khulta
dil shikeba bhi be-qaraar bhi hai

राज़ उस आँख का नहीं खुलता
दिल शकेबा भी बे-क़रार भी है

I can't find the secret
of her glance.
The heart is stoical
and perturbed.

◆

us se chhut kar ye sochta huun 'firaq'
is mein kuchh apna ikhtiyaar bhi hai

उस से छुट कर ये सोचता हूँ 'फ़िराक़'
इस में कुछ अपना इख़्तियार भी है

After my separation from her,
I've been thinking about Firaq.
Is this a choice
that I made on my own?

With Heart Full of Love, How Do You Speak?

ab aksar chup chup se rahein hain
yuunhi kabhu lab kholein hain

In this emotionally charged ghazal, the poet bares his soul, revealing his vulnerability and the profound impact of love on his life. He confesses to his silence and occasional outbursts, suggesting a retreat into himself due to deep-seated pain. The poet cautions those who encounter him in daylight not to be deceived by his dry eyes, as he surrenders to tears at night, a stark contrast to his daytime façade of strength. Firaq muses on his inherent nature to love, yet his destiny is solitude, acknowledging his belonging to someone while still yearning for the love he craves. He paints a vivid picture of cool, dark, fragrant shadows enveloping land and water, questioning the enchantments his ghazals perform to unravel the night's bun, evoking a rich and sensual image. The poet directly addresses the reader, stating that the vibrancy found in the embellishments of his ghazal should be accepted as the tears of the universe before being infused into his poetry. On these nights, the state of the beloved's abode becomes his companion, and in his solitude, her soft fingers open the knots of his garment, creating a private, erotic moment. Firaq asks those who want to hear a sad story to rest at night's end, promising to repeat the tale but pleading for sleep as if exhausted from the weight of his emotions (*gham ka fasaana sunne vaalo aakhir-e shab aaraam karo / kal ye kahaani phir chherein ge ham bhi zara ab so lein hain*). The final verse is poignant, with the poet and the beloved now like strangers, and he pleads for her to acknowledge his condition and devotion despite their estrangement.

ab aksar chup chup se rahein hain yuunhi kabhu lab kholein hain
pehle 'firaq' ko dekha hota ab to bahut kam bolein hai

अब अक्सर चुप चुप से रहें हैं यूँही कभू लब खोलें हैं
पहले 'फ़िराक़' को देखा होता अब तो बहुत कम बोलें हैं

He opens his lips sometimes.
You should have seen him before.
Firaq doesn't speak much nowadays.

◆

din mein ham ko dekhne vaalo apne apne hain aukaat
jaao n tum in khushk aankhon par ham raaton ko ro le hain

दिन में हम को देखने वालो अपने अपने हैं औक़ात
जाओ न तुम इन ख़ुश्क आँखों पर हम रातों को रो लें हैं

During the day,
Everything looks normal.
Don't be misled by my dry eyes.
I do all my crying during the night.

◆

fitrat meri i'shq o mohabbat qismat meri tanhaii
kehne ki naubat hi na aaii ham bhi kisu ke ho lein hain

फ़ितरत मेरी इ'श्क़ ओ मोहब्बत क़िस्मत मेरी तंहाई
कहने की नौबत ही न आई हम भी किसू के हो लें हैं

Love, my disposition,
My fate is loneliness.
'I belong to someone'
goes without saying.

◆

khunak siyaah mahke hue saaye phail jaaein hain jal thal par
kin jatnon se meri ghazlein raat ka juuda kholein hain

ख़ुनुक सियह महके हुए साए फैल जाएँ हैं जल-थल पर
किन जतनों से मेरी ग़ज़लें रात का जूड़ा खोलें हैं

The blessed, fragrant, black shadows
spread across land and water.
What tricks my ghazals perform
to untie the night's braid.

◆

uff vo labon par mauj-e tabassum jaise karvatein lein kaunde
haaye vo aa'lam-e jumnbash-e mizghaan jab fitne par tolein hain

उफ़ वो लबों पर मौज-ए तबस्सुम जैसे करवटें लें कौंदे
हाए वो आ'लम-ए जुम्बिश-ए मिज़्गाँ जब फ़ित्ने पर तौलें हैं

Behold the wave of a smile,
as she changes her side while sleeping,
becoming a ray of light.
Look at the movement of her eyelashes
which makes naughtiness open its wings.

◆

naqshe nigaar-e ghazal mein jo tum ye shaadaabi paao ho
ham ashkon mein kaayenaat ke nok-e qalam ko dabo lein hain

नक़्श ओ निगार-ए ग़ज़ल में जो तुम ये शादाबी पाओ हो
हम अश्कों में काएनात के नोक-ए क़लम को डुबो लें हैं

The fluorescence that you will find
in the embellishments of my ghazal,
I will accept it as tears of the universe
before I immerse the tip of my pen in them.

◆

in raaton ko hariim-e naaz ka ik aa'lam hue hai nadiim
khalvat mein vo narm ungliyaan band-e qaba jab kholein hain

इन रातों को हरीम-ए नाज़ का इक आ'लम हुए है नदीम
ख़ल्वत में वो नर्म उँगलियाँ बंद-ए क़बा जब खोलें हैं

During these nights,
the state of the abode of the beloved
has become my companion.
In my solitude, those soft fingers
open the knots of my garment.

◆

gham ka fasaana sunne vaalo aakhir-e shab aaraam karo
kal ye kahaani phir chherein ge ham bhi zara ab so lein hain

ग़म का फ़साना सुनने वालो आख़िर-ए शब आराम करो
कल ये कहानी फिर छेड़ेंगे हम भी ज़रा अब सो लें हैं

Those who want to hear a poignant melody,
rest in the last moments of the night.
I will tell this tale again.
Let me sleep for a while.

◆

ham log ab to ajnabi se hain kuchh to bataao haal-e 'firaq'
ab to tumhein ko pyaar karein hain ab to tumhein se bolein hain

हम लोग अब तो अजनबी से हैं कुछ तो बताओ हाल-ए 'फ़िराक़'
अब तो तुम्हीं को प्यार करें हैं अब तो तुम्हीं से बोलें हैं

We are like strangers.
Please say something about Firaq.
He is in love with you.
Now, he speaks only to you.

A Smoke-Filled Evening

narm faza ki karvatein dil ko dukkha ke rah gaaein

Firaq explores the impact of love on the heart, using impactful imagery to convey the complex display of feelings that arise from the beloved's presence and absence. The poet describes how even the soft vibrations of the atmosphere can ache the heart, and the cold breeze can carry thoughts of the beloved as if the very air is infused with the pain and memory of love. Firaq sets the scene of a smoke-filled evening and a dispirited beauty, where the heart recalls many stories triggered by the atmosphere. The poet vividly describes the transformative power of the beloved's presence, causing flowers to bloom wherever she walks, their vibrant colours a stark contrast to the world's dullness. In comparison, spring crops fly by like dust, insignificant in the face of her radiance. He acknowledges the complex and contradictory effects of love, with the beloved's eyes having the power to both lull troubles to sleep and awaken them. Even the poet's cries of pain move the stars to tears, echoing his longing throughout the universe. Firaq reflects on how forgotten stories can resurface, causing pain to already-lost hearts, and how love's powerful emotion shakes the essence of life. In a night of waiting for the beloved who never comes, the stars spread their eyes like a carpet, a poignant image of longing and disappointment. The poet contrasts his inner pain with the outer jollity of gatherings seeking fun and questions who can comfort those wounded by the sorrows of love, as even the soaking nights end up causing blazing fires.

narm faza ki karvatein dil ko dukkha ke rah gaaein
thandi havaaein bhi teri yaad dila ke rah gaaein

नर्म फ़ज़ा की करवटें दिल को दुखा के रह गईं
ठंडी हवाएँ भी तिरी याद दिला के रह गईं

My heart aches as the gentle breeze shifts.
Even the cold breeze
carried your thought
back to me.

◆

shaam bhi thi dhuaan dhuaan husn bhi tha udaas udaas
dil ko kaii kahaaniyaan yaad si aa ke rah gaaein

शाम भी थी धुआँ धुआँ हुस्न भी था उदास उदास
दिल को कई कहानियाँ याद सी आ के रह गईं

The evening was smoke-filled
and the beauty was dispirited.
My heart reminisced about
many forgotten tales.

◆

mujh ko kharaab kar gaaein niim-nigaahiyaan teri
mujh se hayaat o maut bhi aankhein chura ke rah gaaein

मुझ को ख़राब कर गईं नीम-निगाहियाँ तिरी
मुझ से हयात ओ मौत भी आँखें चुरा के रह गईं

Your veiled gaze
was ruinous for my heart.
Both life and death walked away
without glancing at me.

◆

husn-e nazar-fareb mein kis ko kalam tha magar
teri adaaein aaj to dil mein sama ke rah gaaein

हुस्न-ए नज़र-फ़रेब में किस को कलाम था मगर
तेरी अदाएँ आज तो दिल में समा के रह गईं

Who could say anything
about your enticing gaze?
Your coquetry
pleased my heart today.

◆

tere khiraam-e naaz se aaj vahaan chaman khile
faslein bahaar ki jahaan khaak uda ke rah gaaein

तेरे ख़िराम-ए नाज़ से आज वहाँ चमन खिले
फ़सलें बहार की जहाँ ख़ाक उड़ा के रह गईं

The romantic advances of your stroll
made the flowers bloom in many places.
The crops of spring flew by like dust.

◆

puuchh n un nigaahon ki turfa karishma-saaziyaan
fitne sula ke rah gaaein fitne jaga ke rah gaaein

पूछ न उन निगाहों की तुर्फ़ा करिश्मा-साज़ियाँ
फ़ित्ने सुला के रह गईं फ़ित्ने जगा के रह गईं

Please don't ask me
about the miraculous layers of her eyes.
They put tribulations to sleep
and let the disquiet arise.

◆

taaron ki aankh bhi bhar aaii meri sada-e dard par
un ki nigaahein bhi tera naam bata ke rah gaaein

तारों की आँख भी भर आई मेरी सदा-ए-दर्द पर
उन की निगाहें भी तिरा नाम बता के रह गईं

Even the eyes of the stars were dampened
when they heard my shrieks of pain.
They shouted your name and rested.

◆

yaad kuchh aaein is tarah bhuli hui kahaaniyaan
khoye hue dilon mein aaj dard utha ke rah gaaein

याद कुछ आईं इस तरह भूली हुई कहानियाँ
खोए हुए दिलों में आज दर्द उठा के रह गईं

I reminisced about
the long-forgotten tales today,
and even the stone-hearted
were left in agony.

◆

saaz-e nishaat-e zindagi aaj larz larz utha
kis ki nigaahein i'shq ka dard suna ke rah gaaein

साज़-ए नशात-ए ज़िंदगी आज लरज़ लरज़ उठा
किस की निगाहें इश्क़ का दर्द सुना के रह गईं

The music of the ecstasy of life
quivered strangely today.
Who was that person
whose eyes voiced over
the agony and suffering of love?

◆

tum nahien aaye aur raat rah gaaii raah dekhti
taaron ki mehfilien bhi aaj aankhein bichha ke rah gaaein

तुम नहीं आए और रात रह गई राह देखती
तारों की महफ़िलें भी आज आँखें बिछा के रह गईं

You didn't come.
The night kept waiting.
Even the stars had spread out
the carpet of their eyes
to welcome you.

◆

phir hain vahi udaasiyaan phir vahi suuni kaayenaat
ahl-e tarab ki mahfilien rang jama ke rah gaaein

फिर हैं वही उदासियाँ फिर वही सूनी काएनात
अहल-ए तरब की महफ़िलें रंग जमा के रह गईं

Once again, gaping sadness.
Once again, the bleak macrocosm.
Even the gathering of the
cheerful ones fell short.

◆

kaun sukuun de saka gham-zadgaan-e i'shq ko
bhiigti raatein bhi 'firaq' aag laga ke rah gaaein

कौन सुकून दे सका ग़म-ज़दगान-ए इश्क़ को
भीगती रातें भी 'फ़िराक़' आग लगा के रह गईं

Who could provide comfort to those
wounded by the sorrows of love?
Firaq, even the soaking nights ended up causing
blazing infernos.

Night, Sleep and a Story

raat bhi niind bhi kahaani bhi

Firaq's ghazal showcases his poetic ability to convey profound truths about life. With mastery over both long and short *behar* formats, Firaq goes straight into the depths of the human heart, exploring the enigmatic threads of love, life, and transitory beauty. He captures the enchanting vigor of youth, the heart's secrets and burdens, and the tempestuous nature of life that engulfs the soul in fiery tempests while also providing moments of soothing respite. Firaq's words paint a picture of unfulfilled yearnings, the combination of happiness and triumph, and the bittersweet essence of life—a delicate balance between the beloved's presence and the ache of separation. Through his masterful use of language and imagery, Firaq invites readers to explore the depths of life, leaving an indelible mark on the souls of all who walk into his poetic landscape.

raat bhi niind bhi kahaani bhi
haae kya chiiz hai javaani bhi

रात भी नींद भी कहानी भी
हाए क्या चीज़ है जवानी भी

Night, sleep and a story.
How wonderful is the
the spring of life.

◆

dil ko apne bhi gham the duniya mein
kuchh balaayein thiin aasmaani bhi

दिल को अपने भी ग़म थे दुनिया में
कुछ बलाएँ थीं आसमानी भी

The heart had maladies of its own.
But some of its afflictions
were legacies of the unknown.

◆

dil ko sho'lon se karti hai sairaab
zindagi aag bhi hai paani bhi

दिल को शो'लों से करती है सैराब
ज़िंदगी आग भी है पानी भी

It saturates the heart
with firestorms.
Life is fire, and life is water.

◆

i'shq-e naakaam ki hai parchhaaii
shaadmaani bhi kaamraani bhi

इ'श्क़-ए नाकाम की है परछाईं
शादमानी भी कामरानी भी

A shadow of love's failure,
both happiness and success.

◆

khalq kya kya mujhe nahien kahti
kuchh sunuun main teri zabaani bhi

ख़ल्क़ क्या क्या मुझे नहीं कहती
कुछ सुनूँ मैं तिरी ज़बानी भी

People say a lot about me.
I want to hear it from you,
in your own words.

◆

apni ma'suumiyat ke parde mein
ho gaaii voh nazar siyaani bhi

अपनी मासूमियत के पर्दे में
हो गई वो नज़र सियानी भी

Under the pretense
of being unsuspecting,
her eyes took on
the appearance of discernment.

◆

din ko suuraj-mukhi hai vo nau-gul
raat ko hai vo raat raani bhi

दिन को सूरज-मुखी है वो नौ-गुल
रात को है वो रात-रानी भी

By day she is the sunflower,
by the hours of darkness
she is the night-blooming jasmine.

◆

dil-e badnaam tere baare mein
log kahte hain ik kahaani bhi

दिल-ए बद-नाम तेरे बारे में
लोग कहते हैं इक कहानी भी

O my notorious heart,
people tell a story
about you.

◆

paas rahna kisi ka raat ki raat
mahmaani bhi mezbaani bhi

पास रहना किसी का रात की रात
मेहमानी भी मेज़बानी भी

When she stays for the night,
it is like welcoming a guest
and being entertained as a guest
at the same time.

◆

zindagi a'in diid-e yaar 'firaq'
zindagi hijr ki kahaani bhi

ज़िंदगी ऐ'न दीद-ए यार 'फ़िराक़'
ज़िंदगी हिज्र की कहानी भी

Firaq, life is both
a soothing sight of the beloved
and an agonizing tale of separation.

Listening to Firaq's Story

kabhi jab teri yaad aa jaaye hai

Firaq discusses the paradoxical nature of love, where the memory of the beloved surges forth like a tidal wave, engulfing hearts and casting a veil of melancholy. He finds himself suspended between life and death, unable to surrender to either in the throes of this all-consuming love. The agonies that kept him restless now provide a reprieve, lulling him into a slumber. The ghazal, a vessel of bittersweet sorrow, beckons to the brave who dare to immerse themselves in its intoxicating essence and emerge transformed. As his beloved's memory threatens to desert him, Firaq questions the stability of his existence, wondering if her fading presence is the cause or if the very foundation of his being is crumbling. His tale, woven with love's triumphs and tribulations, begs to be shared, yet he ponders who possesses the fortitude to truly comprehend the depths of his experience. Through this profound ghazal, Firaq invites readers on a journey through the landscape of love, illuminating the universal truths within the human heart and reminding us of love's power to elevate and shatter the soul.

kabhi jab teri yaad aa jaaye hai
dilon par ghata ban ke chha jaaye hai

कभी जब तेरी याद आ जाय है
दिलों पर घटा बन के छ जाय है

When your memory hits
my imagination,
a mass of cloudiness
shrouds many hearts.

◆

mohabbat mein ae maut ae zindagi
mra jaaye hai ya jiya jaaye hai

मोहब्बत में ऐ मौत ऐ ज़िन्दगी
मरा जाय है या जिया जाय है

O Death, O Life,
while I'm in love,
I can't die or live.

◆

jo be-khwaab rakkhe hai ta-zindagi
vohi gham kisi din sula jaaye hai

जो बे-ख्वाब रक्खे है ता-ज़िन्दगी
वही ग़म किसी दिन सुला जाय है

Something
that keeps you dreamless
each moment,
those agonies
one day put you to sleep.

◆

ghazal meri khenche hai gham ki sharaab
piye hai vo jis se piya jaaye hai

ग़ज़ल मेरी खींचे है ग़म की शराब
पिए है वो जिस से पिया जाय है

My ghazal extracts
a wine of sadness.
Only the enduring ones can relish it.

◆

mujhe chhor kar jaaye hai teri yaad
k jiine ka ik aasra jaaye hai

मुझे छोड़ कर जाय है तेरी याद
कि जीने का इक आसरा जाय है

Did you exit
my imagination,
or the support
that I need for living
is quitting me?

◆

sunaaein tumhein daastaan-e 'firaq'
magar kab kisi se suna jaaye hai

सुनाएं तुम्हें दास्तान-ए 'फ़िराक़'
मगर कब किसी से सुना जाय है

Should I recite Firaq's story?
But who exactly could bear
listen to it?

Embracing the Unknown

yaqiin laayein to kya laayein
jo shak laayein to kya laayein

Firaq explores the paradoxical nature of love, presenting it as a challenging journey marked by contradictions and complexities. Drawing from his own experience, he asserts that finding joy in love's depths is neither insurmountable nor effortless, requiring unwavering dedication, a willingness to embrace the unknown, and the courage to navigate the heart's turbulent waters. Yet, this transformative journey reshapes our understanding of ourselves and our world. Firaq emphasizes the power of love not only as a personal force but also as a societal one, capable of igniting revolutions and redefining the boundaries of what is possible. In a world where pain and suffering are inescapable, Firaq acknowledges the existence of countless healers claiming to possess the ultimate remedy for the aching soul. However, he reminds us that this complex world cannot provide a panacea for every wound inflicted upon the human spirit. Through his words, Firaq invites us to confront the intricacies of love and the human condition, serving as a beacon that illuminates the path to self-discovery. He encourages us to embrace the challenges, find solace in love's transformative power, and recognize that, while pain may be inevitable, it is through the crucible of suffering that we emerge stronger, wiser, and more alive than ever.

yaqiin laayein to kya laayein jo shak laayein to kya laayein
k baaton mein teri sach jhuut ka imkaan nahien hota

यक़ीं लाएँ तो क्या लाएँ जो शक लाएँ तो क्या लाएँ
कि बातों में तिरी सच झूट का इम्काँ नहीं होता

To believe or to disbelieve?
Your words are bereft
of hints of truth or deception.

◆

hamaara tajarba ye hai k khush hona mohabbat mein
kabhi mushkil nahien hota kabhi aasaan nahien hota

हमारा तजरबा ये है कि ख़ुश होना मोहब्बत में
कभी मुश्किल नहीं होता कभी आसाँ नहीं होता

It's my experience
that happiness in love
is never difficult
and never easy.

◆

nigaah-e ahl-e dil se inqilaab aaye hain duniya mein
yaqiin rakh i'shq itna be-sar o saamaan nahien hota

निगाह-ए अहल-ए दिल से इंक़लाब आए हैं दुनिया में
यक़ीं रख इ'श्क़ इतना बे-सर ओ सामाँ नहीं होता

The insight of the believers of love
sparked many revolutions.
Have faith, love is not
needy and impoverished.

◆

'Firaq' ik ik se barh kar chaara-saaz-e dard hain lekin
ye duniya hai yahaan har dard ka darmaan nahien hota

'फ़िराक़' इक इक से बढ़ कर चारा-साज़-ए दर्द हैं लेकिन
ये दुनिया है यहाँ हर दर्द का दरमाँ नहीं होता

Firaq, there are sympathizers
each one better than the other.
But in this world
where there is no cure
for every kind of agony.

The Night Is Too Depressing

ghazal ke saaz uthaao bari udaas hai raat

Firaq reveals a deep spiritual affinity with the poet Mir Taqi Mir (1723–1810), urging readers to seek comfort in poetry and music during the depths of a melancholy night (*nava-e 'mir' sanaao bari udaas hai raat*). He implores us to let the strains of Mir's timeless melodies pierce through the veil of despair, while the breeze carrying whispers from idols' abodes beckoned to find its way to the poet's dwelling. Firaq yearns for a confidant to share his anguish, turning to the shadows of his beloved's raven tresses for comfort in her absence. The night becomes a repository for the poet's unspoken grief as friends gather to contemplate the distant promise of dawn, yet Firaq reminds them that the night's despair is far from over. The clouds of sadness loom overhead, casting innumerable shades of darkness upon the world below. Through this ghazal, Firaq invites readers to immerse themselves in despair and confront the night's melancholy head-on, testifying to the power of poetry and music to provide solace amidst overwhelming sorrow. He encourages us to find meaning and purpose in feeling, embracing the full spectrum of human experience and understanding that we truly live in our highs and lows.

ghazal ke saaz uthaao bari udaas hai raat
nava-e 'mir' sanaao bari udaas hai raat

ग़ज़ल के साज़ उठाओ बड़ी उदास है रात
नवा-ए मीर सुनाओ बड़ी उदास है रात

Pick up the ghazal's instruments
because the night
is too distressing.
Tune in one of Mir's melodies,
for the night
is too despairing.

◆

jo ho sake to idhar ki bhi raah bhuul paro
sanam-kade ki havaao bari udaas hai raat

जो हो सके तो इधर की भी राह भूल पड़ो
सनम-कदे की हवाओ बड़ी उदास है रात

O, the breeze that comes
from the idol-houses,
don't forget to come my way,
if possible,

for the night
is too despairing.

◆

kahein n tum se to phir aur ja ke kis se kahein
siyaah zulf ke saayo bari udaas hai raat

कहें न तुम से तो फिर और जा के किस से कहें
सियाह ज़ुल्फ़ के सायो बड़ी उदास है रात

O, the shadows of the black tresses,
with whom should I share it
but with you,
for the night
is too despairing.

◆

abhi to zikr-e sahar dosto hai duur ki baat
abhi to dekhte jaao bari udaas hai raat

अभी तो ज़िक्र-ए सहर दोस्तो है दूर की बात
अभी तो देखते जाओ बड़ी उदास है रात

Friends, we haven't reached
the point where we should be talking
about the coming dawn.
Just wait and watch,
for the night
is too despairing.

◆

koi shumaar bhi rakhti hai zulmaton ki tahein
bataao gham ki ghataao bari udaas hai raat

कोई शुमार भी रखती हैं ज़ुल्मतों की तहें
बताओ ग़म की घटाओ बड़ी उदास है रात

O, the layers of the clouds of sadness,
do you keep a count?
Say it , for the night
is too despairing.

What Eyes Communicate

aankhon mein jo baat ho gaaii hai

Firaq explores the deep connection between the beloved's gaze and the unveiling of life's mysteries. He invites readers into the depths of human life, where the heart's final breath plunges the world into an all-encompassing darkness. Paradoxically, the release from grief brings a new form of anguish as Firaq questions the nature of his liberation and the silence of his heart. The beloved's gaze transforms the mundane into a vivid portrayal of life, imbuing every object with purpose and meaning. Firaq finds himself lost in the darkness of his beloved's tresses, yearning for a dawn that seems forever obscured. Death becomes the fabric of Firaq's existence, offering a strange comfort and unity with the inevitable cycle of life. The beloved's presence holds sway over time, her arrival heralding the descent of darkness. Firaq marvels at the metamorphosis of her gaze, finding it a reflection of the passion that consumes his heart. In the final verse, he contemplates his beloved's essence, recognizing that to know her is to understand the nature of existence. Through this ghazal, Firaq invites readers to explore love, loss, and the human condition, testifying to the transformative power of the gaze and the eternal search for meaning in a world shrouded in darkness.

aankhon mein jo baat ho gaaii hai
ik sharhe hayaat ho gaaii hai

आँखों में जो बात हो गई है
इक शरह-ए हयात हो गई है

What eyes communicate,
they reveal a secret of life.

◆

jab dil ki vafaat ho gaaii hai
har chiiz ki raat ho gaaii hai

जब दिल की वफ़ात हो गई है
हर चीज़ की रात हो गई है

When my heart died,
everything turned into
a night.

◆

gham se chhut kar ye gham hai mujh ko
kyon gham se najaat ho gaaii hai

ग़म से छुट कर ये ग़म है मुझ को
क्यूँ ग़म से नजात हो गई है

A release from sorrow
caused deep remorse.
Why did I liberate myself
from grief?

◆

muddat se khabar mili n dil ki
shaayad koi baat ho gaaii hai

मुद्दत से ख़बर मिली न दिल की
शायद कोई बात हो गई है

I haven't heard from my heart
in quite a while
Perhaps some sad thing
has happened to it!

◆

jis shaye pe nazar pari hai teri
tasviir-e hayaat ho gaaii hai

जिस शय पे नज़र पड़ी है तेरी
तस्वीर-ए हयात हो गई है

Any object
that attracted your gaze
became a portrayal of life.

◆

ab ho mujhe dekhiye kahaan subaah
un zulfon mein raat ho gaaii hai

अब हो मुझे देखिए कहाँ सुब्ह
उन ज़ुल्फ़ों में रात हो गई है

I don't know what I should do
to regain my morning.
The night has made an appearance
in her tresses.

◆

jo chiiz bhi mujh ko haath aaii
teri saugaat ho gaaii hai

जो चीज़ भी मुझ को हाथ आई
तेरी सौग़ात हो गई है

Anything
I laid my hands on,
became an offering
from you.

◆

kya jaaniye maut pehle kya thi
ab meri hayaat ho gaaii hai

क्या जानिए मौत पहले क्या थी
अब मेरी हयात हो गई है

I can't say what death
was like before.
But now it is my life.

◆

us chashm-e siyaah ki yaad yaksar
shaam-e zulmaat ho gaaii hai

उस चश्म-ए-सियह की याद यकसर
शाम-ए-ज़ुल्मात हो गई है

When I remember
her deep black eyes,
the evening reveals
its streaks of darkness.

◆

is daur mein zindagi basar ki
biimaar ki raat ho gaaii hai

इस दौर में ज़िंदगी बसर की
बीमार की रात हो गई है

Life in this era
is no different
from the dreadful night
of an ailing person.

•

vo chaahein to vaqt bhi badal jaaye
jab aaye hain raat ho gaaii hai

वो चाहें तो वक़्त भी बदल जाए
जब आए हैं रात हो गई है

She can alter the cycle of time
Lo, as she arrived
it is dark all over.

•

pehle vo nigaah ik kiran thi
ab barq-sifaat ho gaaii hai

पहले वो निगाह इक किरन थी
अब बर्क़-सिफ़ात हो गई है

Her gaze
used to be a streak of light.
Now it is lightning—
bright and flashy.

•

ek ek sifat 'Firaq' us ki
dekha hai to zaat ho gaaii hai

एक एक सिफ़त 'फ़िराक़' उस की
देखा है तो ज़ात हो गई है

Every facet of her personality, Firaq,
when I look carefully,
is a hallmark of her identity.

The Caravan of Love Is Moving

aaj bhi qaafila-e i'shq ravaan hai ke jo tha

Firaq explores the timeless essence of love, depicting it as the most fundamental and enduring force in the universe. Through imagery and masterful repetition of *ke jo tha* (as before), the poet invites readers to immerse themselves in the unchanging nature of love, which weaves through the fabric of existence, untouched by external forces. The caravan of love traverses the vast desert of time, each milestone a testament to its enduring legacy. The poet engages the senses with rich metaphors, such as the wisps of candle smoke and the apocalyptic ache of separation, serving as windows into the depths of human emotion. The ghazal captures the bittersweet symphony of love in its myriad forms, from the piercing ache of longing to the tender embrace of cherished memories. Although the ghazal's cultural nuances may appear daunting to some, its universal themes of love and longing transcend linguistic barriers, speaking directly to the heart. Firaq's mastery of the form shines through in every stanza, weaving a narrative that resonates with the essence of the human experience.

aaj bhi qaafila-e i'shq ravaan hai ke jo tha
vohi miil aur vohi sang-e nishaan ke jo tha

आज भी क़ाफ़िला-ए इश्क़ रवाँ है कि जो था
वही मील और वही संग-ए निशाँ है कि जो था

The caravan of love continues to move
just like it did before.
It is the same milestone and
the same mark.

◆

phir tera gham vohi rusva-e jahaan hai ke jo tha
phir fasaana ba-hadiis-e digraan hai ke jo tha

फिर तिरा ग़म वही रुस्वा-ए जहाँ है कि जो था
फिर फ़साना ब-हदीस-ए दिगराँ है कि जो था

The sadness that you gave me
is disgracefully well-known in the world
and it is the same story everyone recites.

◆

manzlein gard ki maanind uri jaati hain
vohi andaaz-e jahaan-e guzraan hai ke jo tha

मंज़िलें गर्द के मानिंद उड़ी जाती हैं
वही अंदाज़-ए जहान-ए गुज़राँ है कि जो था

Signs of disembarkation
vanish like dust.
Did the same thing
happen to the people
who lived before?

◆

zulmat o nuur mein kuchh bhi n mohabbat ko mila
aaj tak ek dhundhalke ka samaan hai ke jo tha

ज़ुल्मत ओ नूर में कुछ भी न मोहब्बत को मिला
आज तक एक धुँदलके का समाँ है कि जो था

Love did not gain anything
either in darkness or light.
It is always twilight
just like it used to be.

◆

yuun to is daur mein be-kaif si hai bazm-e hayaat
ek hungaama sar-e ritl-e giraan hai ke jo tha

यूँ तो इस दौर में बे-कैफ़ सी है बज़्म-ए हयात
एक हंगामा सर-ए रित्ल-ए गिराँ है कि जो था

Although the gathering of life
lacks all joy,
there is a tumult in the glass of wine
as before.

◆

laakh kar jaur o sitam laakh kar ehsaan o karam
tujh pe ai dost vohi vahm o gumaan hai ke jo tha

लाख कर जौर ओ सितम लाख कर एहसान ओ करम
तुझ पे ऐ दोस्त वही वहम ओ गुमाँ है कि जो था

Inflict on me umpteen atrocities
or show me kindness.
O friend, the misgivings and
leeriness persist as before.

◆

i'shq afsurda nahien aaj bhi afsurda bahut
vohi kam kam asr-e soz-e nihaan ke jo tha

इश्क़ अफ़्सुर्दा नहीं आज भी अफ़्सुर्दा बहुत
वही कम कम असर-ए सोज़-ए निहाँ है कि जो था

Love is not sad,
though it is filled with anguish.
There is a bit of heart-burning
and it seethes precisely as before.

◆

phir teri chasm-e sukhan-sanj ne chheri koi baat
vohi jaadu hai vohi husn-e biyaan hai ke jo tha

फिर तिरी चश्म-ए सुख़न-संज ने छेड़ी कोई बात
वही जादू है वही हुस्न-ए बयाँ है कि जो था

Once again,
your expressive eyes gesticulated
something new.
It is the same magic
as before.

◆

raat bhar husn par aaye bhi gaaye sau sau rang
shaam se i'shq abhi tak nigraan ke jo tha

रात भर हुस्न पर आए भी गए सौ सौ रंग
शाम से इश्क़ अभी तक निगराँ है कि जो था

Beauty in hundreds of colours
radiated the whole night
under the guardianship of love,
just like it did before.

◆

aankh jhapki ke idhar khatm hua roz-e visaal
phir bhi is din pe qayaamat ka gumaan hai ke jo tha

आँख झपकी कि इधर ख़त्म हुआ रोज़-ए विसाल
फिर भी इस दिन पे क़यामत का गुमाँ है कि जो था

I blinked,
and the meeting ended,
but it felt like an apocalypse.

◆

qurb hi kam hai n duuri hi zayaada lekin
aaj voh rabt ka ehsaas kahaan hai ke jo tha

क़ुर्ब ही कम है न दूरी ही ज़ियादा लेकिन
आज वो रब्त का एहसास कहाँ है कि जो था

We are neither too close
nor too far,
but it doesn't feel
like a relationship
as it did before.

◆

tiira bakhti nahien jaati dil-e sozaan ki 'firaq'
sham'a ke sar pe vohi aaj dhuaan hai ke jo tha

तीरा-बख़्ती नहीं जाती दिल-ए सोज़ाँ की 'फ़िराक़'
शम्अ के सर पे वही आज धुआँ है कि जो था

The distress of my burning heart
is not lessened.
The same smoke
hovers over the candle
as before.

Love Kills before the Cure

mujh ko maara hai har ik dard o dava se pehle

Love possesses both life-giving qualities and the power to proclaim death for the lover, as exemplified in the stories of great lovers like Majnuun and Farhad. The central theme of this ghazal revolves around the notion that love itself can cause pain and suffering, even before any wrongdoing or heartbreak occurs. The poet suggests that the mere act of falling in love is enough to inflict suffering, as the intensity of the emotion consumes the lover entirely. Throughout the ghazal, imagery and metaphors convey the all-consuming nature of love. Visuals in the second couplet portray love as an uncontrollable force capable of causing physical pain and suffering (*hont julte hain mohabbat mein dua se pehle*). In contrast, the metaphor in the fourth couplet suggests that love's intensity can expose even the most private aspects of the lover's life. The poet also touches upon the idea that union with the beloved, though sought as a cure, is ultimately like a mirage—something seen in the distance that proves to be different from what was desired.

mujh ko maara hai har ik dard o dava se pehle
di saza i'shq ne har jurm o khata se pehle

मुझ को मारा है हर इक दर्द ओ दवा से पहले
दी सज़ा इ'श्क़ ने हर जुर्म ओ ख़ता से पहले

I was killed before
any cure for my pain.
Love punished me
before I was guilty
of any crime or
indiscretion.

◆

aatish-e i'shq bharakti hai hava se pehle
hont julte hain mohabbat mein dua se pehle

आतिश-ए इ'श्क़ भड़कती है हवा से पहले
होंट जुलते हैं मोहब्बत में दुआ से पहले

The flames of love rise
before the breeze comes in.
Lips burn in love
before prayer.

◆

i'shq-e bebaak ko daa've the bahut khalvat mein
kho diya saara bharam sharm o haya se pehle

इ'श्क़-ए बेबाक को दा'वे थे बहुत ख़ल्वत में
खो दिया सारा भरम शर्म ओ हया से पहले

The fearless love
made many claims while in solitude.
I lost my reputation before I overcame
my shyness.

◆

fitne barpa hue har ghuncha-e sar basta se
khul gaya raaz-e chaman chaak-e qaba se pehle

फ़ित्ने बरपा हुए हर ग़ुंचा-ए सर-बस्ता से
खुल गया राज़-ए चमन चाक-ए क़बा से पहले

There was mutiny in
every bud that was closed.
The garden's secret was revealed
before the garb was torn.

◆

khud-ba-khud chaak hue pairahan-e laala o gul
chal gaaii kaun hava baad-e saba se pehle

ख़ुद-बख़ुद चाक हुए पैरहन-ए लाला ओ गुल
चल गई कौन हवा बाद-ए सबा से पहले

The garbs of tulips and roses were
torn apart on their own.
What kind of breeze started before
the morning breeze?

◆

maut ke naam se darte the ham ae shauq-e hayaat
tu ne to maar hi daala tha qaza se pehle

मौत के नाम से डरते थे हम ऐ शौक़-ए हयात
तू ने तो मार ही डाला था क़ज़ा से पहले

I was afraid of death's name,
O, my love life!
But you almost killed me
before death arrived.

◆

be-takuluff bhi tera husn-e khud-aara tha kabhi
ik ada aur bhi thi husn-e ada se pehle

बे-तकल्लुफ़ भी तिरा हुस्न-ए-ख़ुद-आरा था कभी
इक अदा और भी थी हुस्न-ए-अदा से पहले

Your self-adorning beauty
was once informal
and unceremonious.
There was a gesture before
the beauty's graceful expression.

◆

ham unhein pa ke 'firaq' aur bhi kuchh khoye gaye
ye takaluff to n the ahd-e vafa se pehle

हम उन्हें पा के 'फ़िराक़' और भी कुछ खोए गए
ये तकल्लुफ़ तो न थे अहद-ए वफ़ा से पहले

Firaq, I became more distracted
after I made her mine.
These formalities were absent
before the promise of constancy.

Love, Agony and Punishment

apne gham ka mujhe kahaan gham hai

Firaq goes into the depths of love, exploring the complexities of life through a fabric of religious and mythological allusions. Each couplet peels back layers of raw emotion, philosophical quandaries, and timeless truths, drawing readers into the lover's world of selfless devotion and the agony of separation. He skillfully weaves references to Adam's original sin and the concept of a world of love within the larger world, highlighting love's ancient roots and power to elevate and destroy (*i'shq karna gunah-e aadam hai).* The poet confronts life's harsh realities, including the transient nature of existence and the inherent sadness that permeates our days, while also celebrating moments of breathtaking beauty through imagery that engages the senses. As the ghazal unfolds, Firaq's voice serves as a guiding light, testifying to the enduring power of art to outlast our mortal selves. The ghazal becomes a map of the human heart, inviting readers to walk alongside the poet and lose themselves in the winding paths of love and life. Through this journey, Firaq reminds us of our shared joys, sorrows, hopes, and fears, emphasizing the profound connection that binds us in the grand apparel of existence.

apne gham ka mujhe kahaan gham hai
ae k teri khushi muqaddam hai

अपने ग़म का मुझे कहाँ ग़म है
ऐ कि तेरी ख़ुशी मुक़द्दम है

My agony is not the cause
of my anguish.
Above everything,
your contentment
is important to me.

◆

us ke shaitaan ko kahaan taufiiq
i'shq karna gunah-e aadam hai

उस के शैतान को कहाँ तौफ़ीक़
इ'श्क़ करना गुनाह-ए आदम है

Satan doesn't get it.
Falling in love was
Adam's original sin.

◆

is mein thahraao ya sakuun kahaan
zindagi inqilaab-e paiham hai

इस में ठहराव या सुकून कहाँ
ज़िंदगी इंक़लाब-ए पैहम है

No steadiness, no tranquility.
An unending process
of change and adaptation.
That's what life is.

◆

rahti duniya mein i'shq ki duniya
naye unvaan se munazzam hai

रहती दुनिया में इ'श्क़ की दुनिया
नए उन्वान से मुनज़्ज़म है

There is a world of love
within the world
and it is put in order
under a new placard.

◆

uthne vaali hai bazm maazi ki
raushni kam hai zindagi kam hai

उठने वाली है बज़्म माज़ी की
रौशनी कम है ज़िंदगी कम है

The old order
is going to change
and its light is fading.
Its life is diminishing.

◆

ye bhi nazm-e hayaat hai koi
zindagi zindagi ka maatam hai

ये भी नज़्म-ए हयात है कोई
ज़िंदगी ज़िंदगी का मातम है

It's sad to look at life
the way it is.
Life is grieving for life.

◆

ik mua'mma hai zindagi ae dost
ye bhi teri adaa-e mubham hai

इक मुअ'म्मा है ज़िंदगी ऐ दोस्त
ये भी तेरी अदा-ए मुबहम है

Life is a puzzle, my friend.
Or is this an expression
of your perplexing charm?

◆

ae mohabbat tu ik azaab sahi
zindagi be-tere jahannum hai

ऐ मोहब्बत तू इक अज़ाब सही
ज़िंदगी बे तिरे जहन्नम है

O love, you are an agony and torment.
But without you, life is hell.

◆

phirne ko hai rasiili niim-nigaah
aahu-e naaz maa'il-e ram hai

फिरने को है रसीली नीम-निगाह
आहू-ए नाज़ मा'इल-ए रम है

Your moist and luscious eyes,
half-open, always seeking.
It is like a deer that is coaxing,
and it is likely to go wild.

◆

ruup ke jot zer-e pairaahan
gulistaan par rida-e shabnam hai

रूप के जोत ज़ेर-ए पैराहन
गुल्सिताँ पर रिदा-ए शबनम है

Beauty hidden
under your apparel
is like a veil of dewdrops
in a garden.

◆

mere sine se lag ke so jaao
palkein bhaari hain raat bhi kam hai

मेरे सीने से लग के सो जाओ
पलकें भारी हैं रात भी कम है

Get close to me and go to sleep.
Your eyelids are heavy,
and there is not much of a night
left to go through.

◆

narm o doshiiza kis qadar hai nigaah
har nazar daastaan-e mariyam hai

नर्म ओ दोशीज़ा किस क़द्र है निगाह
हर नज़र दास्तान-ए मरयम है

Your eyes,
how soft and how pure.
Each time you look,
it is like a tale of Mary.

◆

diye jaati hai lau sadaa-e 'Firaq'
haan vohi soz o saaz kam kam hai

दिए जाती है लौ सदा-ए 'फ़िराक़'
हाँ वही सोज़ ओ साज़ कम कम है

Firaq's reverberating voice
is still the source of light.
There is ongoing suffering and affliction,
though it is decreasing.

The Bud of Heart Had to Crackle

jahaan-e ghuncha-e dil ka faqat chatakna tha

Firaq takes readers on a journey through the depths of love, exploring the fragility and transience of life through powerful metaphors and colourful imagery. The poet describes the overwhelming power of a single glance, the human tendency to live consciously yet carelessly, and the cyclical nature of hope and despair. Amidst these darker musings, moments of breathtaking beauty emerge, such as the laughing buds in a garden and the beloved's awe-inspiring beauty, reminding us of the wonder that persists even in times of pain and confusion. Firaq grapples with profound questions about love, life, and death. He suggests that the pain and sadness experienced in love may hold the key to understanding life's deepest secrets, reflecting on love's all-consuming nature, and emphasizing the lover's unwavering devotion (*n koi vaa'da n koi yaqiin n koi ummiid / magar hamein to tera intizaar karna tha)*. The final couplet metaphorizes the restlessness and impatience caused by love, comparing the lover's agony of separation to the writhing of someone on their deathbed. Through masterful language and structure, Firaq enhances the emotional impact of his words, creating a haunting melody that echoes the ebb and flow of the human heart.

jahaan-e ghuncha-e dil ka faqat chatakna tha
usi ki buu-e pareshaan vujuud-e duniya tha

जहान-ए गुंचा-ए दिल का फ़क़त चटकना था
उसी की बू-ए परेशाँ वजूद-ए दुनिया था

The world of the bud of the heart
had to crackle.
The flowing fragrance of that bud
was the mark of existence
of this world.

◆

ye keh ke kal koi be-ikhtiyaar rota tha
vo ik nigaah sahi kyon kisi ko dekha tha

ये कह के कल कोई बे-इख़्तियार रोता था
वो इक निगाह सही क्यूँ किसी को देखा था

After saying this,
someone cried beyond control.
That was an eye.
But why did he cast a glance?

◆

har ik ke haath faqat ghaflatein thiin hosh-numa
k apne aap se be-gaana-vaar jiina tha

हर इक के हाथ फ़क़त ग़फ़लतें थीं होश-नुमा
कि अपने आप से बेगाना-वार जीना था

The carelessness of each
and everyone
was consciously observed.
One had to live life,

away from the self,
like an alien.

◆

yahi hua k fareb-e ummiid o yaas mite
vo pa gaye tere haathon hamein jo paana tha

यही हुआ कि फ़रेब-ए उमीद ओ यास मिटे
वो पा गए तिरे हाथों हमें जो पाना था

It happened.
The deceptions of hope
and despair disappeared.
We got from you
what we deserved.

◆

chaman mein ghuncha-e gul khil-khila ke murjhaae
yahi vo the jinhein hans hans ke jaan dena tha

चमन में ग़ुंचा-ए गुल खिलखिला के मुरझाए
यही वो थे जिन्हें हँस हँस के जान देना था

Buds of flowers in the garden laughed
heartily and then faded.
These were the ones that had to die
while smiling.

◆

jahaan tu jalva-numa tha larazti thi duniya
tere jamaal se kaisa jalaal paida tha

जहाँ तू जल्वा-नुमा था लरज़ती थी दुनिया
तिरे जमाल से कैसा जलाल पैदा था

Wherever you showed your charms,
the world looked at you
and quivered.
From your beauty
arose exceptional loftiness.

◆

hayaat o marg ke kuchh raaz khul gaye hon ge
fasaana-e shab-e gham varna dosto kya tha

हयात ओ मर्ग के कुछ राज़ खुल गए होंगे
फ़साना-ए शब-ए ग़म वर्ना दोस्तो क्या था

Some secrets of life and death
must have been revealed.
What was the worth otherwise,
friends,
of the evening of sadness?

◆

kuchh aisi baat n thi tera duur ho jaana
ye aur baat k rah rah ke dard uth-ta tha

कुछ ऐसी बात न थी तेरा दूर हो जाना
ये और बात कि रह रह के दर्द उठता था

That you moved away
was not a giant shock
and it is another matter
that pain persisted.

◆

lagaavatein vo tere husn-e be-niyaaz ki aah
main teri bazm se jab na-ummid utha tha

लगावटें वो तिरे हुस्न-ए बे-नियाज़ की आह
मैं तेरी बज़्म से जब ना-उमीद उट्ठा था

Alas!
My fondness for your uncaring love!
I realized it when I left your place
without any hope.

◆

tujhe ham ae dil-e dard-aashna kahaan dhuundhein
ham apne hosh mein kab the koi jab utha tha

तुझे हम ऐ दिल-ए दर्द-आश्ना कहाँ ढूँडें
हम अपने होश में कब थे कोई जब उट्ठा था

Where should I find you,
my pain-knowing heart?
I was not in my senses
when someone left me.

◆

ye iztiraab o skuun bhi thi ik fareb-e hayaat
k apne haal se be-gaana-vaar jiina tha

ये इज़तिराब ओ सुकूँ भी थी इक फ़रेब-ए हयात
कि अपने हाल से बेगाना-वार जीना था

Distress and tranquility were
allurements of life.
I had to live like an alien,
disconnected from my authentic self.

◆

ye koi yaad hai ye bhi hai koi mahviyat
tere khayal mein tujh ko bhi bhuul jaana tha

ये कोई याद है ये भी है कोई महि्वय्यत
तिरे ख़याल में तुझ को भी भूल जाना था

Is this a memory
or sheer fascination?
I had to forget you
while I was still thinking of you.

◆

visaal us se main chaahuun kahaan ye dil mera
ye ro raha huun k kyuun us ko main ne dekha tha

विसाल उस से मैं चाहूँ कहाँ ये दिल मेरा
ये रो रहा हूँ कि क्यूँ उस को मैं ने देखा था

To seek union with her—
where is the courage in my heart?
Crying, I ask:
Why did I see her in the first place?

◆

ummid yaas bani yaas phir ummid bani
us ik nazar mein fareb-e nigaah kitna tha

उमीद यास बनी यास फिर उमीद बनी
उस इक नज़र में फ़रेब-ए निगाह कितना था

Hope turned into despair,
and then sadness turned into hope.
In that eye, how much deception
was loaded in one glance?

◆

n koi vaa'da n koi yaqiin n koi ummiid
magar hamein to tera intizaar karna tha

न कोई वा'दा न कोई यक़ीं न कोई उमीद
मगर हमें तो तिरा इंतिज़ार करना था

There was no promise,
there was no assurance,
and there was no hope.
But I had to wait for you.

◆

kisi ke sabr ne be-sabr diya sab ko
'Firaq' niz'a mein karvat koi badalta tha

किसी के सब्र ने बे-सब्र दिया सब को
'फ़िराक़' नज़्अ' में करवट कोई बदलता था

Someone's patience
gave restlessness to all.
Moments before dying, Firaq,
someone lying on the bed
was changing his side.

A Journey through the Depths of the Human Heart

kho diya tum ko to ham puuchhte phirte hain yahi

Firaq explores the profound trials and tribulations of love, opening with a poignant expression of loss and bewilderment as the poet grapples with the pain of losing a beloved. The theme of the star-crossed lover reverberates throughout the ghazal as Firaq describes the wounds that bind lover and cherished, the coexistence of antipathy and affection, and the disillusionment that can accompany the pursuit of love and beauty. Firaq also boldly shifts his gaze to religion, critiquing the hypocrisy of those claiming spiritual authority and suggesting that hidden desires and sins often lurk beneath the veneer of piety. This adds depth and complexity to the ghazal, inviting readers to contemplate the nature of true spirituality. The poet's mastery shines through his breathtaking imagery, skillful use of metaphor and symbolism, and the ghazal structure, which mirrors the ebb and flow of the lover's emotions. A sense of total surrender permeates the ghazal, capturing the essence of the romantic ideal—a love that transcends the self and willingly endures pain for the beloved's sake. As the ghazal concludes, Firaq presents a haunting image of the lover as a canvas of wounds, finding bittersweet pleasure in the pain of separation.

kho diya tum ko to ham puuchhte phirte hain yahi
jis ki taqdiir bigar jaaye to vo kaya karta hai

खो दिया तुम को तो हम पूछते फिरते हैं यही
जिस की तक़दीर बिगड़ जाए वो करता क्या है

When I lost you,
I went around asking–
what is the fate
of a star-crossed person?

◆

tujh ko ho jaaein ge shaitaan ke darshan vaa'iz
daal kar munh ko garebaan mein kabhi dekha hai

तुझ को हो जाएँगे शैतान के दर्शन वाइ'ज़
डाल कर मुँह को गरेबाँ में कभी देखा है

Preacher, you will see
the devil face to face.
Did you ever put your face
under your garb and look?

◆

zeenat-e dosh tera naama-e aamaal n ho
teri dastaar se vaa'iz ye latakta kaya hai

ज़ीनत-ए दोश तिरा नामा-ए आमाल न हो
तेरी दस्तार से वाइ'ज़ ये लटकता क्या है

Maybe it is an adornment of your desires.
What is it, preacher, that is hanging
by the side of your high turban?

◆

dil ka ik kaam jo hota nahien ik muddat se
tum zara haath laga do to hua rakkha hai

दिल का इक काम जो होता नहीं इक मुद्दत से
तुम ज़रा हाथ लगा दो तो हुआ रक्खा है

The troubles of my heart
have stayed unattended for a long while.
If you touch me with your hand,
it will be done.

◆

nigaah-e shokh mein aur dil mein chotein hain kaya kaya
aaj tak ham n samajh paaye k jhagra kaya hai

निगह-ए शोख़ में और दिल में हैं चोटें क्या क्या
आज तक हम न समझ पाए कि झगड़ा क्या है

Between her bold eyes and my heart,
there is a bond of wounds.
I have failed until now to understand
the basis of this antipathy.

◆

i'shq se toba bhi hai husn se shikve bhi hazaar
kahiye to hazrat-e dil aap ka mansha kaya hai

इश्क़ से तौबा भी है हुस्न से शिकवे भी हज़ार
कहिए तो हज़रत-ए दिल आप का मंशा क्या है

I have given up on love.
Beauty, I have thousands of complaints against you.
My noble heart, you must speak up.
What would you prefer to do?

◆

haan abhi vaqt ka aaina dikhaaye kya kya
dekhte jaao zamaana abhi dekha kaya hai

हाँ अभी वक़्त का आईना दिखाए क्या क्या
देखते जाओ ज़माना अभी देखा क्या है

The time's mirror will show many things.
Keep looking.
You haven't seen much so far.

◆

n yagaane hain n begaane teri mahfil mein
n koi ghair yahaan hai n koi apna hai

न यगाने हैं न बेगाने तिरी महफ़िल में
न कोई ग़ैर यहाँ है न कोई अपना है

The unrivalled and the unknown—
they find a place in your assembly.
No one here is unnamed,
and no one here
whom I can call my own.

◆

un se barh-charh ke to ae dost hain yaadein in ki
naaz o andaaz o ada mein teri rakkha kya hai

उन से बढ़-चढ़ के तो ऐ दोस्त हैं यादें इन की
नाज़ ओ अंदाज़ ओ अदा में तिरी रक्खा क्या है

Her memories are far more precious.
There is no substance in style,
flair and flirtatious manners.

◆

aisi baaton se badalti hai kahien fitrat-e husn
jaan bhi de de agar koi to kaya hota hai

ऐसी बातों से बदलती है कहीं फ़ितरत-ए हुस्न
जान भी दे दे अगर कोई तो क्या होता है

These things don't change
the nature of beauty.
Even if you give away your life,
it doesn't matter.

◆

teri aankhon ko bhi inkaar teri zulf ko bhi
kis ne ye i'shq ko diivaana bana rakkha hai

तिरी आँखों को भी इंकार तिरी ज़ुल्फ़ को भी
किस ने ये इ'श्क़ को दीवाना बना रक्खा है

Your eyes and your tresses—
both are in denial.
What else has made the lover
as crazy as she is?

◆

dil bhi tera jaan teri aah teri ashk tere
jo hai ae dost vo tera hai hamaara kya hai

दिल तिरा जान तिरी आह तिरी अश्क तिरे
जो है ऐ दोस्त वो तेरा है हमारा क्या है

Heart, breath, sighs, and tears—
whatever exists, my friend, belongs to you.
I don't own anything.

◆

yahi gar aankh mein rah jaaye to hai chingaari
qatra-e ashk jo bah jaaye to ik darya hai

यही गर आँख में रह जाए तो है चिंगारी
क़तरा-ए अश्क जो बह जाए तो इक दरिया है

If it remains in your eye,
it's a spark.
If it flows as a teardrop,
it's a river.

◆

zulf-e shab-guun ke siva nargis-e jaadu ke siva
dil ko kuchh aur balaaon ne bhi aa ghera hai

ज़ुल्फ़-ए शब-गूँ के सिवा नर्गिस-ए जादू के सिवा
दिल को कुछ और बलाओं ने भी आ घेरा है

It wasn't only dark locks
and the narcissus-like magic of eyes,
my heart was surrounded
by other phantoms as well.

◆

zakhm hi zakhm huun main sub-h ki maanind 'Firaq'
raat bhar hijr ki lazzat se maza luuta hai

ज़ख़्म ही ज़ख़्म हूँ मैं सुब्ह की मानिंद 'फ़िराक़'
रात भर हिज्र की लज़्ज़त से मज़ा लूटा है

I'm nursing one wound after another
like the daybreak, Firaq.
How much did I enjoy the pleasure
of the night of separation!

The Heart of Love's Madness

kuchh ishaare the jinhein duniya samajh baithe the ham

Firaq explores the complexities and paradoxes of love, opening with an admission of misunderstanding that lays bare the poet's vulnerability and self-doubt. As the ghazal unfolds, the poet describes the madness of love, the surrender of the senses that comes with true devotion, and the all-consuming nature of passionate love. Love is portrayed not only as a source of joy and ecstasy but also as one of sorrow and misunderstanding. The poet reflects on gestures misinterpreted, kindnesses mistaken for anger, and the pain of separation that can feel like a shield against the world. The ghazal takes a darker turn when the message of death arrives amidst conversation, and the poet admits to mistaking his beloved's eyes for a source of life, when in fact they were harbingers of mortality—a stark reminder of the fragility of life and love. Yet, even in these moments of darkness, the poet recognizes the universal nature of love's pain, comparing his suffering to the legendary tales of Farhad and Majnun. As the ghazal concludes, the poet acknowledges that his perceptions of his beloved were mere illusions and that love is a complex dance of light and shadow. The refrain *samajh baithe the ham* is a powerful anchor, reminding readers of the central theme of misunderstanding and echoing in the mind long after the ghazal ends.

kuchh ishaare the jinhein duniya samajh baithe the ham
us nigaah-e aashnaa ko kya samajh baithe the ham

कुछ इशारे थे जिन्हें दुनिया समझ बैठे थे हम
उस निगाह-ए आश्ना को क्या समझ बैठे थे हम

There were signs
that I mistakenly understood
as the essence of this world.
Was it the gaze of my friend?
What I thought and what it meant.

◆

hosh ki taufiiq bhi kab ahl-e dil ko ho saki
i'shq mein apne ko diivaana samajh baithe the ham

होश की तौफ़ीक़ भी कब अहल-ए दिल को हो सकी
इश्क़ में अपने को दीवाना समझ बैठे थे हम

Those with the heart
never understood the significance
of being in control of their senses.
But once in love,
being crazy was the correct diagnosis.

◆

parda-e aazurdagi mein thi vo jaan-e iltifaat
jis ada ko ranjish-e beja samajh baithe the ham

पर्दा-ए आज़ुर्दगी में थी वो जान-ए इल्तिफ़ात
जिस अदा को रंजिश-ए बेजा समझ बैठे थे हम

In the veil of sorrow,
there was that kindness
and a gesture that I misread.
There was nothing
other than a misunderstanding.

◆

bhuul baithi vo nigaah-e naaz ahd-e dosti
us ko bhi apni tabii'ayat ka samajh baithe ham

भूल बैठी वो निगाह-ए नाज़ अहद-ए दोस्ती
उस को भी अपनी तबीअ'त का समझ बैठे थे हम

The gaze of love
that assured me of friendship,
I thought it was no different
from my disposition.

◆

saaf alag ham ko januun-e aa'shiqi ne kar diya
khud ko tere dard ka parda samajh baithe ham

साफ़ अलग हम को जुनून-ए आशिक़ी ने कर दिया
ख़ुद को तेरे दर्द का पर्दा समझ बैठे थे हम

The madness of love
separated me from others, and
I looked upon myself as fully shielded
by the pain of your love.

◆

baaton baaton mein payaam-e marg bhi aa hi gaya
un nigaahon ko hayaat-afza samajh baithe the ham

बातों बातों में पयाम-ए मर्ग भी आ ही गया
उन निगाहों को हयात-अफ़्ज़ा समझ बैठे थे हम

The message of death arrived
during conversation.
I thought her eyes were stimulants
for a healthier and happier life.

◆

ek duniya dard ki tasviir nikli i'shq ko
koh-kan aur qais ka qissa samajh baithe the ham

एक दुनिया दर्द की तस्वीर निकली इ'श्क़ को
कोह-कन और क़ैस का क़िस्सा समझ बैठे थे हम

The world of pain and suffering
came out as a portrait of love.
Why did I consider it
a tale of Farhad and Majnuun?

◆

rafta rafta i'shq maanuus-e jahaan hota chala
khud ko tere hijr mein tanha samajh baithe the ham

रफ़्ता रफ़्ता इ'श्क़ मानूस-ए जहाँ होता चला
ख़ुद को तेरे हिज्र में तन्हा समझ बैठे थे हम

Slowly and gradually,
my passionate love helped me
to know this world.
I thought I was the only one
caught in the misery of your love!

◆

husn ik husn hi samjhe nahien aur ae "Firaq'
mehrbaan na-mehrbaan kya kya samajh baithe the ham

हुस्न को इक हुस्न ही समझे नहीं और ऐ 'फ़िराक़'
मेहरबाँ ना-मेहरबाँ क्या क्या समझ बैठे थे हम

Beauty was not just beauty for Firaq.
She was kind, unkind,
and many more things.
All those were false impressions!

A Compact and Compressed Love

kami n ki tere vahshi ne khaak uraane mein

Firaq boldly declares the lover's wild and reckless behavior, recognizing that this madness is universal and woven into the fabric of the human experience. The love portrayed is intense and compressed, filled with deep pain that the poet bears witness to, reminding us of the vulnerability we all share in matters of the heart. Despite the pain, there is a glimmer of hope, a beacon suggesting that even the deepest wounds can heal and give way to new growth. Firaq explores the enduring qualities of true love, the essence that remains even when passion has withered. He questions the blurred lines between joy and pain, using strong imagery such as blooming flowers, bruises of the heart, and the veiled melody of the nightingale. The image of a burning candle is a striking metaphor for the self-destructive nature of intense love, with its shimmering signifying pleasure in dying (*bayaan-e sham'a hai haasil yahi hai jalne ka / fana ki kaifiatein dekh jhil-milaane mein).* Yet, amid this intensity, there is a sense of shared experience and connection, reminding us that we are not alone in our struggles with love. As the ghazal concludes, Firaq presents an image of the poet identifying himself as the rose, nightingale, and garden breeze in a jailhouse—a powerful dream of the freedom and beauty found in love, even amid confinement or hardship.

kami n ki tere vahshi ne khaak uraane mein
junuun ka naam uchhalta raha zamaane mein

कमी न की तिरे वहशी ने ख़ाक उड़ाने में
जुनूँ का नाम उछलता रहा ज़माने में

Your wild lover did his best
as he raised the dust.
Craziness thus earned a place for itself
in this world.

◆

'Firaq', daur gaaii ruuh si zamaane mein
kahaan ka dard bhara tha mere fasaane mein

'फ़िराक़' दौड़ गई रूह सी ज़माने में
कहाँ का दर्द भरा था मिरे फ़साने में

Firaq, something akin to the spirit
enveloped the whole world.
My story had a lot of pain—
very compact and compressed.

◆

junuun se bhuul hui dil pe chot khaane mein
'Firaq' der abhi thi bahaar aane mein

जुनूँ से भूल हुई दिल पे चोट खाने में
'फ़िराक़' देर अभी थी बहार आने में

My craziness was quick to hurt
my hapless heart.
Firaq, there was still time
for spring's arrival.

◆

vo koi rang hai ud n jaaye ae gul-e tar
vo koi buu hai jo rusva n ho zamaane mein

वो कोई रंग है जो उड़ न जाए ऐ गुल-ए तर
वो कोई बू है जो रुस्वा न हो ज़माने में

There is a colour,
O fresh flower,
that should not fade.
There is a fragrance
that should not lose face.

◆

ye gul khile hain ke chotein jigar ki ubhari hain
nihaan bahaar thi bulbul tere taraane mein

ये गुल खिले हैं कि चोटें जिगर की उभरी हैं
निहाँ बहार थी बुलबुल तिरे तराने में

Are these flowers blooming
or bruises of my heart
becoming visible?
Spring was veiled
in the nightingale's melody.

◆

bayaan-e sham'a hai haasil yahi hai jalne ka
fana ki kaifiatein dekh jhil-milaane mein

बयान-ए शम्अ है हासिल यही है जलने का
फ़ना की कैफ़ियतें देख झिलमिलाने में

A statement—that's what remained
after it burned.
The pleasure of dying was visible
in the shimmer of the candle.

◆

kisi ki haalat-e dil sun ke uth gaaii aankhein
ke jaan pad gaaii indag bhare fasaane mein

किसी की हालत-ए दिल सुन के उठ गईं आँखें
कि जान पड़ गई हसरत भरे फ़साने में

The condition of someone's heart
raised eyebrows.
Or did it bring a dynamic flourish
to a lonely tale?

◆

usi ki sharah hai ye uth-te dard ka aalam
jo daastaaan thi nihaan tere aankh uthaane mein

उसी की शरह है ये उठते दर्द का आलम
जो दास्ताँ थी निहाँ तेरे आँख उठाने में

This state of suffering
is an explication of the story
that was hidden behind
the lifting of her eyes.

◆

garz ke kaat diye indagi ke din ae dost
vo teri yaad mein hon ya tujhe bhulaane mein

ग़रज़ कि काट दिए ज़िंदगी के दिन ऐ दोस्त
वो तेरी याद में हों या तुझे भुलाने में

Merrily or otherwise,
I passed the days of my life, friend!
In thinking about you
or trying to forget you.

◆

hamiin hain gul hamiin bulbul hamiin hava-e chaman
'firaq' khwaab ye dekha hai qaid-khaane mein

हमीं हैं गुल हमीं बुलबुल हमीं हवा-ए-चमन
'फ़िराक़' ख़्वाब ये देखा है क़ैद-ख़ाने में

I'm the rose and I'm the nightingale,
I'm the breeze of the garden.
Firaq saw this dream in the jailhouse!

six

DHAIVATA (DHA)

Vedas have recognized, and contemporary science has validated, that every minute particle exists in a pair of opposite characters, constantly in communion with each other. They remain in balance, dominated by one or the other, depending upon their environment. Yoga and meditation train us to maintain balance for survival. I love nature, seek oneness with nature, and feel ecstatic by being with and in nature, not as an outside spectator but as an integral part of it, or, I may say, an actor in the contradictory behavior of nature in its vagaries and its pleasantries. Thus, like nature, I may appear contradictory. Still, I am as harmonious with my contradictions as nature's contradictory features, such as ice-cold and charring heat, dreadful droughts, and merciless floods. Even the virtues of God in different religions are given in conflicting terms. Read the Gita, read my essays, read my verses in Ruuh-e Kaaenaat.[12]

–Firaq

[12]Mansingh, Ajai, *Firaq Gorakhpuri: The Poet of Pain & Ecstasy*, Roli Books, 2015.

FIRAQ AND TUFAIL'S CORRESPONDENCE

Mohammad Tufail, editor of the highly regarded Lahore-based literary magazine *Naquush*, started correspondence with Firaq in the early nineteen-fifties. His objective was to get to know the poet better, or it was an attempt, in his own words, to put 'the leviathan inside the bottle.' When this process began, Firaq was unaware that Tufail was using these letters to obtain a publication. That is why Firaq's style of writing was very easygoing and unpretentious. The letters were published in 1962 under *Man Anam*[13], meaning 'I Am.' These letters offer a unique and uncensored glimpse into Firaq's persona, values, beliefs, and reflections on his work. Below are selected excerpts from these letters to share with the readers another opening into his thinking and presumably into his psyche:[14]

> During my childhood, I was different from my brothers and sisters. I was very emotional. I found within me a tremendous capacity to love and hate. Nature was my passion. When I looked at the natural scenery, I lost myself. I had friends and was so passionate about sports that it puzzled my parents. They made fun of me. When I was just two or three years old, I refused to be picked up by an ugly man or woman. I didn't want ugly people to enter our home. By the age of nine or ten, I had developed a sense of beauty, and I could not resist the company of those I considered handsome or beautiful.
>
> I have a special fascination with the night and the element of mystery that accompanies darkness. The

---

[13]Gorakhpuri, Firaq, *Man Anam*. Saqi Book Depot, Delhi, 1997.

[14]Translations by the author.

imagery of night gives my poetry a distinct flavor, and you will not find this emotional state in any other poet. Based on a portion of my work, some critics call me a poet of the midnight.

Being virtuous does not mean that you have given up on sex; it means that you can look at sexual relations through the prism of ecstasy, rapture, and aesthetics. When sensual thoughts merge with your personality and become a part of your character, and when your need for aesthetic living becomes greater than your sexual need, your sexuality is no longer longing for sex; it becomes a pursuit of passionate love (*i'shq*).

If a poet is obsessed with sensual love, they can create good romantic poetry. Still, the creation of high-level love poetry requires that the poet transcend the traditional boundaries of love and sex and adopt a broader concept of what binds people and what higher values unite them.

I have endeavoured to incorporate a profound element into my romantic poetry: unwavering faith in life and nature. I did not feel the need to bring my religious faith or my conception of God into this discussion. My verse is filled with pain and agony, tears and loss, failure and disappointment; yet, at the same time, I have retained my faith in the goodness of life and the wonders of the universe. Without supporting Sufi's viewpoint, I have tried to present what is good and what role truth plays in our lives. This is a fundamental aspect of my worldview.

I remember a poem by the English poet Keats in which he mentioned a parallel between a poet's work and a spider's work. As the spider weaves a net, with one thread at a time, the poet creates his web with one line of verse, and slowly and gradually, he establishes his citadel of love.

The concept of the world that the writers of the past presented in their writings is not relevant to us. But we do celebrate the achievements of Valmiki, Homer, Virgil, Kali Dasa, Firdausi, Hafiz, Tulsidas and Shakespeare. The past has two aspects: one that persists in some form and the other that has lost its relevance. The poet of today must embrace both these aspects in their living form. The consciousness of the past brings about a balance to our lives. We can ask what use is past. If we fail to understand history, we can't make sense of our present. We are not trying to turn our present into our past, but we must understand the connection between the two. If we were to lose the great literature of the past, we would face many obstacles in building what is important to us today.

When I look back at my work, I must retouch my ghazal couplets and ruba'is. I can hear the whispering of hundreds of ghazals in my subconscious mind. However, I don't understand what they are exactly saying. There is a lot of lyrical commotion. That's all.

We can't infuse life into our poetry by writing something new or astonishing. Because many brilliant minds are creating poetry, there is also no guarantee of its continuous existence. Contemporary poetry will sustain itself if it reflects our civilization and draws upon past literary treasures. We must renew our poetry with help from our world views and the literary heritage of humankind. Great literature is seldom literary. Great literature is the language of life, and the poet needs to do this work, which I have been doing. What is the real significance of language? It brings literature closer to life and its exploration in all its facets.

The origin of sorrow can often be linked to a significant life event. However, if it persists, it becomes necessary to thoroughly understand the profound meaning of life. Accepting suffering strengthened my faith in life and the universe, and it didn't weaken me in any way. Elements of sorrow and happiness are mixed up in our daily lives. When these two things come closer and merge, we feel unity and oneness with the whole. It strengthens our actions, creating thoughtfulness and balance. Veils of doubt are lifted.

I fell in love on 12 December 1914 and this affair lasted a few weeks before it ended unsuccessfully, but I suffered its impact for ten or twelve years. The second one lasted about two years, finishing without any bitterness. The third time it happened was in 1929, which went on for a year. This was followed by something terrible that made me cry a lot. What happens is that the break-up has severe consequences. Memories can last a long time, and my couplets hide these stories at their core.

I have been associated with the progressive writers' movement, but I can tell you what is wrong with it. Some of these shortcomings can be overcome if the people involved recognize that not every participant shares the same ideas. There are fundamental issues on which there is general agreement.

1. Literature is a powerful tool for raising public awareness, helping us escape the threat of a Third World War.
2. The movement can help to end slavery and colonialism wherever they exist.

3. We can rid our institutions of corruption, injustice, and inadequate administrative policies.

I want to comment on progressive poetry. As in other movements, whatever the progressives produce is of a lower quality. There are some essential artistic requirements that a poet must fulfill. However, some of our best progressive poets are ignorant about what constitutes good art. There are lousy uses of words, metaphors, and similes, but they are correct and ineffective ways of expressing thoughts. This is true even for the leaders of this movement. No progressive writer has scaled the heights of Ghalib, Mir, Iqbal, Milton, Wordsworth, Keats, Tennyson, etc. Some people have assumed the role of enforcers of rules, acting as de facto godfathers.

It is hard to find the proper meaning of the word 'dimension' in an Urdu dictionary. This shortcoming reflects our weakness; our imagistic and aesthetic poetry has been two-dimensional. There is no third dimension that Einstein talked about (the dimension of time-space curvature). In my Ruba'is collection, *Roop,* I attempted to add a third dimension to emphasize the body, particularly the female form. Additionally, Urdu poetry lacks a sense of colour. I have tried to rectify this shortcoming by paying attention to colour (darkness, light, and the general play of colours in any situation). My poetry's visual side, especially the imagistic aspects, is strong, but I'm nowhere near the best in classical literature. Imagery is not simple photography; it combines feelings, emotions, and aesthetic elements with brushwork. When we combine our emotions with aesthetics, we reach the pinnacle of poetry.

LITERATURE TRANSCENDS THE TWO-NATION THEORY

Our country is not the private property of Hindus or Muslims. It is the motherland of the first human beings. Even today, our breathing contains the signs of the early mornings of human civilization. Our consciousness is still troubled by the collective pain. Atheism and Faith stand here side by side, looking at each other. The ideas of Unity and Oneness bring tears to our eyes. Our collective consciousness has been enriched by the Buddha walking around on his two feet, preaching his enlightenment ideas, Krishna playing the flute, the sound of temple bells, and the call to prayer from the mosques. Life is a much bigger truth than our political differences. Literature transcends the two-nation theory.

Breaking Free from Heart's Prison

shaam-e gham kuchh us nigaah-e naaz ki baatein karo

Firaq takes readers on a unique journey where words hold the power to heal, and conversation becomes a balm for the wounded heart. Each couplet serves as a gentle nudge, encouraging the sharing of love's secrets and sorrows. The poet invites us to speak of the beloved's alluring eyes amid grief, recognizing that the memory of love can light the way in times of darkness. As the heart becomes intoxicated with longing, Firaq urges us to go deeper into its mysteries, even when faced with the silence of the beloved's grace and the shattering of the lover's heart. The metaphor of a broken and mute musical instrument captures the anguish of unfulfilled love. At the same time, the fragrance of the (*aaj us ki nargis-e ghammaaz ki baatein karo*). The poet also yearns for freedom from the heart's confines, using the image of light filtering through a cage's bars to evoke the sense of being trapped. Yet, even in this confinement, there is a desire to soar on love's wings. Firaq acknowledges the beloved's power to transform love, giving it new life with her presence.

shaam-e gham kuchh us nigaah-e naaz ki baatein karo
bekhudi barhti chali hai raaz ki baatein karo

शाम-ए ग़म कुछ उस निगाह-ए नाज़ की बातें करो
बे-ख़ुदी बढ़ती चली है राज़ की बातें करो

During this night of grief,
let's talk about the one
with alluring eyes.
Insobriety is increasing,
let's talk about the secrets of love.

◆

ye sakuut-e naaz ye dil ki ragon ka tuutna
khaamshi mein kuchh shikast-e saaz ki baatein karo

ये सुकूत-ए नाज़ ये दिल की रगों का टूटना
ख़ामुशी में कुछ शिकस्त-ए साज़ की बातें करो

Her enticing silence
and breaking of the heart's veins.
In this silence, let's talk about
the instrument's shattering.

◆

nikhat-e zulf-e pareshaan daastaan-e shaam-e gham
sub-h hone tak isi andaaz ki baatein karo

निकहत-ए ज़ुल्फ़-ए परेशाँ दास्तान-ए शाम-ए ग़म
सुब्ह होने तक इसी अंदाज़ की बातें करो

The fragrance of her untidy tresses
was the story of a sorrowful evening.
Waiting for the daybreak,
let's continue to talk about this.

◆

har rag-e dil vajd mein aati rahe dukhti rahe
yuunhi us ke jaa o bejaa naaz ki baatein karo

हर रग-ए दिल वज्द में आती रहे दुखती रहे
यूँही उस के जा ओ बेजा नाज़ की बातें करो

I wish every vein of the heart
continues to reach
the heights of ecstasy causing suffering.
We should hear more about
her profusion of beauty and grace.

◆

jo adam ki jaan hai jo hai payaam-e zindagi
us sakuut-e raaz us aavaaz ki baatein karo

जो अदम की जान है जो है पयाम-ए ज़िंदगी
उस सुकूत-ए राज़ उस आवाज़ की बातें करो

What is beyond this existence
is a message of life.
Let's talk about the voice of silence
and its secrets.

◆

i'shq rusva ho chala be-kaif sa bezaar sa
aaj us ki nargis-e ghammaaz ki baatein karo

इ'श्क़ रुस्वा हो चला बे-कैफ़ सा बेज़ार सा
आज उस की नर्गिस-ए ग़म्माज़ की बातें करो

Love is disgraced,
joyless and sickly.
Let's talk about her narcissus-like eyes.

•

naam bhi lena hai jis ka ik jahaan-e rango o bu
dosto us nau-bahaar-e naaz ki baatein karo

नाम भी लेना है जिस का इक जहान-ए रंग ओ बू
दोस्तो उस नौ-बहार-ए नाज़ की बातें करो

Talking about her is just like opening
a world of colour and fragrance.
Friends, let's talk about the glamorous beloved.

•

kuchh qafas ki tiiliyon se chhan raha hai nuur sa
kuchh faza kuchh hasrat-e parvaaz ki baatein karo

कुछ क़फ़स की तीलियों से छन रहा है नूर सा
कुछ फ़ज़ा कुछ हसरत-ए परवाज़ की बातें करो

Some rays of light are getting
through the bars of the jailhouse.
Let's talk about the ambiance
and our desire to fly away.

•

i'shq-e beparva bhi ab kuchh na-shakeba ho chala
shokhi-e husn-e karishma-saaz ki baatein karo

इ'श्क़-ए बे-परवा भी अब कुछ ना-शकेबा हो चला
शोख़ी-ए हुस्न-ए करिश्मा-साज़ की बातें करो

Careless love is becoming impatient.
Let's talk about the mischief
of that charismatic beauty.

◆

jis ki furqat ne palat di i'shq ki kaaya 'firaq'
aaj us iisa-nafas dam-saaz ki baatein karo

जिस की फ़ुर्क़त ने पलट दी इ'श्क़ की काया 'फ़िराक़'
आज उस ईसा-नफ़स दम-साज़ की बातें करो

Her separation has altered
the advent of love, Firaq.
Let's talk about the one
whose breath is a life-giver
like a caring soothsayer.

Life's Transient Nature

ye maana zindagi hai chaar din ki

Firaq invites readers to pause and consider the meaning found in even the briefest moments of life. The poet acknowledges the transient nature of our existence yet finds wonder and potential in this brevity, suggesting that a short period can hold a wealth of experiences. The ghazal invites us to cherish the present and appreciate the value of each fleeting moment, while underscoring the fundamental importance of human connection. Firaq questions the value of spiritual attainment in the face of our basic human needs for one another, reminding us that the presence and support of our fellow humans truly sustain us in times of hardship. The poet explores the mysteries of human connection, speaking of the power of a single glance from the beloved that can communicate volumes to the heart. Love, however, is not a straightforward path; it is a consuming force that leaves us grappling with the tumultuous landscape of the heart, evoking emotions that neither joy nor sorrow can adequately encompass. Firaq's masterful use of language amplifies the impact of the ghazal's concise form, distilling complex emotions and profound insights into a few poignant lines. The experiences he describes are universal, providing solace in the shared understanding of our human condition.

ye maana zindagi hai chaar din ki
bahut hote hain yaaro chaar din bhi

ये माना ज़िन्दगी है चार दिन की
बहुत होते हैं यारो चार दिन भी

I know life lasts a short while,
but a brief period
can compress a lot, too.

◆

khuda ko pa gaya vaa'iz magar hai
zaruurat aadmi ko aadmi ki

खुदा को पा गया वाइ'ज़ मगर है
ज़रूरत आदमी को आदमी की

What matters if
the preacher attained godhood.

At this moment, humans need
other humans.

◆

basa-auqaat dil se kah gaii hai
bahut kuchh vo nigaah-e mukhtasar bhi

बसा-औक़ात दिल से कह गई है
कुछ वो निगाह-ए मुख़्तसर भी

Sometimes, she conversed a lot
with my heart—
that eye which doesn't
communicate much.

◆

mohabbat mein karein kya haal dil ka
khushi hi kaam aati hai n gham bhi

मोहब्बत में करें क्या हाल दिल का
ख़ुशी ही काम आती है न ग़म भी

How do we manage ourselves
when we fall in love?
Neither joy nor sorrow
is of any use.

A Wandering Man Named I'shq

meri navaayein sun ke sitaare sub-h
azal se vajd mein hain

Firaq establishes himself as a figure of immense spiritual and artistic significance, claiming that his songs can send the stars into a state of mystical ecstasy. However, as the ghazal unfolds, it becomes clear that the love he speaks of is not a gentle force but a destructive one, personified as a wandering man named *I'shq* who brings devastation in his wake. Firaq warns of love's perils, invoking the tragic tale of Majnun and Laila, where Majnun's all-consuming passion leads him to madness and death in the wilderness (*ek tha majnuun aa'shaq-e laila viiraane mein maut hui*). This serves as a poignant reminder of the sacrifices that love may demand and the price of total devotion. Despite the warnings, Firaq finds himself caught in love's thrall. He speaks of his own experiences of frustration and confusion when lovers fail to understand each other. This moment of vulnerability and doubt is universal, resonating with anyone caught in the throes of love.

meri navaayein sun ke sitaare sub-h azal se vajd mein hain
kitni naaii aavaaz hai meri phir bhi kitni puraani hai

मेरी नवायें सुन के सितारे सुब-ह अज़ल से वज्द में हैं
कितनी नई आवाज़ है मेरी फिर भी कितनी पुरानी है

Stars are in a mystical state
since the dawn of time
after listening to my songs.
Completely fresh is my voice,
yet it is ancient in its essence.

◆

ek aadmi i'shq naam ka phirta hai galiyon-galiyon
dekho us se bach ke rahna vo shakhs bara nuksaani hai

एक आदमी इ'श्क़ नाम का फिरता है गलिओं-गलिओं
देखो उस से बचे रहना वो शख़्स बड़ा नुकसानी है

There is someone
named i'shq, and
he is roaming the streets.
Beware!
That person could hurt you a lot.

◆

ek tha majnuun aa'shaq-e laila viiraane mein maut hui
aur agar tafsiil se puuchho ye qissa tuulaani hai

एक था मजनूँ आ'शिक़े लैला वीराने में मौत हुई
और अगर तफ़सील से पूछो ये क़िस्सा तूलानी है

There was Majnu,
the lover of Laila,
and he died in the wilderness.
And if you want to know
details of his story,
it is rather too long a narrative.

◆

vo bhi na samjhe baat haamari ham bhi na samjhe us ki baat
ya to 'firaq' hamien diivaane ya duniya diivaani hai

वो भी न समझे बात हमारी हम भी न समझे उस की बात
या तो 'फ़िराक़' हमीं दीवाने या दुनिया दीवानी है

She doesn't get it,
and I, too, fail to understand this.
Firaq, either we are crazy,
or the world is out of its mind.

The Hidden Realm of Love

pehron-pehron tak ye duniya bhuula sapna ban jaaye hai

Firaq unveils the enigmatic nature of his craft, acknowledging that the muse inspiring his songs remains a mystery even to himself. He implores readers never to seek the identity of the one who sets his heart ablaze, for a poet's love is a secret that dances on the edge of revelation, leaving all intrigued and captivated. Amidst the shadows of this world, the poet beckons readers to join him in seeking the hidden realm of love, the elusive essence of true love that dwells within the folds of existence (*is duniya hi mein sune hain ik duniya-e mohabbat bhi / ham bhi usi jaanib jaavein hain bolo tum bhi aao ho*). As the ghazal climaxes, Firaq is consumed by a state that defies description, a testament to the profound and complex emotions surging through his being. Though the translation may not fully capture the subtle nuances of the original, the ghazal's core themes of love, yearning, and self-discovery resonate with universal power. Each verse is an invitation to embark on a transformative journey, to lose oneself in the rapture of emotion and emerge changed.

pehron-pehron tak ye duniya bhuula sapna ban jaaye hai
main to sarasar kho jaauun huun yaad kyon itna aao ho

पहरों-पहरों तक ये दुनिया भूला सपना बन जाए है
मैं तो सरासर खो जाऊं हूँ याद क्यों इतना आओ हो

For long moments,
this world appears to be a forgotten dream.
I'm completely lost.

Why do you come to me
with such traction?

◆

mere naghme kis ke liye hain khud mujh ko maa'luum nahien
kabhi n puuchho ye shaa'yir se tum kis ka gun gaao ho

मेरे नग़मे किस के लिए हैं खुद मुझ को मालूम नहीं
कभी न पूछो ये शा'इर से तुम किस का गुन गाओ हो

For whom do I write my songs,
I've no idea who she is.
Never ask a poet for whom
he goes into rapture.

◆

is duniya hi mein sune hain ik duniya-e mohabbat bhi
ham bhi usi jaanib jaavein hain bolo tum bhi aao ho

इस दुनिया ही में है सुने हैं इक दुनिया-ए महब्बत भी
हम भी उसी जानिब जावें हैं बोलो तुम भी आओ हो

Deep within this world,
there is a world of love.
I'm going in that direction.
Speak up if you wish to join.

◆

aksar gahri soch mein un ko khoya khoya paavein hain
ab hai 'firaq' ka kuchh rozon se jo aalam kya puuchho ho

अक्सर गहरी सोच में उन को खोया खोया पावें हैं
अब है 'फ़िराक़' का कुछ रोज़ों से जो आलम क्या पूछो हो

In deep reflection,
he loses awareness of everything.
Firaq has been in a condition
that is hard to describe.

The Unbearable Night

tum juda ho jaao ge to ho jaaye gi ye raat pahaar

Firaq weaves a fabric of love, each verse unveiling the poet's innermost desires and profound connection with his beloved. The poet's plea echoes through the night, a desperate cry for his beloved to remain by his side, as the mere thought of separation renders the night an insurmountable mountain of darkness. Yet, with the beloved's presence, the night transforms into a delightful journey, a sacred space where love blossoms and time loses grip. The poet likens the memory of his beloved to the shimmering stars reflected in the flowing Ganges, offering solace and comfort to aching hearts that yearn for connection (*jaise taaron ki chamak bahti hui ganga mein / ahl-e gham ko yuun-hi yaad aao k kuchh raat kate*). The power of love transcends the boundaries of time and space as the Easterly breezes carry whispers of bygone days. The poet beckons the listener to sing a ghazal by Mir, as if the melody holds the key to unlocking the secrets of the night and momentarily lifting the burden of existence. In the final verse, Firaq stands silent amidst the gathering, his voice stilled by the weight of his emotions, imploring someone to summon his beloved, for only their presence can alleviate his pain.

tum juda ho jaao ge to ho jaaye gi ye raat pahaar
raat ki raat thahar jaao k kuchh raat kate

तुम जुदा हो गे तो ये हो जाए गी ये रात पहाड़
रात की रात ठहर जाओ कि कुछ रात कटे

If you leave me, this night will be unbearable.
Please stay for the night.
This way, the night will pass delightfully.

◆

jaise taaron ki chamak bahti hui ganga mein
ahl-e gham ko yuun-hi yaad aao k kuchh raat kate

जैसे तारों की चमक बहती हुई गंगा में
अहल-ए ग़म को यूँही याद आओ कि कुछ रात कटे

Just like the shining stars are reflected
in the flowing Ganges.
Be in the thoughts of those who are suffering.
Perhaps the night may pass quickly.

◆

yaad-e ayyam ki purvaaiio dheeme-dheeme
'mir' ki koi ghazal gaao k kuchh raat kate

याद-ए अय्याम की पुरवाइओ धीमे-धीमे
'मीर' की कोई ग़ज़ल गाओ कि कुछ रात कटे

The easterly breezes of times past slow down.
Sing a ghazal by Mir!
This way, the night may pass effortlessly.

◆

aa ke mahfil mein 'firaq' aaj nahien naghma-sara
ja ke us ko bhi bulaao k kuchh raat kate

आ के महफ़िल में 'फ़िराक़' आज नहीं नग़मा सरा
जा के उस को भी बुलाओ कि कुछ रात कटे

Firaq came to the meeting,
but he was not singing a song.
Call the one he loves.
This way, the night may pass painlessly.

Forgotten Tales

yaad n kar dil-e haziin bhuuli hui kahaniyaan

Each verse of this ghazal unveils the poet's innermost struggles and invites readers to empathize with the indelible marks left by the memories of love. The poet's plea to his suffering heart reverberates through the lines, urging it to release the forgotten tales of yesteryears. The echoes of youth in bloom and the intoxicating joys of beauty threaten to consume him. In contrast, recognizing beauty's fleeting nature and the prime of life invites contemplation on the transience of existence. Through strong imagery and metaphors, Firaq likens love to an unstoppable wave, a force that, once unleashed, cannot be contained. The restlessness permeating the lover's soul becomes a constant companion, a testament to love's all-consuming nature (*mauj thahar saki kahien saath pe ho ke tahnashiin / i'shq mein be-sakuun yuunhi kat-ti hai zindgaaniyaan*). The poet's memories of his beloved resurface in unexpected moments, reminding us that the soul remembers even when the mind may forget. The gloomy setting mirrors the poet's inner turmoil, with the darkness of the night reflecting the shadows that haunt his heart. The rising clouds and fleeting brilliance of lightning symbolize the transient nature of beauty's favors and kindness. Amidst the melancholy, there is a glimmer of hope as Firaq reflects on the evolving nature of love, acknowledging its transformation and the wisdom that comes with experience.

yaad n kar dil-e haziin bhuuli hui kahaniyaan
uth-ti hui javaniyaan husn ki shaadmaaniyaan

याद न कर दिल-ए हज़ीं भूली हुई कहानियां
उठती हुई जवानियाँ हुस्न की शादमानियाँ

Don't remember,
O my suffering heart,
forgotten tales of the days gone by.
Youth reaching its prime and
the pleasures and charms
of beauty.

♦

mauj thahar saki kahien saath pe ho ke tahnashiin
i'shq mein be-sakuun yuunhi kat-ti hai zindgaaniyaan

मौज ठहर सकी कहीं साथ पे हो के तःनशीं
इ'श्क़ में बे-सकूं यूंही कटती है ज़िंदगानियाँ

Once it was settled,
the wave could not be stopped.
You spend your life like this
when you're in love.

♦

aaj faza ki khaamushi kuchh use phir suna gaaii
bhuuli hui thi i'shq ko husn ki khush-bayaaniyaan

आज फ़ज़ा की ख़ामुशी कुछ उसे फिर सुना गई
भूली हुई थी इ'श्क़ को हुस्न की खुशबयानियाँ

The silence of the ambiance
repeated to him,
although he had forgotten
the beauty's eloquence.

◆

uff ye faza udaas-udaas aah ye mauj-e duud-e shaam
yaad si aa ke rah gaein dil ko kaaii kahaaniyaan

उफ़ ये फ़ज़ा उदास-उदास आह ये मौजे दूदे-शाम
याद सी आ के रह गईं दिल को कई कहानियां

Alas, this setting is filled
with extreme sadness.
Oh, this wave of night's darkness.
Rushed to the heart at this moment
a bunch of stories.

◆

umdi ghataaein bijliaan jaise chamak ke rah gaein
aaj to yaad aa gaein husn ki meharbaaniyaan

उमड़ी घटाएँ बिजलियाँ जैसे चमक के रह गयीं
आज तो याद आ गयीं हुस्न की मेहरबानियां

Rising clouds and lightning
brightened the sky,
but then they were gone.
Today, I remembered beauty's favors
and kindness.

◆

aks sa par ke rah gaya jaise teri nigaah ka
yaad si aa ke rah gaein bhuuli hui kahaaniyaan

अक्स सा पड़ के रह गया जैसे तेरी निगाह का
याद सी आ के रह गयीं भूली हुई कहानियां

There was a reflection
like that of your eyes.
It refreshed stories that were
no longer stored in my mind.

◆

aur hi rang hai 'Firaq' ab to shu-uure i'shq ka
ab n khush-gumaaniyaan ab n vo bad-gumaaniyaan

और ही रंग है 'फ़िराक़' अब तो शुऊरे-इ'श्क़ का
अब न वो खुशगुमानियाँ अब न वो बदगुमानियां

I'shq nowadays, Firaq,
has a different awareness and colour.
There are no longer any misconceptions
and wrong presumptions.

The Unspoken Truths

ye to nahien k gham nahien

In this ghazal, each verse is a mirror held up to the soul, reflecting the poet's innermost struggles and the universal truths that reside within us all. The poet's words transform into a silent plea for comprehension in a world that frequently fails to see beyond outward appearances. He contemplates the nature of life and death, acknowledging the finality of death while affirming the significance of life itself (*maut agarche maut hai / maut se ziist kam nahien*). This comparison is a powerful reminder that every moment of our lives is imbued with meaning, and the joys and sorrows we experience are no less profound than the ultimate destiny that awaits us all. The poet's emotional landscape shifts, revealing a sense of numbness that has settled over his soul, with the once vibrant hues of happiness and sorrow fading into a canvas of subdued grays. This emotional disengagement reflects the exhaustion that can overwhelm us when the burden of life's trials and tribulations becomes too great. Yet, the poet's words remind us of the inescapable nature of the human condition as we grapple with the consequences of our actions, the burdens of our sins, and the search for meaning in a world that often seems indifferent to our struggles. Through his honest and unflinching exploration of these themes, Firaq creates an apparel of emotions that resonates with the essence of being human.

ye to nahien k gham nahien
haan meri aankh nam nahien

ये तो नहीं कि ग़म नहीं
हाँ मेरी आँख नम नहीं

There is no lack of grief.
But my eyes are not moist.

◆

maut agarche maut hai
maut se ziist kam nahien

मौत अगरचे मौत है
मौत से ज़ीस्त कम नहीं

Death, after all,
is death.
But life is no less
in comparison.

◆

ab n khushi ki hai khushi
gham ka bhi ab to gham nahien

अब न ख़ुशी की है ख़ुशी
ग़म का भी अब तो ग़म नहीं

Happiness nowadays
provides no pleasure.
Sorrow, too, is not causing
any suffering.

◆

somo-salaat se 'firaq'
mere gunaah kam nahien

सौमो-सलात से 'फ़िराक़'
मेरे गुनाह कम नहीं

Prayers and ablutions
are fine
but the gravity of my sins
is also severe.

This Breeze, This Night

ye nik-haton ki narm-ravi ye hava ye raat

Firaq depicts his innermost struggles and the indelible marks left by the memories of a shattered love. Each verse, laden with emotion, transports readers to a realm where the echoes of a lost love reverberate through the fabric of existence, with the gentle caress of fragrances, the whisper of the breeze, and the night's embrace serving as catalysts for stirring memories of broken bonds. The poet personifies love as fragile, revealing the despair that threatens to consume it as it lies gasping for breath in the lap of sorrow. The plea for intervention becomes a desperate cry, reminding us that love, like any living thing, requires nurturing and care to survive life's trials and tribulations. The depth of the poet's devotion is laid bare in a verse that speaks of a lifetime spent waiting for a beloved who never arrived, highlighting the sacrifices that genuine love demands. The poet delves deeply into the mysterious and profound nature of love, describing inexplicable events that baffle even the most grief-stricken soul, testifying to love's irrational and all-consuming power. In the final verse, the metaphor of sleep and wakefulness symbolizes the timeless, all-consuming state of love, where the boundaries between day and night dissolve, and the lover becomes a prisoner of their emotions.

ye nik-haton ki narm-ravi ye hava ye raat
yaad aa rahe hain i'shq ko tuute tu'allqaat

ये निकहतों की नर्म-रवी ये हवा ये रात
याद आ रहे हैं इ'श्क़ को टूटे तअ'ल्लुक़ात

This tip-toying of fragrances,
this breeze, and this night.
Love is reminiscing
broken relationships.

◆

mayuusion ki god mein dam torta hai i'shq
ab bhi koi bana le to bigri nahien hai baat

मायूसियों की गोद में दम तोड़ता है इ'श्क़
अब भी कोई बना ले तो बिगड़ी नहीं है बात

In the lap of despair,
love is losing its breath.
If someone can avert this tragedy,
all can be saved.

◆

ik u'mr kat gaii hai tere intizaar mein
aise bhi hain k kat n saki jin se ek raat

इक उ'म्र कट गई है तिरे इंतिज़ार में
ऐसे भी हैं कि कट न सकी जिन से एक रात

I've spent all my life
waiting for you.
Some couldn't spend
one night doing that.

◆

jin ka suraagh pa n saki gham ki ruuh bhi
naadaan hue hain i'shq mein aise bhi saanehaat

जिन का सुराग़ पा न सकी ग़म की रूह भी
नादाँ हुए हैं इ'श्क़ में ऐसे भी सानेहात

Even the soul of grief
couldn't find their trace.
O, the foolish ones,
there have occurred
such events in love.

◆

kya niind aaye us ko jise jaagna n aaye
jo din ko din kare vo kare raat ko bhi raat

क्या नींद आए उस को जिसे जागना न आए
जो दिन को दिन करे वो करे रात को भी रात

How can one get to sleep
who doesn't know
how do you wake up from sleep?
For such a person,
a day is just a day,
a night is just a night.

If This Happened Differently

raaz ko raaz hi rakkha hota

Each verse in this ghazal is a poignant revelation and a deeply emotional confession that resonates through the heart's chambers, inviting readers to empathize with the poet's experience. The opening verse is tinged with regret, a silent plea for the heart's secrets to remain hidden as the weight of the revealed burdens weighs heavily on the soul. As the ghazal progresses, the poet paints a grim picture of solitude, where the heart and loneliness intersect, and the beloved's absence becomes a consuming void that yearns for completion. The poet's words transform into a desperate invocation, longing for the presence that would make the world magnificent. Firaq confronts the inescapable nature of love's agony, emphasizing that even in the act of forgetting, the pain of separation intensifies, a testament to the indelible mark left by true love. The memory of the beloved becomes an eternal flame, forever searing the heart. As the ghazal reaches its climax, the poet bears his human vulnerability, grappling with the essence of love and the futility of abandonment through the lens of his pen name, Firaq.

raaz ko raaz hi rakkha hota
kya kahna agar aisa hota

राज़ को राज़ ही रक्खा होता
क्या कहना अगर ऐसा होता

I wish the concealed
had not been revealed.
It would have been wonderful
if it had happened this way.

◆

main huun dil hai tanhaaii hai
tum bhi jo hote achha hota

मैं हूँ दिल है तन्हाई है
तुम भी जो होते अच्छा होता

I'm here, and my heart is here.
So is the loneliness.
It would have been magnificent
if you were here too.

◆

ham jo tujhe kuchh bhuul bhi jaate
dard-e mohabbat duuna hota

हम जो तुझे कुछ भूल भी जाते
दर्दे-मोहब्बत दूना होता

Even if I had forgotten you,
the agony of my heart
would have been double.

◆

ham bhi 'Firaq' insaan the aakhir
tark-e mohabbat se kya hota

हम भी 'फ़िराक़' इंसान थे आखिर
तरके-मुहब्बत से क्या होता

Firaq, after all, I was human.
What would I have gained
by falling out of love.

Image after Image

raat aadhi se ziaada ho gaaii thi saara aa'lam sota tha

Firaq weaves a tale that transcends the boundaries of a simple story, inviting readers to embark on a profound journey into the mysteries of the heart and the complexities of human existence. Each verse serves as an invitation, urging us to go deeper into a world where the boundaries between sleep and wakefulness blur and the anguish of a lonely soul pierces the silence of the night. The intensity of the lover's longing resonates within us, challenging our understanding of love and its place in our lives. The poet confronts those who have turned their backs on love, reminding them of the hollow comfort of a life devoid of passion and emphasizing the pursuit of love as an essential part of our humanity (*tark-e mohabbat karne vaalo kaun aisa jag jiit liya / i'shq se pehle ke din socho kaun bara sukh hota tha*). Through his words, Firaq dares us to awaken the magic of beauty in a world often shrouded in ignorance and indifference, reminding us of beauty's transformative power and ability to illuminate even the darkest corners of our souls. The lament for the unheard tears and sighs of the lover, combined with the beauty of gardens and the tumultuous wailing of rivers, serves as a reminder of the duality of our existence, where joy and sorrow are inextricably intertwined. As the ghazal reaches its climax, the image of Firaq stringing pearls of poetry under the starlit sky emerges as a powerful metaphor for the transformative nature of art, reminding us of our power to create beauty and meaning even in our darkest hours.

raat aadhi se ziaada ho gaaii thi saara aa'lam sota tha
naam tera le-le kar koi dard ka maara rota tha

रात आधी से ज़्यादा हो गई थी सारा आ'लम सोता था
नाम तेरा ले-ले कर कोई दर्द का मारा रोता था

It was past midnight,
and the whole world was asleep.
Repeatedly calling your name
someone is stricken with pain
was wailing.

◆

tark-e mohabbat karne vaalo kaun aisa jag jiit liya
i'shq se pehle ke din socho kaun bara sukh hota tha

तरके-मोहब्बत करने वालो कौन ऐसा जग जीत लिया
इश्क़ से पहले के दिन सोचो कौन बड़ा सुख होता था

Those who gave up loving,
what did they achieve?
Remember the days
before love commenced,
what kind of comfort was there?

◆

duniya-duniya ghaflat taari aa'lam-aa'lam be-khabri
husn ka jaadu kaun jagaaye ek zamaana sota tha

दुनिया-दुनिया ग़फ़लत तारी आ'लम-आ'लम बे-खबरी
हुस्न का जादू कौन जगाये एक ज़माना सोता था

The world is clueless,
and there is unawareness all around.
Who could dare rouse the magic of beauty?
The whole world was asleep.

◆

us ke aansu kis ne dekhe us ki aahein kis ne suniin
chaman-chaman tha husn bhi lekin dariya-dariya rota tha

उस के आंसू किस ने देखे उस की आहें किस ने सुनी
चमन-चमन था हुस्न भी लेकिन दरिया-दरिया रोता था

Who had seen his tears?
And who had heard his cries?
Gardens were filled with beauty,
but the wailing of rivers
was tumultuous.

◆

pichhla pahar tha hijr ki shab ka jaagta rabb sota sansaar
taaron ki chhaaon mein koi 'firaq' sa jaise moti pirota tha

पिछला पहर था हिज्र की शब् का जागता रब्ब सोता संसार
तारों की छाओं में कोई 'फ़िराक़' सा जैसे मोती पिरोता था

It was the last stretch
of the night of loneliness.
God was awake,
but the world was asleep.
Under the silhouette of the stars,
someone like Firaq was busy
beading a string of pearls.

Like a Prayer

koi paighaam-e mohabbat lab-e ai'jaaz to de

Firaq's exploration of beauty and love in this ghazal intoxicates readers. The plea for a secret to be conveyed through the eyes of the beloved is a masterful stroke, reminding us of the profound intimacy between lovers, where a glance can speak volumes and carry the weight of a thousand unspoken truths. The poet boldly embraces pain as a catalyst for creativity. The clear sense of anticipation in the air testifies to his unwavering dedication to his craft. With pain as their muse and a melodic instrument in hand, the poet stands ready to unleash his emotional turmoil upon the world. In the final verse, the poet's words strike a chord that resonates with the essence of the human condition. Despite being prisoners in our way, confined by the limitations of our circumstances and the chains of our desires, the poet reminds us of the indomitable spirit within us all. With the power to start a fire and the yearning to soar beyond our cages, we are urged to seize the moments of respite that allow us to compose the songs of our souls and nurture the flames of our passion.

koi paighaam-e mohabbat lab-e ai'jaaz to de
maut ki aankh bhi khul jaaye gi aavaaz to de

कोई पैग़ाम-ए मोहब्बत लब-ए एजाज़ तो दे
मौत की आँख भी खुल जाएगी आवाज़ तो दे

Give me a message of love
these magical lips.
Even the death's eye will open,
you have to say something.

◆

ik zara ho nasha-e husn mein andaaz-e khumaar
ik jhalak i'shq ke anjaam ko aaghaaz to de

इक ज़रा हो नशा-ए हुस्न में अंदाज़-ए ख़ुमार
इक झलक इ'श्क़ के अंजाम को आग़ाज़ तो दे

If there is some style of insobriety in beauty,
one could get a preview
of the start and the end of our love affair.

◆

jo chhupaaye n chhupe aur bataaye n bane
dil-e aa'shiq ko in aankhon se koi raaz to de

जो छुपाए न छुपे और बताए न बने
दिल-ए आ'शिक़ को इन आँखों से कोई राज़ तो दे

What he can't hide or share with others,
give your lover's heart a secret
with the movement of your eyes.

◆

muntazir itni kabhi thi n faza-e aafaak
chherne hi ko huun pur-dard ghazal saaz to de

मुंतज़िर इतनी कभी थी न फ़ज़ा-ए आफ़ाक़
छेड़ने ही को हूँ पुर-दर्द ग़ज़ल साज़ तो दे

The ambiance of the vast sky
never showed such a sense of expectation.
I'm ready to start,
Let the pain give me a melodic instrument.

◆

ham asiiraan-e qafas aag laga sakte hain
fursat-e naghma kabhi hasrat-e parvaaz to de

हम असीरान-ए क़फ़स आग लगा सकते हैं
फ़ुर्सत-ए नग़्मा कभी हसरत-ए परवाज़ तो दे

We are the caged prisoners
and we can start a fire.
Let the interlude give us
the time to compose a song
and a desire to fly.

Just as It Was

gham tera jalva-gah-e kaun o makaan hai k jo tha

Each verse of this ghazal pulsates with the intensity of a love that consumes and transforms, leaving an indelible mark on the fabric of our lives. Immersed in a world where the anguish of separation from the beloved saturates every particle of the universe, human life becomes a testament to the enduring strength of love and its capacity to mold our essence. Firaq's words serve as a beacon, reminding us that the pain of love is not fleeting but a steadfast companion throughout time. The ghazal captivates readers with the unchanging essence of love's expression, celebrating its eternal nature as a force that transcends the boundaries of time and space. Yet, amidst the ecstasy of love, Firaq reveals its darker undercurrents, portraying the beloved as a foe of the heart and life and highlighting the duality of love's potential to both uplift and annihilate. Firaq confronts the sobering reality that even the purest of loves can be corrupted by the pursuit of selfish gain. It serves as a reminder that the human heart is a battleground where love and greed collide. The poet's words are a call to guard against the erosion of love's essence and hold fast to the purity of emotion that defines our humanity. Despite the fading intensity of desire over time, Firaq emphasizes love's enduring magic with the power of poetry, the beauty of recitation, and the intoxicating atmosphere of the tavern of love, remaining constant sources of solace and inspiration. In the final verse, Firaq leaves readers with a beautiful image of the fire that burns within the human heart, the smoke rising from our chests as a testament to the enduring presence of love and pain.

gham tera jalva-gah-e kaun o makaan hai k jo tha
yaa'ni insaan vohi shola b jaan k jo tha

ग़म तिरा जल्वा-गह-ए कौन ओ मकाँ है कि जो था
या'नी इंसान वही शो'ला-ब-जाँ है कि जो था

The grief of your separation
has enveloped the universe
just as it was.
Human's life is aflame
just as it was.

◆

phir vohi rang-e takallum nigaah-e naaz mein hai
vohi andaaz vohi husn-e biyaan hai k jo tha

फिर वही रंग-ए तकल्लुम निगह-ए नाज़ में है
वही अंदाज़ वही हुस्न-ए बयाँ है कि जो था

Once again,
it's the same colour of speech
in the glance of love.
The exact manner and
the sheer beauty of the description
just as it was.

◆

kab hai inkaar tere lutf-e karam se lekin
tu vohi dushman-e dil dushman-e jaan hai k jo tha

कब है इंकार तिरे लुत्फ़ ओ करम से लेकिन
तू वही दुश्मन-ए दिल दुश्मन-ए जाँ है कि जो था

I don't deny the pleasure
of earning your reward, but
you are the same enemy
of my heart and my life,
just as it was.

◆

i'shq afsurda nahien aaj bhi afsurda bahut
vohi kam kam asr-e soz-e nihaan hai k jo tha

इ'श्क़ अफ़्सुर्दा नहीं आज भी अफ़्सुर्दा बहुत
वही कम कम असर-ए सोज़-ए निहाँ है कि जो था

Love is not melancholy,
but it is depressing a lot.
There is a feeling
of deep hidden sorrow,
just as it was.

◆

jaan de baithe the ik baar havas vaale bhi
phir vohi marhala-e suud o ziaan hai k jo tha

जान दे बैठे थे इक बार हवस वाले भी
फिर वही मरहला-ए सूद ओ ज़ियाँ है कि जो था

Once, even the lustful folks
had fallen in love with you.
But very soon,

it was a matter of gain and loss,
just as it was.

◆

husn ko khench to leta hai abhi tak lekin
vo asar jazb-e mohabbat mein kahaan hai k jo tha

हुस्न को खींच तो लेता है अभी तक लेकिन
वो असर जज़्ब-ए मोहब्बत में कहाँ है कि जो था

Although it can still attract beauty,
the preceding force of desire
isn't there,
just as it was.

◆

phir teri chashm-e sukhan-sanj ne chheri koi baat
vohi jaadu hai vohi husn-e biyaan hai k jo tha

फिर तिरी चश्म-ए सुख़न-संज ने छेड़ी कोई बात
वही जादू है वही हुस्न-ए बयाँ है कि जो था

Once again,
your poetic eye has started to converse.
It is the same magic
and the beauty of recitation,
just as it was.

◆

phir sar-e mai-kada-e i'shq hai ik baarish-e nuur
chhalke jaamon se charaghaan ka samaan hai k jo tha

फिर सर-ए मय-कद-ए इ'श्क़ है इक बारिश-ए नूर
छलके जामों से चराग़ाँ का समाँ है कि जो था

Once again,
in the tavern of love,
light is raining.
The overflowing glasses of wine
create an atmosphere,
just as it was.

◆

aaj bhi aag dabi hai dil-e insaan mein 'firaq'
aaj bhi siinon se uth-ta vo dhuaan k jo tha

आज भी आग दबी है दिल-ए इंसाँ में 'फ़िराक़'
आज भी सीनों से उठता वो धुआँ है कि जो था

Even today, there is a fire hidden
in the hearts of humans, Firaq.
Smoke is rising from the chests,
just as it was.

Tears That Pierce a Stone

ash'aar nahien hain ye meri ruuh ki hai pyaas

Firaq immerses readers in his inner world, where the boundaries between poetry and the soul's thirst dissolve. His words are not mere ink on paper; they spring from his core, a torrential outpouring of the yearning that defines his existence. His tears are a force of nature, capable of piercing the hardest of hearts with their diamond-like intensity. The line between sorrow and ecstasy blurs, and weeping is a testament to love's transformative power. Firaq's verses loom large with the beloved's absence, a void threatening to consume him. The assembly of love becomes a hollow shell without the radiant presence of the one who holds the key to his heart, serving as a reminder of the aching emptiness at the core of every lover's soul. Yet, amid this desolation, Firaq finds hope in his heart, a hidden oasis sustaining him with its ceaseless flow of emotion. His eyes' moistness becomes the lifeblood coursing through his veins, a reminder that love endures even in the darkest times. The ghazal draws us into a world where the physical and metaphysical boundaries blur. The fragrance of the beloved's tresses becomes tangible, and a ghostly whisper is carried on the morning breeze, reminding us that true love transcends the limitations of the flesh. At the center lies Firaq's heart, capable of navigating life's treacherous waters with grace and fortitude.

ash'aar nahien hain ye meri ruuh ki hai pyaas
jaari hue sar-chashme meri tishna-labi se

अशआ'र नहीं हैं ये मिरी रूह की है प्यास
जारी हुए सर-चश्मे मिरी तिश्ना-लबी से

It is not my verse;
It is the thirst of my soul.
These are springs of water
that flow
from my inner longing.

◆

aansu ko mere khel-tamaasha n samajhna
kat jaata hai patthar isi hiire ki kani se

आँसू को मिरे खेल-तमाशा न समझना
कट जाता है पत्थर इसी हीरे की कनी से

These are my tears.
It is not a show of amusement.

It is the pearl
that can pierce a stone.

◆

aaj anjuman-e i'shq nahien anjuman-e i'shq
kis darja kami bazm mein hai teri kami se

आज अंजुमन-ए इ'श्क़ नहीं अंजुमन-ए इ'श्क़
किस दर्जा कमी बज़्म मैं है तेरी कमी से

The assembly of love today
is not like an assembly of love.
How much you have been missed
is hard to describe.

◆

is vaadiye viraan mein hai sar-chashma-e dil bhi
hasti meri sairaab hai aankhon ki nami se

इस वादी-ए वीराँ में है सर-चश्मा-ए दिल भी
हस्ती मिरी सैराब है आँखों की नमी से

In this deserted valley,
some springs arise from my heart.
The moistness of my eyes
supports my existence.

◆

khud mujh ko bhi taa-der khabar ho nahien paayi
aaj aaii teri yaad is aahista-ravi se

ख़ुद मुझ को भी ता-देर ख़बर हो नहीं पाई
आज आई तिरी याद इस आहिस्ता-रवी से

Even I didn't feel its arrival.
Your memory came
with such slow movement.

◆

vo duundhne nikli hai teri nikhat-e gaisu
ik roz mila tha main nasiim-e sahri se

वो ढूँढने निकली है तिरी निकहत-ए-गेसू
इक रोज़ मिला था मैं नसीम-ए-सहरी से

He has gone out in search
of the fragrance of your tresses.
One day, I met the morning breeze.

◆

ik dil ke siva paas haamare nahien kuchh bhi
jo kaam ho le lete hain ham log isi se

इक दिल के सिवा पास हमारे नहीं कुछ भी
जो काम हो ले लेते हैं हम लोग इसी से

Nothing except the heart
is my most precious possession,
and it is an all-purpose device.

◆

rahta huun 'Firaq' is liye vaarafta k duniya
kuchh hosh mein aa jaaye meri be-khabari se

रहता हूँ 'फ़िराक़' इस लिए वारफ़्ता कि दुनिया
कुछ होश में आ जाए मिरी बे-ख़बरी से

Firaq, I spend my time
walking around crazily.
I expect that the world
would gain awareness
with my outpourings
while I lose my consciousness.

Then Again...

kisi ka yuun to hua kaun u'mr bhar phir bhi

In this ghazal, considered one of Firaq's finest by his fans, the poet combines contrasting notions using the refrain *phir bhi* (then again), evoking a pervasive sense of ambivalence and poignant irony that lingers long after the final verse. The ghazal explores the transient nature of human connections, the seductive yet illusory essence of love and beauty, and the searing anguish of separation (*hazaar baar zamaana idhar se guzra hai /naaii naaii si hai kuchh teri rahguzar phir bhi*). Firaq's verses depict the heart's eternal struggle, desperately clinging to the fragments of a bond even as they slip through the fingers like grains of sand. The imagery of a caravan poised for departure symbolizes life's journey, forever propelled by the winds of change. Yet, amidst this constant motion, the beloved's captivating gaze remains an anchoring force, its power undiminished by time or distance, forever ensnaring the poet's soul (*jhapak rahi hai zamaan o makaan ki bhi aankhein / magar hai qaafila aamaada-e safar phir bhi*). With his *takhallus* woven seamlessly into the final couplet, Firaq leaves an indelible mark on the ghazal's form. Each *she'r* is a self-contained universe, inviting readers to lose themselves within its depths and emerge forever changed.

kisi ka yuun to hua kaun u'mr bhar phir bhi
y husn o i'shq to dokha hai sab magar phir bhı

किसी का यूँ तो हुआ कौन उ'म्र भर फिर भी
ये हुस्न ओ इ'श्क़ तो धोका है सब मगर फिर भी

No one belongs to anyone for life,
then again.

This beauty, this love—
these are all deceptions,
then again.

◆

hazaar baar zamaana idhar se guzra hai
naaii naaii si hai kuchh teri rahguzar phir bhi

हज़ार बार ज़माना इधर से गुज़रा है
नई नई सी है कुछ तेरी रहगुज़र फिर भी

People have trampled this pathway—
it seems one too many times.
Then again,
it looks new and unused.

◆

kahuun ye kaise idhar dekh ya n dekh udhar
k dard dard hai phir bhi nazar nazar phir bhi

कहूँ ये कैसे इधर देख या न देख उधर
कि दर्द दर्द है फिर भी नज़र नज़र फिर भी

How can I tell you
to look here, not there.
Then again,
sorrow is sorrow,
an eye is an eye.

◆

jhapak rahi hai zamaan o makaan ki bhi aankhein
magar hai qaafila aamaada-e safar phir bhi

झपक रही हैं ज़मान ओ मकाँ की भी आँखें
मगर है क़ाफ़िला आमादा-ए सफ़र फिर भी

Eyes of the time and place
are narrowing,
then again.
The caravan is ready
for its journey.

◆

palat rahe hain ghariib-ul-vatan palatna tha
vo kuucha ru-kash-e jannat ho ghar hai ghar phir bhi

पलट रहे हैं ग़रीब-उल-वतन पलटना था
वो कूचा रू-कश-ए जन्नत हो घर है घर फिर भी

The wanderers are coming back.
They had no choice.
Those avenues were like paradise,
then again, home is home.

◆

teri nigaah se bachne mein u'mr guzri hai
utar gaya rag-e jaan mein ye neshtar phir bhi

तिरी निगाह से बचने में उ'म्र गुज़री है
उतर गया रग-ए जाँ में ये नेश्तर फिर भी

I spent my life trying to save myself
from the charms of your eyes.
Then again, I couldn't protect
my neck from your lancet.

◆

ghame-e firaq ke kushton ka hashar kya ho ga
ye shaam-e hijr to ho jaaye gi sahar phir bhi

ग़म-ए-फ़िराक़ के कुश्तों का हश्र क्या होगा
ये शाम-ए हिज्र तो हो जाएगी सहर फिर भी

Those who died
for the grief of separation,
what would happen to them?
Then again,
this night of separation
would become a new dawn.

◆

agarche bekhudi-e i'shq ko zamaana hua
'Firaq' karti rahi kaam vo nazar phir bhi

अगरचे बे-ख़ुदी-ए इ'श्क़ को ज़माना हुआ
'फ़िराक़' करती रही काम वो नज़र फिर भी

Love's rapture ended
a long time ago.
Then again, Firaq,
her eyes continued
to allure me.

Polarities of Love

samajhta huun k tu mujh se juda hai

Firaq grapples with the agony of being torn from his beloved, his being shattered by this devastating loss. Yet even in darkness, memories of their love shine through as a beacon of hope. His verses oscillate between the extreme polarities of love—one moment basking in joyful reminiscence, the next drowning in tears. This duality encapsulates the lover's journey, testifying to the heart's capacity for ecstatic heights and aching depths.

Firaq glimpses a betrayal of his perceptions, realizing love's spectacle is often cloaked in deception. Still, he is irresistibly drawn to its flame, willing to risk searing pain to bask in its warmth. The beloved's indifference is an ever-present torment, a reminder of the price of devotion. His words bleed with the intensity of a love that refuses silence, a throbbing pain with each beat of his weary heart. Yet, amid this relentless torment, the poet discovers an inner resilience forged in the fires of adversity. Love's ultimate lesson is that true salvation lies within, and the human spirit can endure even the most crushing blows. Firaq's final verse offers hope and acceptance, a balm reminding us that love's trials are inevitable.

samajhta huun k tu mujh se juda hai
shab-e furqat mujhe kya ho gaya hai

समझता हूँ कि तू मुझ से जुदा है
शब-ए फ़ुर्क़त मुझे क्या हो गया है

I do understand it.
We have been separated.
Something has happened to me
that I can't comprehend.

◆

kabhi khush kar gaaii mujh ko teri yaad
kabhi aankhon mein aansu aa gaya hai

कभी ख़ुश कर गई मुझ को तिरी याद
कभी आँखों में आँसू आ गया है

Sometimes, your thought
is a source of contentment.
Sometimes, a tear appears in my eyes.

◆

hijaabon ko samajh baitha main jalva
nigaahon ko bara dhoka hua hai

हिजाबों को समझ बैठा मैं जल्वा
निगाहों को बड़ा धोका हुआ है

I mistook veils
for a spectacle.
Something has betrayed
my eyes.

◆

kabhi tarpa gaya hai dil tera gham
kabhi dil ko sahaara de gaya hai

कभी तड़पा गया है दिल तिरा ग़म
कभी दिल को सहारा दे गया है

Sometimes, my heart was hurt
by the sorrow you caused.
Sometimes, my heart found itself
supported by the same thing.

◆

na ji khush kar saka tera karam bhi
mohabbat ko bara dhoka hua hai

न जी ख़ुश कर सका तेरा करम भी
मोहब्बत को बड़ा धोका रहा है

Even your kindness
didn't bring any joy—
and my love was shortchanged.

◆

jise chaunka ke tu ne pher li aankhein
vo tera dard ab tak jaagta hai

जिसे चौंका के तू ने फेर ली आँखें
वो तेरा दर्द अब तक जागता है

Something that you stirred
and then paid no heed to it.
That ache you
gave is still awake.

◆

mohabbat mein 'firaq' itna n gham kar
zamaane mein yahi hota raha hai

मोहब्बत में 'फ़िराक़' इतना न ग़म कर
ज़माने में यही होता रहा है

God willing!
In this life of mine,
I'm my rescuer
and protector.

◆

khuda hafiz magar ab zindagi mein
faqat apna sahaara rah gaya hai

ख़ुदा-हाफ़िज़ मगर अब ज़िंदगी में
फ़क़त अपना सहारा रह गया है

Firaq, don't be too regretful
and despondent in love.
It is how the world works!

Sound from the Broken Strings

ashk bhar laaye kisi ne jo tera naam liya

Each couplet of this ghazal is a raw, searing testament to the unbridled power of emotion—a cry from the depths of a heart consumed by all-encompassing passion. The mere whisper of the beloved's name shatters the lover's composure, unleashing a torrent of tears from his torn-apart heart. This is love's affliction, a plague ravaging the soul, forever altering the sufferer who yearns for his beloved's solacing presence. Yet amid this tempest, the lover's spirit stands unyielding. Though his heart lies in ruins, he rises resolutely, pouring devotion in an eternal melody. This is the true lover's testament—unwavering dedication, ready to expose his soul despite insurmountable challenges. His plea is a cry from his depths, a desperate invocation of the binding bond, disregarding trivial concerns of agreement for love renders all else insignificant. All that matters is the hunger for the beloved's presence lingering at his core. In the final couplet, the poet paints a portrait of utter desolation—the lover adrift in despair, bereft of companions, reduced to pouring grief into unhearing walls unable to comprehend his profound pain.

ashk bhar laaye kisi ne jo tera naam liya
aur kya hijr mein hota tere biimaaron se

अश्क भर लाए किसी ने जो तिरा नाम लिया
और क्या हिज्र में होता तिरे बीमारों से

My eyes filled with tears
when someone mentioned your name.
What else could be expected

from those who are sick
in your love during separation?

◆

chher naghma koi go dil ki shikasta hain ragein
ham nikaalein ge sada tuute hue taaron se

छेड़ नग़मा कोई गो दिल की शिकस्ता हैं रगें
हम निकालेंगे सदा टूटे हुए तारों से

Please start a melody,
although the veins of the heart are impaired.
We shall produce the sound
from the broken strings.

◆

ham ko teri hai zaruurat n ise bhuul ae dost
tere iqraaron se matlab hai n inkaaron se

हम को तेरी है ज़रूरत न इसे भूल ऐ दोस्त
तेरे इक़रारों से मतलब है न इन्कारों से

I want you, dear friend,
please don't forget this.
I'm not concerned
with your agreements or
disagreements.

◆

ham hain vo bekas o be-yaar k baithe baithe
apna dukh-dard kaha karte hain diivaaron se

हम हैं वो बेकस ओ बे-यार कि बैठे बैठे
अपना दुख-दर्द कहा करते हैं दीवारों से

We are the useless ones
without friends
and while sitting in a corner
we narrate our pain
and grief to the walls.

Tinkling of Footsteps

bahut pahle se un qadmon ki aahat jaan lete hain

From the outset, the poet establishes a profound intuition and connection to life's rhythms, one that transcends mere understanding. He revels in this deep knowing yet remains acutely aware of the human heart's dangers. Love is revealed as a force that can be both a source of creation and destruction, elevating or damning the soul. The lover's gaze becomes a metaphor for the seductive, life-stealing allure of passion. The poet grapples with the true nature of success, suggesting that pursuing worldly acclaim often extracts a terrible cost paid in the soul's currency. He imparts wisdom on matters of the heart, urging readers to look beyond the superficial charm of those seeking to beguile, recognizing the deceptive power of silver-tongued words. Yet even amid such challenges, the poet finds strength in cherished memories. In lonely hours, he wraps himself in a shroud of remembrance, finding solace in the lingering echoes of departed love. Confronting death, he personifies it as a friend and a source of gratitude, recognizing the essential duality of existence where one journey's end marks another's beginning. The poet reflects on the power of his art to touch hearts and minds, recognizing the universal hunger to find meaning and connection in suffering. However, he warns of the disguised enemy wearing the mask of friendship while harbouring malice, highlighting the vulnerability of intimate bonds to betrayal.

bahut pahle se un qadmon ki aahat jaan lete hain
tujhe ae zindagi ham duur se pehchaan lete hai

बहुत पहले से उन क़दमों की आहट जान लेते हैं
तुझे ऐ ज़िंदगी हम दूर से पहचान लेते हैं

I know the tinkling
of those footsteps well,
in advance.
I do recognize you,
O life, from some distance.

◆

meri nazrein bhi aise qaatlon ka jaan o ii'man hain
nigaahein milte hi jo jaan aur iimaan lete hain

मिरी नज़रें भी ऐसे क़ातिलों का जान ओ ईमाँ हैं
निगाहें मिलते ही जो जान और ईमान लेते हैं

My power of sight knows
the winsome killers
and what they believe.
When we meet face to face,
they sweep away
both my life and my faith.

◆

jise kahte hai duniya kaamyaabi vaae naadaani
use kin qiimton par kaamyaab insaan lete hain

जिसे कहती है दुनिया कामयाबी वाए नादानी
उसे किन क़ीमतों पर कामयाब इंसान लेते हैं

What the world calls success
in its total incomprehension
people pay a high price
for attaining it.

◆

nigaah-e baada-guun yuun teri baton ka kya kehna
teri har baat lekin ehtiyaatan chhaan lete hain

निगाह-ए बादा-गूँ यूँ तो तिरी बातों का क्या कहना
तिरी हर बात लेकिन एहतियातन छान लेते हैं

Your speech, my friend
with wine-coloured intoxicated eyes,
is worthy of praise,
but I do exercise restraint
as a matter of caution.

◆

tabii'yat apni ghabraati hai jab sunsaan raaton me
ham aise mein teri yaadon ki chaadar taam lete hain

तबीअ'त अपनी घबराती है जब सुनसान रातों में
हम ऐसे में तिरी यादों की चादर तान लेते हैं

When my mind is troubled
during desolate nights—
in such a miserable situation,
I wrap and drown myself
in the shroud of your thoughts.

◆

khud apna faisla bhi i'shq mein kaafi nahien hota
use bhi kaise kar guzrein jo dil mein thaan lete hain

ख़ुद अपना फ़ैसला भी इ'श्क़ में काफ़ी नहीं होता
उसे भी कैसे कर गुज़रें जो दिल में ठान लेते हैं

Decisions don't matter
when you are in love.
How do I get past
my determination?
It's a challenge.

◆

jise suurat bataate hain pata deti hai siirat ka
ibaarat dekh kar jis tarah maa'ni jaan lete hain

जिसे सूरत बताते हैं पता देती है सीरत का
इबारत देख कर जिस तरह मा'नी जान लेते हैं

It is a gateway to the inner self,
and not just facial appearance.
I look at the writing and
know its meaning.

◆

rafiiq-e zindagi thi ab aniis-e vaqt-e aakhir hai
tera ae maut ham ye duusra ehsaan lete hain

रफ़ीक़-ए ज़िंदगी थी अब अनीस-ए वक़्त-ए आख़िर है
तिरा ऐ मौत हम ये दूसरा एहसान लेते हैं

She was a friend in my life.
Now, towards its end,
she has become a confidante.
Death, I'm doubly indebted to you.

◆

zamaana vaardaat-e qalb sun-ne ko tarasta hai
isi se to sar-aankhon par mera diivaan lete hain

ज़माना वारदात-ए क़ल्ब सुनने को तरसता है
इसी से तो सर आँखों पर मिरा दीवान लेते हैं

People are thirsty to know
how my heart was wounded—
and that is why they cherish
the collection of my ghazals.

◆

'Firaq' aksar badal kar bhes milta hai koi kaafir
kabhi ham jaan lete hain kabhi pehchaan lete hain

'फ़िराक़' अक्सर बदल कर भेस मिलता है कोई काफ़िर
कभी हम जान लेते हैं कभी पहचान लेते हैं

In disguise, a *kafir* often tries
to meet me, Firaq.
Sometimes, I guess his intent,
and sometimes, I know
that he is here to kill.

Bliss and Grief

faza tabussum-e sub-h-e bahaar thi lekin

Each couplet in this ghazal is a testament to the poet's melodic prowess. From the start, he combines a radiant spring morning smile with tears reaching his beloved's abode—a duality that reflects how bliss and profound grief are often intertwined in life's grand tapestry. He grapples with existence's profound, volatile nature, finding jubilant gatherings one moment yet starkly confronted by lurking death the next—the truth of the essential human condition. Yet amid existential uncertainty, the poet finds solace in love's transformative power. He speaks of lovers' union stripping away pretense to reveal inner beauty—a transcendent, divine glimpse found only in another's embrace. The ghazal takes us through the cycles of life and death, the dance of endings and beginnings. The night of death threatens to consume all we cherish, yet glimmers the promise of a new dawn's chance to begin anew. But the path demands courage and fortitude—a willingness to bear the weight of our humanity. Only the sensitive soul's passion and fire can embrace being fully alive in ecstasy and agony. As the end nears, the poet's reflection on memory's bittersweet nature grows poignant—joy and sorrow come with remembrance, love's imprint lingering like sweet heartache. This ghazal celebrates the enduring human spirit, the beauty, and the pain shaping who we are. Firaq invites us to embrace the fullness of our experiences, find purpose amid life's great mysteries, and live with an open heart.

faza tabussum-e sub-h-e bahaar thi lekin
pahunch ke manzil-e jaanaan pe aankh bhar aaii

फ़ज़ा तबस्सुम-ए सुब्ह-ए बहार थी लेकिन
पहुँच के मंज़िल-ए जानाँ पे आँख भर आई

The morning of spring
brimmed with smiles.
When I reached
my beloved's place,
my eyes filled with tears.

◆

kisi ki bazm-e tarab mein hayaat bat-ti thi
umiid-vaaron mein kal maut bhi nazar aaii

किसी की बज़्म-ए तरब में हयात बटती थी
उमीद-वारों में कल मौत भी नज़र आई

In someone's happy gathering,
life was the gift for a giveaway.
Among the hopefuls,
we saw even death waiting.

•

zara visaal ke baa'd aaiina to dekh ae dost
tere jamaal ki doshiizgi nikhar aaii

ज़रा विसाल के बा'द आइना तो देख ऐ दोस्त
तिरे जमाल की दोशीज़गी निखर आई

My love, look at the mirror
after our union.
The maidenhood of your beauty
showed itself in sharp contours.

•

ruki ruki si shab-e marg khatm par aaii
vo pau phati vo naaii zindagi nazar aaii

रुकी रुकी सी शब-ए मर्ग ख़त्म पर आई
वो पौ फटी वो नई ज़िंदगी नज़र आई

Slowly and gradually,
the evening of my demise ended.
Lo, the dawn appeared,
and I saw traces of a new life.

•

ye mor vo hai k parchhaayiaan bhi deingi n saath
musafaron se kaho us ki rahguzar aaii

ये मोड़ वो है कि परछाइयाँ भी देंगी न साथ
मुसाफ़िरों से कहो उस की रहगुज़र आई

It is the bend where your shadow
will leave you alone.
Tell the passengers
that her pathway has arrived.

◆

kahaan har ek se insaaniyat ka baar utha
k ye bala bhi tere aa'shiqon ke sar aaii

कहाँ हर एक से इंसानियत का बार उठा
कि ये बला भी तिरे आशिक़ों के सर आई

No, not everyone could lift
the burden of humanness.
Even this calamity
had to be borne by your lovers.

◆

dilon mein aaj teri yaad muddaton ke baa'd
b-chehra-e mutabasumm b-chasm-e tar aaii

दिलों में आज तिरी याद मुद्दतों के बा'द
ब-चेहरा-ए मुतबस्सिम ब-चश्म-ए तर आई

Your thoughts in my heart
after such a long time!
With a smiley face
and a tearful eye, it came.

◆

naya nahien hai mujhe marg-e na-gahaan ka pyaam
hazaar rang se apni mujhe khabar aaii

नया नहीं है मुझे मर्ग-ए ना-गहाँ का पयाम
हज़ार रंग से अपनी मुझे ख़बर आई

The message
of untimely death
is not new to me.
I came to know
about my well-being
in thousands of colours.

◆

faza ko jaise koi raag chiirta jaaye
teri nigaah dilon mein yuun utar aaii

फ़ज़ा को जैसे कोई राग चीरता जाए
तिरी निगाह दिलों में यूँही उतर आई

As if a melody is piercing
the ambiance.
Your eyes struck
innocent hearts
without warning.

◆

ajab nahien k chaman dar chaman bane har phuul
kali kali ki saba ja ke god bhar aaii

अजब नहीं कि चमन-दर-चमन बने हर फूल
कली कली की सबा जा के गोद भर आई

It is not strange
to see flowers
in one garden
after another.
The breeze emanating

from each bud
impregnated one and all.

◆

shab-e 'Firaq' uthe dil mein aur bhi kuchh dard
kahuun ye kaise teri yaad raat bhar aaii

शब-ए-'फ़िराक़' उठे दिल में और भी कुछ दर्द
कहूँ ये कैसे तिरी याद रात-भर आई

Firaq, in this evening of separation,
there is a new pain arising.
With whom do I share
the news that I missed you
the whole night.

Earth on the Brink of Awakening

chhalak ke kam n ho aisi koi sharaab nahien

The poet plunges into the depths of existence, weaving a fabric of passion. Each couplet is revelatory, a window into the profound human experience. He masterfully encapsulates the essence of true passion, likening it to an overflowing, uncontainable wine. The narcissus' glance alone transforms the world, testifying to love's all-consuming nature. As the ghazal unfolds, Firaq grapples with the anticipation of change, the sense that the earth itself awakens. In this charged atmosphere, dreaming takes revolutionary power—the promise of our transformative potential. Yet, amid this fervour, the poet remains acutely aware of the divine omnipotence that holds sway over earth, sky, and the universe's fabric. Love takes a new perspective in the face of such awe-inspiring might, a reminder of human fragility and limitations. But the poet sees transformation's potential, the need for our blood to become pure, life-giving water—a call to action, pursuing a brighter, more luminous existence. And despite challenges, his belief in the resilient human spirit shines through. Even in the darkest times, when life rots from within, hope remains in dreams of a beckoning better future. This ghazal wields the power to hold a mirror to the human soul, reflecting our very essence. Through colourful imagery and expressive language, it invites us to confront the depths of our passions, grapple with swirling change, and find solace in knowing that t we're not alone in our struggles.

chhalak ke kam n ho aisi koi sharaab nahien
nigaah-e nargis-e raa'na tera javaab nahien

छलक के कम न हो ऐसी कोई शराब नहीं
निगाह-ए नर्गिस-ए रा'ना तिरा जवाब नहीं

No wine would survive
the loss of an overflow
A glance at a beautiful narcissus
has no limit to what it can do.

◆

zamiin jaag rahi hai k inqilaab hai kal
vo raat hai koi zarra bhi mahv-e khwaab nahien

ज़मीन जाग रही है कि इंक़लाब है कल
वो रात है कोई ज़र्रा भी महव-ए ख़्वाब नहीं

Is the earth awake,
or is the revolution coming?
Not even a particle is dreaming.
What a night!

◆

zamiin us ki falak us ka kaaenaat us ki
kuchh aisa i'shq tera khaan-maan kharaab nahien

ज़मीन उस की फ़लक उस का काएनात उस की
कुछ ऐसा इ'श्क़ तिरा ख़ानुमाँ-ख़राब नहीं

He owns the earth,
the sky, and the universe.
Your kind of love
is not that godforsaken.

◆

abhi kuchh aur ho insaan ka lahu paani
abhi hayaat ke chehre par aab o taab nahien

अभी कुछ और हो इंसान का लहू पानी
अभी हयात के चेहरे पर आब ओ ताब नहीं

Human blood needs
to be more like water.
Even more.
The face of life so far has not shown
any lustrous brightness.

◆

dikha to deti hai behtar hayaat ke sapne
kharaab ho ke bhi ye zindagi kharaab nahien

दिखा तो देती है बेहतर हयात के सपने
ख़राब हो के भी ये ज़िंदगी ख़राब नहीं

She shows her dreams
of a better future.
Even though it is rotting,
life is not that bad.

Intensity of Inner Sorrow

ye maut o adam kon o makaan aur hi kuchh hai

Firaq often addresses himself in the third person. The closing couplet powerfully asserts the uniqueness of his verse, following in the footsteps of his mentor, Ghalib. While many write great rhymes, Firaq's expression and language are distinct. In this ghazal, he challenges perceptions of reality itself—death, non-existence, and all creation—suggesting that a deeper truth lies beneath appearances, a beckoning mystery to unravel. He grapples with love's enduring power, recognizing the unchanging essence of his beloved's eyes amid his transformed perceptions over time—a testament to the heart's resilience. Yet he remains aware of the inner sorrow's intensity, the hidden pain smoldering like smoke from a flame. The poem reminds us of the depth and complexity of our emotional landscapes, with the profoundest experiences often hidden from view. This complexity is nowhere more evident than in love's paradoxical nature. In the lovers' gathering, boundaries between grief and happiness dissolve into pure, all-consuming sensations. Yet the poet is also attuned to distance's allure, the mysterious appeal of nearness and remoteness—a delicate dance of longing and fulfillment. Weaving rich metaphors and symbolism of eyes, smoke, flames, lightning, wounds, and seasons, each image illuminates hidden human truths. As he delves into these universalities, Firaq showcases his unique voice, distinguishing him from his peers. The finale boldly asserts his individuality, reminding that while others are poets, his recitation and language are unmatched.

ye maut o adam kon o makaan aur hi kuchh hai
sun le k mera naam o nishaan aur hi kuchh hai

ये मौत ओ अदम कौन ओ मकाँ और ही कुछ है
सुन ले कि मिरा नाम ओ निशाँ और ही कुछ है

This death and non-existence,
this whole creation—
it is something else.
Please listen to me and my name.
It is something else.

◆

itna to yaqiin hai k vohi hain teri aankhein
is par bhi magar vahm o gumaan aur hi kuchh hai

इतना तो यक़ीं है कि वही हैं तिरी आँखें
इस पर भी मगर वहम ओ गुमाँ और ही कुछ है

I'm sure about one thing—
your eyes are the same
as they used to be.
Yet this impulse and
my imagination are something else.

◆

sho'lon mein vo andaaz kahaan soz-e nihaan ke
uth-ta hai jo dil se vo dhuaan aur hi kuchh hai

शो'लों में वो अंदाज़ कहाँ सोज़-ए निहाँ के
उठता है जो दिल से वो धुआँ और ही कुछ है

The manner of inner sorrow
inside these flames and
the smoke that is rising
from the heart
it is something else.

◆

ik kaifiyat-e raaz hai gham hai n musarrat
is bazm-e mohabbat mein samaan aur hi kuchh hai

इक कैफ़ियत-ए राज़ है ग़म है न मसर्रत
इस बज़्म-ए मोहब्बत में समाँ और ही कुछ है

It is a state in which
I'm hiding a secret.
There is no grief and no happiness.
In this lovers' gathering,
the spectacle,
it is something else.

◆

jo marhala-e kurbat o duuri se guzar jaaye
sunte hain k vo jazv-e nihaan aur hi kuchh hai

जो मरहला-ए क़ुर्बत ओ दूरी से गुज़र जाए
सुनते हैं कि वो जज़्ब-ए निहाँ और ही कुछ है

The moment that passes
in nearness and remoteness,
is said to hide allurement and
it is something else.

◆

ya dard ke naghmon mein vohi hai teri aavaaz
ya parda-e saaz-e rag-e jaan aur hi kuchh hai

या दर्द के नग़्मों में वही है तिरी आवाज़
या पर्दा-ए साज़-ए रग-ए जाँ और ही कुछ है

Either the painful melodies
have your familiar voice,

or the veil of the instrument
of the vein of life,
it is something else.

◆

bijli ke chamakne mein kahaan i'shq ki garmi
vo sho'la-e larzaan o tapaan aur hi kuchh hai

बिजली के चमकने में कहाँ इ'श्क़ की गर्मी
वो शोला-ए-लर्ज़ाँ ओ तपाँ और ही कुछ है

Where is the heat of love
in the shine of lightning?
This shaking and the wavering flame,
it is something else.

◆

jo zakham khila de jo mera rang ura de
vo fasl-e gul o fasl-e khizaan aur hi kuchh hai

जो ज़ख़्म खिला दे जो मिरा रंग उड़ा दे
वो फ़स्ल-ए गुल ओ फ़स्ल-ए ख़िज़ाँ और ही कुछ है

Something that makes
my wounds blossom,
and something that causes my colour to fade.
That state of spring and
that state of autumn,
it is something else.

◆

shaa'yir hain 'Firaq' aur bhi is daur mein lekin
ye rang-e biyaan rang-e zabaan aur hi kuchh hai

शाइ'र हैं 'फ़िराक़' और भी इस दौर में लेकिन
ये रंग-ए बयाँ रंग-ए ज़बाँ और ही कुछ है

Firaq, there are other poets currently.
But this style of recitation
and this colourfulness of language
it is something else.

Enigma of Life and Death

har naala tere dard se ab aur hi kuchh hai

Firaq grapples with the paradoxical nature of devotion and desire, observing that while the faithful may sacrifice their lives, the yearning for existence is even more profound. It is a yearning unsatisfied by mere gestures but demanding deeper, authentic engagement with the world and ourselves. He invites contemplation of life and death's enigma, the secret cycle of existence's evolution over time—a mystery defying easy explanation, only unravelled through the heart's lens. Yet he remains attuned to the absence of divine retribution, realizing that doomsday's sun and hell's fires are illusions that distract from the true source of our suffering. Instead, he warns of a different rage-fury within the human soul, a testament to the contradictions defining our inner lives. He observes that the world's actual troubles lie beyond religion or ethics in quieter, more intimate corners of the heart. Amidst weighty themes, he remains attuned to the awakening's power to rouse the world and lull non-existence to sleep—the duality of the human experience's longing for action and repose.

har naala tere dard se ab aur hi kuchh hai
har naghma sar-e bazm-e tarab aur hi kuchh hai

हर नाला तिरे दर्द से अब और ही कुछ है
हर नग़मा सर-ए बज़्म-ए तरब और ही कुछ है

Each lamentation
because of the pain
that you gave me
is something else.
Each musical note
for pleasure seekers
is something different.

◆

arbaab-e vafa jaan bhi dene ko hain tayyaar
hasti ka magar husn-e talab aur hi kuchh hai

अरबाब-ए वफ़ा जान भी देने को हैं तयार
हस्ती का मगर हुस्न-ए तलब और ही कुछ है

Those who value fidelity
are ready to sacrifice their lives.
But what the beauty of existence desires
is something different.

◆

ye kaam n le naala o fariyaad o fughaan se
aflaak ulat dene ka dhab aur hi kuchh hai

ये काम न ले नाला ओ फ़र्याद ओ फ़ुग़ां से
अफ़्लाक उलट देने का ढब और ही कुछ है

Don't use your laments
and cries for this.
The way to turn heaven around
is something different.

◆

ik silsila-e raaz hai jiina k ho marna
jab aur hi kuchh tha ab aur hi kuchh hai

इक सिलसिला-ए राज़ है जीना कि हो मरना
जब और ही कुछ था मगर अब और ही कुछ है

The tradition of living
and dying is a secret.
It was different
in the times gone by, and it
is something different.

◆

kuchh mehr-e qiyaamat hai n kuchh naar-e jahannum
hoshiaar k vo qahar o ghazab aur hi kuchh hai

कुछ मेहर-ए क़यामत है न कुछ नार-ए जहन्नम
होश्यार कि वो क़हर ओ ग़ज़ब और ही कुछ है

There is neither the sun
of the doomsday
nor the fires of hell.
Be aware!
This rage rising within
is something different.

◆

mazhab ki kharaabi hai n akhlaaq ki pasti
duniya ke masaa'ib ka sabab aur hi kuchh hai

मज़हब की ख़राबी है न अख़्लाक़ की पस्ती
दुनिया के मसाइब का सबब और ही कुछ है

It is neither the fault of the religion
nor the decline of ethics.
The cause of the world's calamities
is something different.

◆

duniya ko jaga de jo a'dam ko bhi sula de
sunte hain k vo roz vo shab aur hi kuchh hai

दुनिया को जगा दे जो अदम को भी सुला दे
सुनते हैं कि वो रोज़ वो शब और ही कुछ है

Something that wakes up the world
and puts the nonexistence to sleep.
That day and that evening,
I appreciated
is something different.

◆

aankhon ne 'firaq' aaj n puuchho jo dikhaaya
jo kuchh nazar aata hai vo sab aur hi kuchh hai

आँखों ने 'फ़िराक़' आज न पूछो जो दिखाया
जो कुछ नज़र आता है वो सब और ही कुछ है

Firaq, don't ask me
what the eyes showed me.
Whatever you see
is something different.

Inner Landscape

dete hain jaam-e shahaadat mujhe maa'luum n tha

Firaq grapples with love's all-consuming nature, permeating every aspect of existence. Even lifelong weariness of worldly sorrows is linked to the beloved, testifying to love's pervasive influence on the human psyche. Yet the poet remains attuned to love's transformative potential, marvelling at how the ordinary becomes extraordinary, mere wine drops becoming divine sparks in the beloved's hands. This transformative power is most evident in the poet's inner landscape. Since beholding the beloved, he has been plunged into profound turmoil—the complex politics of beauty upending firmly held beliefs. Yet the poet recognizes love's unexpected guises, realizing it can manifest as a human force catalyzing doomsday's upheaval—love's unpredictable nature striking at any moment, leaving us forever changed. With this comes vulnerability, as we acknowledge love's destructive capacity. Once central, the poet's heart lies shattered at the beloved's feet—a devastating consequence he was unprepared for. Yet, amid ruin, clarity emerges—understanding the depths of heartache only in the beloved's absence, their beings eternally intertwined. This leads to a startling conclusion: love's ultimate testament is choosing death over falling in love, a choice that defies previous beliefs, revealing love's sacrificial demands.

dete hain jaam-e shahaadat mujhe maa'luum n tha
hai ye aain-e mohabbat mujhe maa'luum n tha

देते हैं जाम-ए-शहादत मुझे मा'लूम न था
है ये आईन-ए मोहब्बत मुझे मा'लूम न था

They give you
the drink of martyrdom.
I didn't know it.
It is said to be
the code of love.
I didn't know it.

◆

i'shq bas mein hai mashie-at ke aqiida tha mera
us ke bas mein hai mashie-at mujhe maa'luum n tha

इ'श्क़ बस में है मशिय्यत के अक़ीदा था मिरा
उस के बस में है मशिय्यत मुझे मा'लूम न था

Love is in the hands
of the unknown.
That was my belief.
But it controls the unknown.
I didn't know it.

◆

aaj har qatra-e mai ban gaya ik chingaari
thi ye saaqi ki shararat mujhe maa'luum n tha

आज हर क़तरा-ए मय बन गया इक चिंगारी
थी ये साक़ी की शरारत मुझे मा'लूम न था

Today, every drop of wine
has become a spark.
It was Saqi's playful doing.
I didn't know it.

◆

gham-e hasti se jo be-zaar raha main ik u'mr
tujh se bhi thi use nisbat mujhe maa'luum n tha

ग़म-ए हस्ती से जो बेज़ार रहा मैं इक उम्र
तुझ से भी थी उसे निस्बत मुझे मा'लूम न था

Her drunken eye picked up
a sword in the gathering.
How lovers change
their game plans!
I didn't know it.

◆

jab se dekha hai tujhe mujh se hai meri an-ban
husn ka rang-e siyaasat mujhe maa'luum n tha

जब से देखा है तुझे मुझ से है मेरी अन-बन
हुस्न का रंग-ए सियासत मुझे मा'लूम न था

I'm not one with myself
since I saw you.
What was the nature
of beauty's politics?
I didn't know it.

◆

shakl insaan ki ho chaal bhi insaan ki ho
yuun bhi aati hai qiyaamat mujhe maa'luum n tha

शक्ल इंसान की हो चाल भी इंसान की हो
यूँ भी आती है क़यामत मुझे मा'लूम न था

She looks human.
She behaves like a human.
Doomsday comes in this form.
I didn't know it.

◆

sar-e maamuura-e aa'lam ye dil-e khana-kharaab
mit gaya teri badolat mujhe maa'luum n tha

सर-ए मामूरा-ए आलम ये दिल-ए ख़ाना-ख़राब
मिट गया तेरी बदौलत मुझे मा'लूम न था

In front of the neighborhood of
this inhabited world
stands my shattered heart.
It was eradicated because of you.
I didn't know it.

◆

dard-e dil kya hai khula aaj tere larne par
tujh se itni thi mohabbat mujhe maa'luum n tha

दर्द-ए दिल क्या है खुला आज तिरे लड़ने पर
तुझ से इतनी थी मोहब्बत मुझे मा'लूम न था

What is the affliction of the heart?
I realized when you parted with me.
I loved you so very much.
I didn't know it.

◆

dam nikal jaaye magar dil n lagaaye koi
i'shq ki ye thi vasiiyat mujhe maa'luum n tha

दम निकल जाए मगर दिल न लगाए कोई
इ'श्क़ की ये थी वसिय्यत मुझे मा'लूम न था

You can choose to die,
but don't fall in love.
It was love's testament.
I didn't know it.

◆

husn vaalon ko bahut sahl samajh rakkha tha
tujh pe aaye gi tabiiyat mujhe maa'luum n tha

हुस्न वालों को बहुत सहल समझ रक्खा था
तुझ पे आएगी तबीअत मुझे मा'लूम न था

I thought those beautiful ones
were easy to deal with.
I would fall in love with you.
I didn't know it.

Vitality of Spring

ye narm narm hava jhilmila rahe hain charaagh

This tender, enchanting ghazal envelops us in profound intimacy and wonder. The breeze's soft caress and shimmering dance of lights evoke the beloved's fragrant thoughts, filling the air—a heady, intoxicating perfume that transports us to pure, unadulterated bliss. The beloved's radiant smile becomes a luminous leitmotif that weaves through the fabric, illuminating hearts like scintillating temple lights—a divine presence that uplifts the soul. Yet the poet remains attuned to deeper existential currents through the drawn sword's image, evoking tension where life and death profoundly disagree. The vitality of abundant spring-flaming flowers and blooming gardens stretching to the horizon symbolizes unstoppable nature and the promise of new beginnings. Hope resonates in whispers of future love unburdened by past sorrows. But the poet, with a keen sense, perceives the beloved's gaze as a mysterious power—eyes becoming the world's secret, tracking all who fall under their transformative, illuminating spell. As dawn approaches, he senses a collective yearning, a shared horizon-gazing hope burning bright, further illuminating the transformative nature of love. Perhaps love's most profound testament manifests in the beloved's luminous footprints lighting the world, even for those hiding from stars, reminding us that connection and transformation remain possible in the most profound isolation. Inwardly, the poet turns to love's wounding scars ,lighting up hearts daring to open themselves—testaments to the depth of flowing emotions, reminders that even in darkness, we live and feel. The finale invites reveling in the shimmering, overflowing molten beauty of passion—a call to surrender to love's transformative power in all forms and to embrace our full humanity. Firaq offers a glimpse of the divine, a transcendent moment reminding us of infinite inner possibilities.

ye narm narm hava jhilmila rahe hain charaagh
tere khayal ki khushbu se bas rahe hain khwaab

ये नर्म नर्म हवा झिलमिला रहे हैं चराग़
तिरे ख़याल की ख़ुशबू से बस रहे हैं दिमाग़

This soft, very soft breeze.
The lights are shimmering.
With the fragrance of
the presence of your thoughts,
senses are filling up.

◆

dilon ko tere tabassumm ki yaad yuun aaii
k jagmaga uthein jis tarah mandiron mein charaagh

दिलों को तेरे तबस्सुम की याद यूँ आई
कि जगमगा उठें जिस तरह मंदिरों में चराग़

Hearts remembered your smile
like scintillating lights radiate
in the temples.

◆

jhalakti hai khinchi shamshiir mein nai duniya
hayaat o maut ke milte nahien hain aaj dimaagh

झलकती है खिंची शमशीर में नई दुनिया
हयात ओ मौत के मिलते नहीं हैं आज दिमाग़

In the drawn sword
shines a new world.
Life and death today are not thinking
the same thing.

◆

tamaam shola-e gul hai tamaam mauj-e bahaar
k ta-hadd-e nigaah-e shauq lahlahaate hain baagh

तमाम शो'ला-ए गुल है तमाम मौज-ए बहार
कि ता-हद-ए निगह-ए शौक़ लहलहाते हैं बाग़

Flowers are flaming,
spring is everywhere.
As far as the eye could see,
there are blooming gardens.

◆

nai zamiin naya aasmaan nai duniya
suna to hai k mohabbat ko in dinon hai faraagh

नई ज़मीन नया आसमाँ नई दुनिया
सुना तो है कि मोहब्बत को इन दिनों है फ़राग़

New land, new sky,
and a new world.
I've heard that love is free
from care nowadays.

◆

jo chhup ke taaron ki aankhon se paaon dharta hai
usi ke naqsh-e kaf-e pa se jal uthe hain charaagh

जो छुप के तारों की आँखों से पाँव धरता है
उसी के नक़्श-ए कफ़-ए पा से जल उठे हैं चराग़

Her eyes are becoming
the world's secret.
This is the way she keeps
track of the hearts.

◆

jahaan-e raaz hui ja rahi hai aankh teri
kuchh is tarah vo dilon ka laga rahi hai suraagh

जहान-ए राज़ हुई जा रही है आँख तिरी
कुछ इस तरह वो दिलों का लगा रही है सुराग़

All the eyes are fixated
on the coming dawn.
We can find traces of the rays
of the rising sun.

◆

nigaahein matla-e nau par hain ek aa'lam ki
k mil raha hai kisi phuut-ti kiran ka suraagh

निगाहें मतला-ए नौ पर हैं एक आलम की
कि मिल रहा है किसी फूटती किरन का सुराग़

The one who places her feet
hiding from the eyes of the stars.
Say thanks to that person.
Those footprints
have lighted the stars.

◆

dilon mein daagh-e mohabbat ka ab ye aa'lam hai
k jaise niind mein duube hon pichhli raat charaagh

दिलों में दाग़-ए-मोहब्बत का अब ये आ'लम है
कि जैसे नींद में डूबे हों पिछ्ली रात चराग़

This is the state of wounds of love
in the hearts around—
as if the sleep drowned the lights
last night.

◆

'firaq' bazm-e charaaghaan hai mahfil-e rindaan
saje hain pighli hui aag se chhalakte aayaagh

'फ़िराक़' बज़्म-ए-चराग़ाँ है महफ़िल-ए रिंदाँ
सजे हैं पिघली हुई आग से छलकते अयाग़

Firaq, the gathering of drink lovers
looks like the mass of shimmering lights.
Overflowing wine glasses,
beautifully arranged,
are shaped by the molten fire.

Seeing beyond the Surface

ek muddat se teri yaad bhi aaii n hamein

Each couplet in this ghazal is a gem in its own right, shining with profound meaning while seamlessly mixing with the others to create a breathtaking poetic journey. Firaq's words paint pictures of a heart caught between attachment and detachment, yearning for an elusive love. Firaq challenges our perceptions of love and the characters we encounter. He urges us to distinguish between mere kindness and genuine affection, reminding us that even the quietest of hearts can house tumultuous emotions. With metaphors as lush as blooming roses and melodies as haunting as the nightingale's song, Firaq asserts his identity as both the lover and the beloved. He invites us to see beyond the surface and recognize the multifaceted nature of the poet's soul. As we navigate the unpredictable landscapes of love-struck individuals, Firaq's words serve as a compass, guiding us through the intricacies of the heart.

ek muddat se teri yaad bhi aaii n hamein
aur ham bhuul gaye hon tujhe aisa bhi nahien

एक मुद्दत से तिरी याद भी आई न हमें
और हम भूल गए हों तुझे ऐसा भी नहीं

I haven't thought about you
for a very long time.
That I have completely forgotten you,
that is also not the case.

◆

muunh se ham apne ko bura to nahien kahte k 'firaq'
hai tera dost magar aadmi achha bhi nahien

मुँह से हम अपने बुरा तो नहीं कहते कि 'फ़िराक़'
है तिरा दोस्त मगर आदमी अच्छा भी नहीं

Firaq is not a good person.
That's not what I say.
He is your friend, but he is not
an honorable person.

◆

sar mein sauda bhi nahien dil mein tamanna bhi nahien
lekin is tark-e mohabbat ka bharosa bhi nahien

सर में सौदा भी नहीं दिल में तमन्ना भी नहीं
लेकिन इस तर्क-ए मोहब्बत का भरोसा भी नहीं

No madness in my head,
no desire in my heart.
But I am not persuaded
that I have abandoned love.

◆

dil ki ginti n yagaanon mein n begaanon mein
lekin us jalva-gah-e naaz se uth-ta bhi nahien

दिल की गिनती न यगानों में न बेगानों में
लेकिन उस जल्वा-गह-ए नाज़ से उठता भी नहीं

The heart is nothing special,
neither a favorite nor a stranger,
but it is unwilling to leave the place
of beauty's exposition.

◆

mehrbaani ko muhabbat nahien kahte ae dost
aah ab mujh se teri ranjish-e beja bhi nahien

मेहरबानी को मोहब्बत नहीं कहते ऐ दोस्त
आह अब मुझ से तिरी रंजिश-ए बेजा भी नहीं

My friend, let us not call kindness
an act of love.
Alas, the indifference now is such
that you do not have a single grievance
against me.

◆

baat ye hai k sukuun-e dil-e vahshi ka maqaam
kunj-e zindaan bhi nahien vus'at-e sahra bhi nahien

बात ये है कि सुकून-ए दिल-ए वहशी का मक़ाम
कुंज-ए ज़िंदाँ भी नहीं वुसअ'त-ए सहरा भी नहीं

Here is the dilemma—the place
for the peace of my savage heart
is neither the groove of the prison
nor the expanse of the desert.

◆

ar-re sayyaad hamien gul hain hamien bulbul bhi
tu ne kuchh aah suna bhi nahien dekha bhi nahien

अरे सय्याद हमीं गुल हैं हमीं बुलबुल हैं
तू ने कुछ आह सुना भी नहीं देखा भी नहीं

O hunter, I am the rose.
I am the nightingale too.
You haven't heard any such thing.
You haven't seen any such thing.

◆

yuun to hangaame uthaate nahien diivaana-e i'shq
magar ae dost kuchh aison ka thikaana bhi nahien

यूँ तो हंगामे उठाते नहीं दीवाना-ए इ'श्क़
मगर ऐ दोस्त कुछ ऐसों का ठिकाना भी नहीं

Mad lovers are not known
to cause trouble, but, my friend,
you can't be sure about these folks.

A Poignant Farewell

duur duur tak laakh pukaaro us ka suraagh nahien milta

Firaq invites new voices to breathe life into the ancient art of the ghazal. His verses whisper secrets of the heart, exploring the depths of longing and the bittersweet nature of love. In the stillness of the night, Firaq's words come alive with haunting echoes of memories and the piercing pain of absence. Through sharp metaphors and delicate imagery, he unravels the essence of the ghazal—a symphony of suffering and agony, the heartbeat of love. Firaq speaks of the beloved's gaze, a force that penetrates the soul, leaving an indelible mark. He ponders the mysterious forces shaping his poetry and marvels at the transformative power of tears. As his tales spread across the world, Firaq questions who can truly comprehend the depths of his emotions. His words become a mirror, reflecting the universal human condition, offering solace and companionship in the shared language of the heart.

Duur duur tak laakh pukaaro us ka suraagh nahien milta
jo tahziib rasm-e ahd ki vaadiyon mein kho jaati hai

दूर दूर तक लाख पुकारो उस का सुराग़ नहीं मिलता
जो तहज़ीब रस्म-ए कुहन की वादियों में खो जाती है

We can try calling from far away,
but we find no trace of civilizations.
They were laid to rest
in the ravines of redundant routines.

◆

ab tum se rukhsat hota huun aao sambhaalo saaz-e ghazal
naye taraane chhero mere naghmon ko niind aati hai

अब तुम से रुखसत होता हूँ आओ सम्भालो साज़-ए ग़ज़ल
नए तराने छेड़ो मेरे नग़मों को नींद आती है

I'm taking your leave.
Come and take control

of the instruments of ghazal.
Start new tunes and strains.
My melodies will now rest
and take a nap.

◆

jab aankhein jhapkaate hain ahd jab duniya so jaati hai
un raaton ke sannaton mein mujh ko teri yaad aati hai

जब आँखें झपकाते हैं तारे जब दुनिया सो जाती है
उन रातों के सन्नाटों में मुझ को तेरी याद आती है

When the stars are blinking,
and the world goes to sleep,
in the stillness of those nights,
I miss you, mightily.

◆

ae shab-e gham ke jaagne vaalo tum ko to hai khud maa'luum
jaate jaate gham jaata hai aate aate niind aati hai

ऐ शब्-ए ग़म के जागने वालो तुम को तो खुद है मालूम
जाते-जाते ग़म जाता है आते आते नींद आती है

Those who are awake
during this night of distress,
they know it quite well.
Affliction takes time to leave,
and the sleep takes time to get you.

◆

kahne vaalo kahne ki yuun laakhon baatein hain lekin
jis ko ghazal kahiye bas vo to ek baat dohraati hai

कहने वालो कहने की यूं लाखों बातें हैं लेकिन
जिस को ग़ज़ल कहिये बस वो तो एक बात दोहराती है

If we want to talk,
there are millions of topics.
Something that we call ghazal
repeats just one thing—
my suffering and agony.

◆

mujh se puuchho kya hai logo us ki thahri-thahri nigaah
ek chhuri jo chalti nahien aur dil mein utarti jaati hai

मुझ से पूछो कया है लोगो उस की ठहरी-ठहरी निगाह
एक छुरी जो चलती नहीं और दिल में उतरती जाती है

People, you can ask me
about her highly composed eyes.
They are like a blunt cutter
that doesn't gash
but deeply sink into the heart.

◆

main ne us ko nahien dekha hai kaise bataon kaise kahuun
kis ke rukh se mari ghazal ya-rabb ghuunghat sarkaati hai

मैं ने उस को नहीं देखा है कैसे बताऊँ कैसे कहूँ
किस के रुख से मेरी ग़ज़ल या-रब्ब घूँघट सरकाती है

I haven't seen her.
So, what can I say?

Whose force is it, O god,
that my ghazal's grace lifts a veil?

◆

patta patta buuta buuta tab aata hai rang pe jab
apne aansuuon se shabnam gulzaar ka munh dho jaati hai

पत्ता पत्ता बूटा बूटा तब आता है रंग पे जब
अपने आंसूओं से शबनम गुलज़ार का मुँह धो जाती है

Every leaf, every little plant gains colour
when dewdrops with their tears
sprinkle the glow of the garden.

◆

duniya-duniya aa'lam-aa'lam jis ke aaj afsaane hain
us 'firaq' ki raam-kahaani kis ki samajh mein aati hai

दुनिया-दुनिया आलम-आलम जिस के आज अफ़साने हैं
उस 'फ़िराक़' की राम-कहानी किस की समझ में आती है

His stories
have crazily gained traction
in the whole world.
But I wonder who can make sense

of Firaq's tale of woe and
heart-touching narrative.

seven

NISADA (NI)

For Hindus, the concept of vahdat ul vujuud (the complete unity between the Creator and the creation) is not simply an intellectual belief. It is a spiritual experience and a solid inner feeling. In India, religion has always remained the soul of philosophy, and philosophy, in turn, has been the intellectual underpinning of religion. Hindus prefer not to engage in dry academic exercises; their religion is not a collection of beliefs. It is an aggregation of spiritual thoughts and feelings which are expressed in complete unison...

Suppose the soul of Indian-ness is allowed to enter Urdu poetry. In that case, the created verse will gain purpose, integration with life, purity, and spiritual distinctiveness. It will make such melodies that each note will surpass the uniqueness of the whole piece.[15]

–Firaq

FIRAQ AND 'HINDUSTANIYAT' (INDIANNESS)

When Firaq gained consciousness, India was in the grip of British colonialism. At the same time, he was hearing

[15]Hanafi, Shamim, and Suhail Ahmad Faruqi, eds. *Firaq: Dayar-e Shab Ka Musafir,* Maktaba Jamia Limited, New Delhi, 1996, pp. 116 and 146.

voices about the Indian Renaissance. These ideas had originated with Raja Ram Mohan Roy. Sir Syed Ahmad was a small part of it. Thinkers like Swami Vivekananda and Aurobindo Ghosh made significant contributions. When the British enslaved India, an impression gained momentum that Indians had lost control of their destiny. Several movements started to correct this situation. Some aimed at social and cultural rejuvenation, while others focused on gaining some form of self-rule. A poet growing up in this environment could not help but confront the question of his identity. Who am I? What kind of culture do I belong to? What is my cultural heritage? As a young boy, his exposure to India's scriptures and mythologies was due to the religious atmosphere at home. The surrounding environment was filled with natural beauty. Yet there was no answer to the question of what it meant to be an Indian, or what was the essence of Indianness. The past innovations in dance, drama, poetry, music and folktales—these were all part of Indianness. It had been a tremendous creative force. During one period, it offered *Bhagavad Gita,* in another Jataka tales, and then it produced great spiritual pathfinders like Guru Nanak and Kabir, Tulsidas and Surdas.

The great ideas always moved Firaq. He felt that the biggest strength of the Indian civilization lay in its softness (in the sense of peace and tranquility), caring for others, and a belief in the oneness of humanity. The action aimed at suppressing others was alien to the Indian culture. That is why Firaq was impressed by the early Iqbal verse that revealed the true essence of India, rather than the older Iqbal, who was more interested in promoting a narrowly defined religious framework. In general, Urdu poetry had failed to bring out the best aspects of India's cultural heritage. Firaq consciously attempted to rectify this situation by writing poems like *Aadhi Raat, Parchhaayiaan, Dharti Sangiit, Jugnu* and *Hindola. Hindola* (The Cradle) is a remarkable epic poem that encompasses three thousand years of Indian history, ranging from the great scriptures like the Ramayana and Mahabharata to modern-era poets such as Ghalib and Tagore. Firaq weaves his personal story into the more remarkable account of his motherland. He concludes the poem with a plea for better opportunities for India's younger generation, who will one day become the guardians of this great nation.

Firaq believed in the fundamental Hindu assumption that ultimate reality was one, and that it could not be understood with the help of logic or philosophy. To express it in words is equally challenging. It can be realized only through intuition. When an ordinary human being understands this, they become a yogi. The universe was created through a competition between different forces, but upon closer examination, we find nothing but the unity of opposites. Everything that gives the appearance of duality, such as atma and parmatma, man and woman, life and death, and earth and sky, is a reflection of one underlying reality. In the beginning, there was only one. Prajapati, the first divine being, was a single entity, but he was so troubled by loneliness that he divided himself into two parts–one part became male, the other a female. With time, they were separated. Since then, they have yearned to reunite, to regain their oneness. Love poetry is the vehicle that conveys this universal truth.

vo husn o ishq jo subh-e azal se bichhre the
mile hain vaadi-e ghurbat mein phir vatan ke liye

वो हुस्न-ओ इश्क़ जो सुबह ए अज़ल से बिछड़े थे
मिले हैं वादी-ए घुर्बत में फिर वतन के लिए

The beauty and love—
separated at creation,
have found union in an alien land
while looking for
their homeland.

The ultimate reality takes the form of love and encompasses the entire existence within its fold. It reduces the tension between being and becoming; the metaphysical level transforms itself into an infinite state.

It's fair to say that Firaq Gorakhpuri was a poet of *Hindustaniyat* (Indianness), especially when we look at how deeply rooted his poetry was in India's culture, spirit, and soil. At a time when many Urdu poets were drawing heavily from Persian and Arabic traditions, with their rich metaphors, mystical Sufi themes, and ornate romantic imagery, Firaq chose a different path. He grounded his poetic imagination in *'India,'* its diverse landscapes, cultural mingling, and ancient spiritual traditions.

What set him apart was more than just his vocabulary; it was his entire outlook. For Firaq, Hindustaniyat wasn't just a political stance or cultural slogan but an emotional and aesthetic commitment. He saw India as a vast, beautiful tapestry woven from Hindu and Muslim threads, and that sense of unity and shared heritage runs through his poetry.

Unlike most contemporaries, Firaq didn't avoid drawing on Indian sources. His poems are filled with imagery and references from India's philosophical and mythological traditions, a rarity in Urdu poetry of that time. He wasn't afraid to include the Upanishadic idea of the soul seeking union, the eternal love of Krishna and Radha, or the mood and colour of Indian seasons and flowers, not just roses and nightingales borrowed from Persian gardens but Indian fields, monsoons, and mango blossoms. In doing so, he gave Urdu poetry a new language that spoke from and to Indian hearts.

Firaq also passionately believed in the power of the Hindustani language, not the heavily Sanskritized Hindi or the overly Persianized Urdu, but a natural, everyday idiom that ordinary people used, regardless of religion. That belief ran deep. He rejected any narrow or communal view of language and instead saw Urdu as a bridge, a space where India's diverse heritage could thrive and flourish.

Even more striking is how Firaq's philosophical inspiration drew from Indian scriptures, such as the Bhagavad Gita and the Upanishads. His way of thinking about love, death, union, and the self drew on the depth of Advaita Vedanta, but without losing the sensual beauty that made his poetry so emotionally alive. He blended the spiritual with the physical, the timeless with the intimate. Firaq Gorakhpuri stands out in the Urdu literary tradition, not just as a master of language, but as a poet who carried the soul of India in every line. He gave Urdu poetry a distinctly Indian flavor, rich in emotion, rooted in culture, and lit by the light of Hindustaniyat.

Making of India

zer o bam se saaz-e khilqat ke jahaan banta gaya

This ghazal is unique because it addresses an essential and distinctly complex topic: the formation of India as a unified nation. India is not generally recognized as a nation of immigrants, but that is what it has been, if we look at historical records. Aryans were the first to migrate from Central Asia, and they settled near the Indus river about three thousand years ago. These people laid the foundation of Hindu dharma, and the rishis (sages) who accompanied them were the sources of sacred scriptures, including the Vedas, Upanishads, and epic poems such as the Mahabharata and the Ramayana. There were also migrations into southern India in later centuries. Firaq is right when he says:

sar-zamiin-e hind par aqvaam-e aa'lam ke 'firaq'
qaafle baste gaye hindostaan banta gaya

सर-ज़मीन-ए हिंद पर अक़्वाम-ए आलम के 'फ़िराक़'
क़ाफ़िले बसते गए हिन्दोस्ताँ बनता गया

Masses from other homelands
chose this soil, Firaq,
and caravans set up homes.
At a leisurely pace, one day,
India emerged as one nation.

◆

Here is the rest of the ghazal.

zer o bam se saaz-e khilqat ke jahaan banta gaya
ye zamiin banti gaii ye aasmaan banta gaya

ज़ेर ओ बम से साज़-ए ख़िलक़त के जहाँ बनता गया
ये ज़मीं बनती गई ये आसमाँ बनता गया

Slowly and gradually,
with ups and downs,
the magic of creation unfolded.
Land emerged,
and the sky opened.

◆

daastaan-e jaur-e behad khuun se likhta raha
qatra qatra ashk-e gham ka be-karaan banta gaya

दास्तान-ए जौर-ए बेहद ख़ून से लिखता रहा
क़तरा क़तरा अश्क-ए ग़म का बे-कराँ बनता गया

Someone wrote the tale
of extreme inconstancy.
Each drop of sadness
was transformed
into a boundless ocean.

◆

i'shq-e tanha se huii aabaad kitni manzalein
ik musaafir karvaan dar kaarvaan banta gaya

इ'श्क़-ए तन्हा से हुईं आबाद कितनी मंज़िलें
इक मुसाफ़िर कारवाँ-दर-कारवाँ बनता गया

The lonely love created and settled
many points of disembarkation.
One traveler joined the others
and it made caravan after caravan.

◆

main tere jis gham ko apna jaanta tha vo bhi to
zeb-e unvaan-e hadiis-e diirgaan banta gaya

मैं तिरे जिस ग़म को अपना जानता था वो भी तो
ज़ेब-ए उनवान-ए हदीस-ए दीगराँ बनता गया

The sorrow that you gave me
was solely my possession and
it became a beautiful part
of stories which others shared.

◆

baat nikle baat se jaise vo tha tera bayaan
naam tera daastaan dar daastaan banta gaya

बात निकले बात से जैसे वो था तेरा बयाँ
नाम तेरा दास्ताँ दर दास्ताँ बनता गया

One thing always led to another—
that was your style of sharing stories.
Your name became part of a riveting tale.

◆

ham ko hai maa'luum sab ruudaad-e i'lm o falasfa
haan har iimaan o yakiin vahm o gumaan banta gaya

हम को है मालूम सब रूदाद-ए इल्म ओ फ़ल्सफ़ा
हाँ हर ईमान ओ यक़ीं वहम ओ गुमाँ बनता गया

I know the convoluted origin
of knowledge and philosophy.
With passage,
they became the basis of faith,
doubt, skepticism and imagination.

◆

main kitab-e dil mein apna haal -e gham likhta raha
har varaq ik baab-e taariikh-e jahaan banta gaya

मैं किताब-ए दिल में अपना हाल-ए ग़म लिखता रहा
हर वरक़ इक बाब-ए तारीख़-ए जहाँ बनता गया

I wrote the tale of my painful life
in the journal of my heart.
In time, every page was like a chapter
in the history of the world.

◆

bas usi ki tarjmaani hai mere ashaa'r mein
jo sukuut-e raaz rangiin dastan banta gaya

बस उसी की तर्जुमानी है मिरे अशआ'र में
जो सुकूत-ए राज़ रंगीं दास्ताँ बनता गया

My couplets are a representation
of something that became a colourful
chronicle of secrets of silence.

◆

main ne saunpa tha tumhein ik kaam saari u'mr mein
vo bigar-ta hi gaya ae dil kahaan banta gaya

मैं ने सौंपा था तुझे इक काम सारी उम्र में
वो बिगड़ता ही गया ऐ दिल कहाँ बनता गया

In all my life, I assigned you one task.
It became knotty and tricky.
Oh, my heart, what a mix-up!

◆

meri ghutti mein pari thi ho ke hal urdu zabaan
jo bhi main kahta gaya husn-e bayaan banta gaya

मेरी घुट्टी में पड़ी थी हो के हल उर्दू ज़बाँ
जो भी मैं कहता गया हुस्न-ए-बयाँ बनता गया

The Urdu language was part
of my genetic makeup.
Whatever I had to say
it blossomed into delightful recitation.

◆

vaqt ke haathon yahaan kaya kaya khazaane lut gaye
ek tera gham k ganj-e shaaiigaan banta gaya

वक़्त के हाथों यहाँ क्या क्या ख़ज़ाने लुट गए
एक तेरा ग़म कि गंज-ए शाईगाँ बनता गया

Time was cruel.
Treasures were looted.
It was your thought
while in separation from you
that became the treasure
of my well-being.

Endless Dance with Death

jaane kya baat hai kis chiiz ki yaad aati hai

In the evening's descent, the poet is consumed by a profound unease, yearning for something beyond reach. Memories of cherished love, lost to time's relentless march, surge back with consuming force. In the night's hush, he discerns echoes of the universe's pulse, a reminder of the vastness of his emotions. Firaq's verses are a rich canvas, the dawn's mirror reflecting his beloved's resplendent beauty, soothing and tormenting him. Life's voice recedes, a mere murmur against his overpowering love. These meticulously woven metaphors beckon the reader into the poet's realm, where they experience the abyss of anguish and the fervor of love. As the ghazal climaxes, Firaq addresses himself in the final couplet *(maqt'a)*, a powerful testament to the transformative nature of love. When truly in love, life becomes an endless dance with death (*zindagi i'shq ki kya puuchhte ho kya hai 'firaq' / maut hi maut har-ek samt nazar aati hai*). Urdu's subtle nuances, playful wordplay, and melodic flow enchant this mesmerizing piece. Even in our darkest moments, beauty can be found, and the pain of loss testifies to our capacity to love.

jaane kya baat hai kis chiiz ki yaad aati hai
shaam ko roz tabii'yat meri ghabraati hai

जाने क्या बात है किस चीज़ की याद आती है
शाम को रोज़ तबीयत मेरी घबराती है

Wonder what I'm missing!
There is something that bothers me
as the evening arrives.

◆

yaad un zulfon ki aati hai rah-e ghurbat mein
be-jagah aaj mujhe raat hui jaati hai

याद उन ज़ुल्फ़ों की आती है रहे ग़ुरबत में
बेजगह आज मुझे रात हुई जाती है

I remember her tresses
while in exile.
For no reason,
the darkness of night hits me.

◆

koi dukhta hua dil hai k ghazal hai meri
apna dukh-dard kahaani si kahe jaati hai

कोई दुखता हुआ दिल है कि ग़ज़ल है मेरी
अपना दुःख-दर्द कहानी सी कहे जाती है

Is it an afflicted heart
or a ghazal of mine?
It is telling its sorrow and grief
in the form of a story.

◆

sub-h aaiina dikhaati hai faza ko jis vaqt
saaf is mein teri tasviir nazar aati hai

सुब-ह आइना दिखाती है फ़ज़ा को जिस वक़्त
साफ़ इस में तेरी तस्वीर नज़र आती है

When the dawn shows her mirror
to its surroundings
I find your beauty's glow
hidden in it.

◆

sar b sar raaz hui jaati hai hasti apni
zindagi duur ki aavaaz hui jaati hai

सर-ब-सर राज़ हुई जाती है हस्ती अपनी
ज़िन्दगी दूर की आवाज़ हुई जाती है

In its entirety, my existence
is becoming taciturn and silent.
Life sounds like a voice
from far away.

◆

i'shq mein kaun thi vo baat mujhe yaad nahien
zindagi aaj jise soch ke pachhtaati hai

इ'श्क़ में कौन थी वो बात मुझे याद नहीं
ज़िन्दगी आज जिसे सोच के पछताती है

While I was in love,
something happened.
I think about it and
feel great pain.

◆

zindagi i'shq ki kya puuchhte ho kya hai 'firaq'
maut hi maut har-ek samt nazar aati hai

ज़िन्दगी इ'श्क़ की क्या पूछते हो क्या है 'फ़िराक़'
मौत ही मौत हरेक सम्त नज़र आती है

Firaq, please don't ask me
what happens to your life
when you're in love.
Wherever you look,
it is nothing but death.

Time for Change

zamiin badli falak badla mazaaq-e zindagi badla

Firaq reflects on the ever-changing nature of life and the role of poetry in this dynamic landscape. He observes profound transformations in the world, from the earth and sky to the essence of human existence, suggesting that even ancient values and traditions have undergone significant changes. Firaq's poetry is both a passive observation and a call to action, urging readers to recognize their transformative power in shaping reality. He emphasizes the need for new guidance and leadership in this transformed world, as traditional methods of instruction and spiritual guidance may no longer be sufficient. Firaq combines the emergence of new spiritual pathfinders with the presence of centuries-old religious authorities, highlighting the tension between tradition and progress. The penultimate couplet presents a beautiful and enigmatic image of the night, suggesting that change can come quietly but profoundly impact our collective dreams and aspirations. In the final couplet, Firaq acknowledges the need for new melodies and fresh poetic perspectives to reflect these transformations (*'Firaq' ham-navaa-e Miir o Ghaalib ab naye naghme / vo bazm-e zindagi badli vo rang-e shaa'yiri badla).*

zamiin badli falak badla mazaaq-e zindagi badla
tammaddun ke qadiim aqdaar badle aadmi badla

ज़मीं बदली फ़लक बदला मज़ाक़-ए ज़िंदगी बदला
तमद्दुन के क़दीम अक़दार बदले आदमी बदला

The earth changed,
the sky changed,
and the zest for life changed.
Civilization's ancient values changed.
What was considered human
also changed.

◆

badalte ja rahe hain ham bhi duniya ko badalne mein
nahien badli abhi duniya to duniya ko abhi badla

बदलते जा रहे हैं हम भी दुनिया को बदलने में
नहीं बदली अभी दुनिया तो दुनिया को अभी बदला

While we are changing the world,
we are also being transformed.
If the world has not yet changed,
we'll change it just now.

◆

nai manzil ke miir-e kaarvaan bhi aur hote hain
puraane khizr-e rah badle vo tarz-e rahbari badla

नई मंज़िल के मीर-ए कारवाँ भी और होते हैं
पुराने ख़िज़्र-ए रह बदले वो तर्ज़-ए-रहबरी बदला

Caravans need new guides
if they are searching
for a new destination.
The old spiritual mentors
have given up.
The mode of instruction
has changed too.

◆

naye mansuur hain puraane sheikh o qaazi hain
n fatve kufr ke badle n uzr-e daar hi badla

नए मंसूर हैं सदियों पुराने शेख़ ओ क़ाज़ी हैं
न फ़तवे कुफ़्र के बदले न उज़्र-ए दार ही बदला

There are new spiritual pathfinders
along with centuries of sheikhs and qazis.
Neither the fatwas of *kufr* have changed
nor the excuses for sending people
to the gallows.

◆

sitaare jaagte hain raat lat chhatkaaye soti hai
dabe paaon kisi ne aa ke khwaab-e zindagi badla

सितारे जागते हैं रात लट छटकाए सोती है
दबे पाँव किसी ने आ के ख़्वाब-ए-ज़िंदगी बदला

The stars are awake.
The night is asleep
while spreading the braids of her hair.
Walking softly, someone came
and changed the dream of life.

◆

'firaq' ham-navaa-e miir o ghaalib ab naye naghme
vo bazm-e zindagi badli vo rang-e shaa'yiri badla

'फ़िराक़' हम-नवा-ए 'मीर' ओ 'ग़ालिब' अब नए नग़मे
वो बज़्म-ए-ज़िंदगी बदली वो रंग-ए शाइ'री बदला

Firaq, a companion of Mir and Ghalib,
it's time for new melodies.
The conclave of life has changed
and the colour of the poetry has changed too.

A City Is Forlorn and Bereft

kyon chher chher ke puuchhte ho ruudaad meri uftaad meri

Firaq questions an unseen listener's relentless probing into the wounds of his past, cautioning that recounting his trials will only open old scars and leave both speaker and listener awash in regret. His words paint a picture of his former sanctuary, now a shadow of its former self, haunted by torment and sorrow. The desert metaphor symbolizes the void left by loss *(sahra-sahra vahshat ho gi),* while the phrase 'crying like a river' *(dariya dariya ro jaao ge)* underscores the magnitude of his emotions. Firaq employs the vibrant roses metaphor to represent the joys he once held close, only to discover they have metamorphosed into thorns piercing his soul, reminding us of life's capricious nature. Firaq ventures into the profound impact of absence as the ghazal progresses, painting a world that has become a faded memory. The intensity of his longing is clear, striking a universal chord about the transformative power of love and the aching void it leaves in its wake. Firaq reflects on the transitory nature of companionship, offering a glimmer of hope that the presence of the heart and emotional connections truly matter, urging us to cherish the moments we have with those we hold dear. In the end, Firaq pays tribute to his legacy, depicting Allahabad forever altered by his absence, a testament to the enduring impact of individual life and the power of poetry to transcend time and space.

kyon chher chher ke puuchhte ho ruudaad meri uftaad meri
main kah kah ke pachhtaaun ga tum sun sun ke pachhtaao ge

क्यों छेड़-छेड़ के पूछते हो रू-दाद मेरी उफ़ताद मेरी
मैं कह-कह के पछताऊं गा तुम सुन-सुन के पछताओ गे

You are rubbing my wounds
when you are asking me to narrate
the tale of my troubles and hardships.
I'll regret recounting it,
you will repent listening to it.

◆

us gham-khaane se jab guzro ge jis ko mera ghar kahte the
sahra-sahra vahshat ho gi dariya-dariya ro jaao ge

उस ग़म-खाने से जब गुज़रो गे जिस को मेरा घर कहते थे
सहरा-सहरा वहशत हो गी दरिया-दरिया रो जाओ गे

When you pass by that place
of torment and sadness
that was once my home,
you will see the wilderness of a desert
and then you will cry river-like.

◆

siine se laga rakkha tha ae ranga-rang gulo tum ko
ye mujh ko maa'luum nahien tha tum daagh-e jigar ban jaao ge

सीने से लगा रक्खा था ऐ रंगा-रंग गुलो तुम को
ये मुझ को मा'लूम न था तुम दाग़-ए जिगर बन जाओ गे

O colourful roses,
I kept you close to my heart.
I didn't know that you would become
a wound on my heart.

◆

jab se gaye ho rahti duniya hai ik bhuuli-bisri yaad
main ne kabhi ye socha nahien tha tum itna yaad aao ge

जब से गए हो रहती दुनिया है इक भूली-बिसरी याद
मैं ने कभी ये सोचा नहीं था तुम इतना याद आओ गे

When you left me,
my world appeared to me
like a distant memory.
I never thought that
I will miss you so much.

◆

rah-e zindagi mein koi aakhir tak saath nahien deta
dil ka saath is rahguzar mein chhorte ho pachhtaao ge

रहे-ज़िन्दगी में कोई आखिर तक साथ नहीं देता
दिल का साथ इस रहगुज़र में छोड़ते हो पछताओ गे

On the path of life,
no one stays with you until the end.

But if you leave the presence of the heart,
you will regret it.

♦

aaj allahabaad hai suuna shaay'ir ke uth jaane se
sadion sadion dhuundho ge lekin kahaan 'firaq' ko paao ge

आज अल्लाहाबाद है सूना शाइर के उठ जाने से
सदिओं-सदिओं ढूँढो गे लेकिन कहाँ 'फ़िराक़' को पाओ गे

Today Allahabad is forlorn and bereft
because of the poet's demise.
You will search for Firaq for centuries,
but you will not find him.

Those Who Saw Firaq

siine se tujh ko laga kar rakkha apna khuun pilaaya tha

Firaq's words resonate with the universal truth of love's all-consuming nature, demanding complete surrender in this profound ghazal. His deep-seated imagery pierces the soul, speaking of nourishing a beloved with one's lifeblood and cradling the troubles of the heart with tenderness. Firaq grapples with the transitory nature of love and beauty, acknowledging the wealth of indescribable experiences bestowed upon him by the world of passion. He likens these moments to silky threads of a story, blurring the lines between the tangible and intangible. In a moment of breathtaking visual poetry, Firaq imagines an image of his beloved's face unveiling, striking with the force of a shining tempest upon the soul's placid waters. He reflects on the yearning for true companionship, considering himself blessed to have found his beloved, even though the authenticity of their bond remains uncertain. As the ghazal reaches its climax, Firaq pays homage to his legacy, speaking of the envy future generations will harbour at the mere thought of sharing the same air as the poet.

siine se tujh ko laga kar rakkha apna khuun pilaaya tha
dard-e mohabbat dil ne tujh ko kin jatnon se paala tha

सीने से तुझ को लगा कर रक्खा अपना खून पिलाया था
दर्दे मुहब्बत दिल ने तुझ को किन जतनों से पाला था

I kept them close to my bosom,
nourished them with my blood.
O the afflictions of my heart,
do you realize how much my heart
had done for you?

◆

phir bhi husn o i'shq ki duniya de gaii kya kuchh go ae dil
afsaana tha jo bhi tha khwaab tha jo kuchh dekha tha

फिर भी हुस्नो इ'श्क़ की दुनिया दे गई क्या कुछ गो ऐ दिल
अफसाना था जो भी था ख्वाब था जो कुछ देखा था

Even in the end,
the world of love and
beauty offered me a lot.
Whatever it was,
it was no better than a story.
Whatever I saw
was just like a dream.

◆

thahre hue paani mein jaise nuur ka tuufaan aa jaaye
afsaana tha jo bhi tha khwaab tha jo kuchh dekha tha

ठहरे हुए पानी में जैसे नूर का तूफ़ान आ जाए
आईने के सामने उस ने कल जब अपना घूँघट खोला था

Yesterday when she opened her veil
in front of a mirror,
it was like a storm of shining light
hitting a settled body of water.

◆

un ko mubaarak jin logon ko sachche dost aur yaar mile
mere liye to ek vohi tha sachcha tha ya jhuuta tha

उन को मुबारक जिन लोगों को सच्चे दोस्त और यार मिले
मेरे लिए तो एक वोही था सच्चा था या झूठा था

Lucky were those folks
who got true friends.
For me, she was the only one—
whether true or false.

◆

aane vaali naslein tum par rashk karein gi ham-asro
jab ye dhyaan aaye ga un ko tum ne 'firaq' ko dekha tha

आने वाली नस्लें तुम पर रश्क करें गी हम-असरो
जब ये ध्यान आये गा उन को तुम ने 'फ़िराक़' को देखा था

The future generations
will be envious,
dear contemporaries,
when they would realize

that you had seen
Firaq in person.

Love as a Force of Nature

dilon ka soz tere ru-e be-naqaab ki aanch

Firaq's imagery paints a picture of hearts set ablaze by the radiance of his beloved's unveiled face, a gathering kindled by the incandescent prime of her youth. The sheer force of beauty can set the world on fire, leaving the reader weak in the knees. Firaq speaks of wine-flushed faces, sparkling eyes intoxicated with brilliance, and the sun's heat finding refuge within the hearts of those who drink deep of love's elixir. Amidst the fever-pitch of emotion, Firaq strikes a note of poignant contemplation, reminding us of the fleeting nature of earthly pleasures and the need to seek a higher purpose while surrendering to love's intoxicating pull. He weaves together opposites in a dance of exquisite tension, mixing the cool freshness of dawn with the searing heat of the rising sun, the icy perfection of his beloved's glance with the molten fire of her youth. As the ghazal ends, Firaq creates an image of terrifying beauty, describing a moonlit night, a breeze carrying the scent of the impending firestorm, and a passion so intense that it could set the heavens ablaze. He hints at a more profound transformation, suggesting that the most significant changes are born in the crucible of the heart.

dilon ka soz tere ru-e be-naqaab ki aanch
tamaam garmi-e mahfil tere shabaab ki aanch

दिलों का सोज़ तिरे रू-ए-बे-नक़ाब की आँच
तमाम गर्मी-ए महफ़िल तिरे शबाब की आँच

The burning of hearts
and the warmth of your facial veil.
All the snugness in the gathering,
all due to the prime of your youth.

◆

charaah ke saaghar-e mai jagmaga uthe chehre
simat ke aa gaai siinon mein aaftaab ki aanch

चढ़ा के साग़र-ए मय जगमगा उठे चेहरे
सिमट के आ गई सीनों में आफ़्ताब की आँच

After drinking a few glasses of wine,
faces sparkled.
The heat of the sun shrank
and found a place in the bosom.

◆

ye agle vaqton ke hain khush hain baagh-e jannat mein
unhein khabar hi nahien kya hai is svaab ki aanch

ये अगले वक़्तों के हैं ख़ुश हैं बाग़-ए-जन्नत में
उन्हें ख़बर ही नहीं क्या है इस सवाब की आँच

They belong to the times passed,
and they are happy in paradise's gardens.
They are not aware of the mellowness
of this reward for good deeds.

◆

sahir ki taaza-dami charhti dhuup ki garmi
teri nigaah ki dhandak tere shabaab ki aanch

सहिर की ताज़ा-दमी चढ़ती धूप की गर्मी
तेरी निगाह की धनक तेरे शबाब की आँच

The freshness of the dawn
and the warmth of the sunrise.
The coolness of your glance
and the warmness of your youth.

◆

ye raat aag laga de kahien n duniya mein
ye chaandni ye havaayein ye maahtaab ki aanch

ये रात आग लगा दे कहीं न दुनिया में
ये चाँदनी ये हवाएँ ये माहताब की आँच

I'm afraid that this might set fire
to the world
This moonlit night, this breeze,
and the homeliness of the moon.

◆

'firaq' vaqt ke rukh se ulat rahi hai naqaab
zamiin se ta-b-falak hai is inqilaab ki aanch

'फ़िराक़' वक़्त के रुख़ से उलट रही है नक़ाब
ज़मीं से ता-ब-फ़लक है इस इंक़लाब की आँच

Firaq, the veil is being lifted
from the face of time.
From the earth to the sky,
there is the feverishness of a revolution.

Life of Separation

ab daur-e aasmaan hai n daur-e hayaat hai

Firaq challenges the fabric of existence in this ghazal, suggesting that the heavens or life's progression do not dictate the current moment, but rather the pain of separation. He personifies this pain as a source of wisdom, setting an intellectually stimulating tone. Firaq describes love as a separate realm where day and night dissolve, transcending time and conventional reality. He encourages embracing the present and finding meaning in life's ephemeral nature, comparing a fully lived life to the immortality of Khizr. Firaq questions the notion of enlightenment, suggesting that true enlightenment may be found in embracing life's shadows and uncertainties. He explores the devastating impact of love on the heart, transforming existence into a trembling, unstable entity, and acknowledges the difficulty of explaining love's intricacies. Firaq presents a stunning visual metaphor, likening the star-filled night sky to sparks left behind by lightning that have destroyed the restless heart, suggesting that the universe's beauty is born from human pain. In the final couplet, Firaq grapples with existence as a continuous process of non-existence, inviting the reader to embrace life's impermanence and find meaning in the present.

ab daur-e aasmaan hai n daur-e hayaat hai
ae dard-e hijr tu hi bata kitni raat hai

अब दौर-ए आसमाँ है न दौर-ए-हयात है
ऐ दर्द-ए-हिज्र तू ही बता कितनी रात है

It is neither a movement of the heavens
nor that of life.
O pain of separation,
it is your turn now to tell me
how much night is left?

◆

har kaayenaat se ye alag kaayenaat hai
hairat saraa-e i'shq mein din hai n raat hai

हर काएनात से ये अलग काएनात है
हैरत-सरा-ए इ'श्क़ में दिन है न रात है

This universe is different
from all others.
In the amazing house of love,
there is neither day nor night.

◆

jiina jo aa gaya to ajal bhi hayaat hai
aur yuun to u'mr-e khizr bhi kya be-sabaat hai

जीना जो आ गया तो अजल भी हयात है
और यूँ तो उम्र-ए-ख़िज़्र भी क्या बे-सबात है

If one learns the art of living,
death becomes a part of being.
Even the immortal life of Khizr
will look transient.

◆

kion intah-e hosh ko kahte hain be-khudi
khurshiid hi ki aakhri manzil to raat hai

क्यूँ इंतिहा-ए होश को कहते हैं बे-ख़ुदी
ख़ुर्शीद ही की आख़िरी मंज़िल तो रात है

Why do we call
enlightenment
a state of intoxication?
When the sun reaches
its journey's end,
there is darkness.

◆

Hasti ko jis ne zalzala-saamaan bana diya
vo dil qaraar paaye muqaddar ki baat hai

हस्ती को जिस ने ज़लज़ला-सामाँ बना दिया
वो दिल क़रार पाए मुक़द्दर की बात है

Something that turned existence
into a quake,
that heart is hard to alleviate.
It is a matter of luck.

◆

ye mushgaafiaan hain giraan tab-e i'shq par
kis ko dimaagh-e kaavish-e zaat o sifaat hai

ये मुशगाफ़ियाँ हैं गिराँ तब-ए इ'श्क़ पर
किस को दिमाग़-ए काविश-ए ज़ात ओ सिफ़ात है

The trivial details of love
are strenuous to explain.
Who has the brain to separate
one thing from another?

◆

gardu sharaar-e barq-e dil-e beqaraar dekh
jin se ye teri taaron bhari raat raat hai

गर्दूं शरार-ए बर्क़-ए दिल-ए बे-क़रार देख
जिन से ये तेरी तारों भरी रात रात है

Look at the dust of sparks
after lightning destroyed
the restless heart.
What do you think

the star-filled night of yours
is made of?

◆

hasti bajuz fana-e musalsal k kuchh nahien
phir kis liye ye fikr-e qaraar o sabaat hai

हस्ती ब-जुज़ फ़ना-ए मुसलसल के कुछ नहीं
फिर किस लिए ये फ़िक्र-ए क़रार ओ सबात है

If existence itself is nothing more than
continuous non-existence,
why this perturbation about finding
some peace of mind?

◆

unvaan ghaflatlon ke hain qurbat ho ya visaal
bas fursat-e hayaat 'firaq' ek raat hai

उनवान ग़फ़लतों के हैं क़ुर्बत हो या विसाल
बस फ़ुर्सत-ए हयात 'फ़िराक़' एक रात है

Things go wrong,
whether it is separation or union.
The whole duration of life, Firaq,
is no different from one night.

Love's Many Facets

vo chup chaap aansu bahaane ki raatein

Firaq explores the bittersweet nature of love and its profound impact on the human heart. Through a series of evocative vignettes, he captures the essence of love's many facets, from the innocent bloom of youthful passion to the aching sorrow of separation. Central to the poem is the idea that love exists outside the bounds of ordinary reality, creating a world that is both intensely real and strangely dreamlike. Firaq's imagery and emotional depth invite the readers to immerse themselves in this world, to experience the sensory delights and the profound longing that characterizes the journey of the heart. Firaq reflects on the fleeting nature of life's most precious moments, suggesting that the wonderful days and nights of love are a rare and precious gift. This message serves as a reminder to cherish the connections we form and the memories we create, even as we navigate the inevitable ups and downs of existence. Firaq's words speak to the universal human experience of love, offering solace and understanding to all who have loved and lost.

vo chup chaap aansu bahaane ki raatein
vo ik shakhs ke yaad aane ki raatein

वो चुप-चाप आँसू बहाने की रातें
वो इक शख़्स के याद आने की रातें

Those nights
when tears rained from the eyes.
Those nights
when the thought of someone special
just came rushing back.

◆

shab-e maah ki vo thandi anchein vo shabnam
tere husn ke rismasaane ki raatein

शब-ए मह की वो ठंडी आँचें वो शबनम
तिरे हुस्न के रस्मसाने की रातें

The warmth and dew drops
of a moonlit night.
The time of your beauty
to be bathed in fragrance.

◆

javaani ki doshiizgi ka tabussam
gul-e zaar ke vo khilaane ki raatein

जवानी की दोशीज़गी का तबस्सुम
गुल-ए ज़ार के वो खिलाने की रातें

A smile of virgin youth.
The time when flowers bloom
in the garden.

◆

phuvaarin si naghmon ki padti hon jaise
kuchh us lab ke sun-ne suna-ne ki raatein

फुवारें सी नग़्मों की पड़ती हों जैसे
कुछ उस लब के सुनने-सुनाने की रातें

It is like a drizzle of melodies—those nights
when her lips are either listening to
or saying something.

◆

mujhe yaad hai teri har sub-h-e rukhsat
mujhe yaad hain tere aane ki raatein

मुझे याद है तेरी हर सुब्ह-ए रुख़्सत
मुझे याद हैं तेरे आने की रातें

I remember
each morning of your departure—

and I remember
each night of your arrival.

◆

pur-israar si meri arz-e tamanna
vo kuchh zer-e lab muskaraane ki raatein

पुर-असरार सी मेरी अर्ज़-ए तमन्ना
वो कुछ ज़ेर-ए लब मुस्कुराने की रातें

A mysterious expression of desire.
Those nights of smiling under the lip.

◆

sar-e shaam se ta sahar kurb-e jaanaan
n jaane vo thien kis zamaane ki raatein

सर-ए शाम से ता-सहर क़ुर्ब-ए जानाँ
न जाने वो थीं किस ज़माने की रातें

From evening until dawn,
the pain of missing the beloved.
I don't know what period of my life
I'm talking about.

◆

sar-e mai-kada tishnagi ki vo qasmein
vo saaqi se baatein banaane ki raatein

सर-ए मय-कदा तिश्नगी की वो क़स्में
वो साक़ी से बातें बनाने की रातें

Oaths of one's thirst
inside the tavern.
Unending whispering
with the Saqi.

•

'firaq' apni qismat mein shaayad nahien the
thikaane ke din thikaane ki raatein

'फ़िराक़' अपनी क़िस्मत में शायद नहीं थे
ठिकाने के दिन या ठिकाने की रातें

I don't think, Firaq,
they were written in my fate.
Wonderful nights or beautiful days.

Part II

RUBA'IAAT-E FIRAQ

Eight

SUNDARAM (BEAUTY)

Beauty is truth, truth beauty, that is all
Ye know on earth, and all ye need to know.

John Keats
Ode on a Grecian Urn (1819)

RUBA'I AS A POETIC FORM

Ruba'i is a specific sub-genre of Persian and Urdu poetry. It is also a problematic form to practise because it requires great precision. The poet is required to show exactness in the use of language. In addition to the incredible clarity about the subject matter, the poet must exhibit great skill in capturing the idea in four short lines. The word ruba'i comes from the Arabic *rub'a,* which means four. Out of the four lines, three (first, second and fourth) must be rhymed, meaning they use the same rhyming scheme or qafiya. If the third line is also rhymed, that is good. The use of radif is not an essential requirement. The poet picks up an idea or thought in the first line, which is carried forward in the following three lines. The flow of words is like a river rising. The fourth line is the punch line, and it resolves the tension. That is why the last line is the soul or essence of the enterprise. Ruba'i came to Deccan first, where Dakhni poets had used this sub-genre in the seventeenth century, and leading poets from Delhi soon followed in their footsteps.

It is said that ruba'i is an excellent medium for expressing *sringara rasa,* one of the nine *rasas* or flavors used in Sanskrit poetry to express romantic love or appreciate the beauty of the female form. However, the romantic relationship between the ordinary lover and the beloved is a metaphor for the love between human beings and the divine. Myth is used to reinforce this perspective. It is mentioned that Prajapati, the first divine incarnation before other gods appeared on the scene, suffered from feelings of loneliness as he was the only being in the entire universe. To overcome his loneliness, he divided himself into two parts—male and female, love and beauty, or i'shq and *husn.* The two parts shared erotic feelings, but eventually, they were separated. However, they continued to yearn for each other. That is why most of the *sringara rasa* poetry in Urdu and Persian is focused on the union (visaal) and separation (firaq). As the poet captures feelings in the four-line format, inner and outer intermingle. The sense of self and the other disappears. Firaq's use of ruba'i followed this archetype. Firaq explicitly mentioned in his first published book of ruba'is, titled *Roop,* that these were *sringara rasa* rubais. He also clearly drew on mythology to shape his metaphorical structures. He fondly drew on Sita from the epic Ramayana to illustrate the concept of beauty and an unwavering sense of dedication to her marital obligations.

Most readers know about ruba'i because they have read or heard about Edward Fitzgerald's excellent translation of *Rubaiyat* by Omar Khayyam (1048–1131), the famous Persian poet. If we read Khayyam's poetry at the surface level, he appears to be an erotic pagan poet, fond of wine drinking. But that view is false and misleading. *Ruba'iyat* is an excellent work of Sufi mysticism. Wine and the woman serving the drink (*saqi*) are metaphors. Wine and the intoxication offered by it are joys provided by the divine. Wine drinking is an act of surrender to divine love, which is a panacea for human suffering. The great yogi, Paramahansa Yogananda, has compared *Ruba'iyat* to *The Revelation of St. John the Divine.*[16]

Firaq published his collection of ruba'is titled *Roop* in the mid-1940s, and the volume was dedicated to his long-time friend, the poet Josh Malihabadi. Firaq explained how he became involved in ruba'i writing and his friend Josh's role in this endeavour in the preface written for that volume. The starting point was a question that Josh had asked (*Firaq, have you written ruba'is?*) that triggered a response and a desire to write ruba'is. Meanwhile, the two friends misunderstood something that threatened the stability of their eight-year-old friendship. Firaq expressed his feelings in a ruba'i and ended up writing a few hundred of them. He made it clear in his preface that his ruba'is fall in the *sringar rasa* category. He wrote, 'These ruba'is do not contain aspects of poetry that we eagerly look forward to reading. But if our aesthetic need is satisfied by writing about sensual desire or erotic feelings, why don't we consider that verse as beneficial? Why do we think that high-level poetry concerned with beauty and elegance has played no role in the evolution of our civilization? I want a more comprehensive understanding of the meanings of progressivism. We can't separate beauty from sexuality or eroticism.'[17]

---

[16]Yogananda, Paramahansa, *Wine of Mystics: The Rubaiyat of Omar Khayyam, A Spiritual Interpretation*, Self Realization Fellowship Pub, 1996, p. xi.
[17]Gorakhpuri, Firaq, *Roop*, Rajpal & Sons, Delhi, 2017, pp. 14–15.

FIRAQ'S CONCEPT OF BEAUTY

In this chapter, we have tried to collect ruba'is related to Firaq's concept of beauty. He says beauty is found in daily activities of life; both a woman standing in the muddy field doing planting or the one taking a walk in the garden are beautiful in their own ways. Beauty is found in all moods and expressions of feelings—it is present in smiles and the articulation of anger towards loved ones when they fail to meet certain expectations. Beauty is not only found in objects that are seen, but it is also present in all other sensual experiences: hearing a melody, tasting food, sipping wine, touching someone special, and more. Beauty is found in our attitudes towards others, whether we are kind, generous, or compassionate. There is beauty in changing seasons—summer's beauty is destroyed by autumn, but it creates its unique patterns; wintery snow is magnificent to look at, and nothing compares to the magic of blossoming flowers during the spring. There is beauty in the mundane tasks of life and our spiritual aspirations. There is beauty in perfection and imperfection, such as a half-opened bud, a partially formed rainbow. They are beautiful too. There is beauty in both the light and the darkness that we often overlook. The beloved's face is gorgeous when seen without a mask. It becomes even more beautiful or mysterious when veiled. Beauty is everywhere, but to fully experience it, we need the eyes and sensibility of a poet.

RUBA'IS

The Evening's Shadow

The woman we meet in Firaq's quartets is not the same person who shows up as his beloved in his ghazals. The beloved is a paragon of beauty, and her every move is filled with charms; she commands the fragrance of gardens as she walks. Every embellishment is already a part of her persona. The woman in the ruba'is is an ordinary, hard-working, primarily rustic beauty who is utterly earthbound in her household responsibilities, for her children and life partner. Her day starts early and ends late. She must milk the cows, cook the food, and do other chores before the sun has made its presence known in the sky. She might go to the fields to work with her husband or do other labor. This busy schedule doesn't end until the evening arrives, and 'the sun readies its horse for the chariot of fire'.

aa ja k khari hai shaam parda ghere
muddat hui jab hue darshan tere
maghrib se sunehari gard uthi suu-e qaaf
suuraj ne agni rath ke ghore phere

आ जा कि खड़ी है शाम पर्दा घेरे
मुद्दत हुई जब हुए थे दर्शन तेरे
मग़रिब से सुनहरी गर्द उठी सू-ए-क़ाफ़
सूरज ने अग्नी रथ के घोड़े फेरे

Come, the evening is standing here
casting its shadow.
It has been quite a while
that I saw you last.
Golden dust appeared in the west,
spreading end-to-end.
And the sun readied its horses
for the chariot of fire.

The Glance That Made Buds Blossom

The woman mentioned in this ruba'i possesses magical powers due to her dedication to the well-being of her family. The purity of her heart performs wonders; whatever she does has the air of divination, a blessing of sorts that transforms 'poison into nectar'. She doesn't lose her temper, but flowers bloom in fear when she does. Whether it is her kids or her partner, they all get punished if they cross the line of what is allowed. However, all this is done with great love.

amrit vo halahal ko bana deti hai
ghusse ki nazar phuul khila deti hai
maan laadli aulaad ko jaise taare
kis pyaar se premi ko saza deti hai

अमृत वो हलाहल को बना देती है
ग़ुस्से की नज़र फूल खिला देती है
माँ लाडली औलाद को जैसे ताड़े
किस प्यार से प्रेमी को सज़ा देती है

She turns poison into nectar.
Her angry glance
makes the buds blossom.
Like the mother disciplines her kids.
With the same affection,
she punishes her lover.

Her Voice Is a Melody

She is not a musician; she doesn't sing, but there is music in her voice. When she speaks, the words pour out, following a rhythmical movement. Even the air surrounding her makes a note and adds the tinkling of unseen musical instruments.

aavaaz p sangiit ka hota hai bharam
karvat leti hai naram lai mein sargam
ye bol surele tharthraati hai faza
an-dekhe saaz ka khanakana paiham

आवाज़ पे संगीत का होता है भरम
करवट लेती है नर्म लय में सरगम
ये बोल सुरीले थरथराती है फ़ज़ा
अन-देखे साज़ का खनकना पैहम

You will mistake her voice
for a melody.
Soft tone as in a musical note,
moving.
Lyrical singing
while the atmosphere is shivering
The constant tinkling
of an unseen musical instrument.

Eyes as Messages of Love

Once again, a different conception of the female form. Her eyes convey love, and her hair gives the appearance of black snakes in deep slumber. But she is carrying a fawn (something we don't associate with an urban beauty) who is stretching his neck lovingly on her side.

aankhein hain k paighaam mohabbat vaale
bikhri hain latein k niind mein hain kale
pahlu se laga hua hiran ka bachcha
kis pyar se hai baghal mein gardan daale

आँखें हैं कि पैग़ाम मोहब्बत वाले
बिखरी हैं लटें कि नींद में हैं काले
पहलू से लगा हुआ हिरन का बच्चा
किस प्यार से है बग़ल में गर्दन डाले

Are these her eyes
or messages of love?
Are these her disheveled curls
or snakes in deep slumber?
Hugging her bosom is a fawn
stretching its neck lovingly
on her side.

Like Lamps Shimmering in a Temple

This ruba'i celebrates the smile of the rural woman. It is like the gentle breeze touching the rosebud, a musician starting a new melody, or lamps shining inside a temple.

ghunche ko nasiim gud-gudaaye jaise
mutrib koi saaz chher jaaye jaise
yuun phuut rahi hai muskaraahat ki kiran
mandir mein charaagh jhil-milaaye jaise

ग़ुंचे को नसीम गुदगुदाए जैसे
मुतरिब कोई साज़ छेड़ जाए जैसे
यूँ फूट रही है मुस्कुराहट की किरन
मंदिर में चराग़ झिलमिलाए जैसे

A gentle breeze
tickles the rosebud
like a musician
who starts a new strain?
The ray of smiles
is raising itself
like lamps shimmer
inside a temple.

A Sacred Image

The poet reaches lyrical heights as he tries to capture in words the person he sees in his mind's eye: matchless, a dream fulfillment, single-minded, a goddess in disguise, a sacred image.

saani nahien tera n koi teri misaal
kis khwaab ki taa'biir hai ye shaan-e jamaal
siine mein yaksuii ke palte palte
jaise suurat pakar le yazdaan ka khayal

सानी नहीं तेरा न कोई तेरी मिसाल
किस ख़्वाब की ता'बीर है ये शान-ए-जमाल
सीने में यकसूई के पलते पलते
जैसे सूरत पकड़ ले यज़्दाँ का ख़याल

You have no match,
nor is there someone
who is your role model?
The fulfillment of a strange dream
is the majesty of your beauty.
The birth of single-mindedness
in your bosom,
like your appearance,
grabs the idea of a sacred image.

Just Like...

The full power of innovative metaphors is unleashed in describing the youth drenched in sweetness.

jis tarah asaavari ke dil ki dharkan
jaise pichhle pahar ka mahka hua ban
jaise khilte kanval ke sine ki umang
chhalka parta hai mad mein duuba jauban

जिस तरह असावरी के दिल की धड़कन
जैसे पिछले पहर का महका हुआ बन
जैसे खिलते कँवल के सीने की उमंग
छलका पड़ता है मद में डूबा जौबन

Just like the heartbeat
of an Asavari raga,
just like the fragrant forest
of the latter part of the night,
just like the aspiration
of a blossoming lotus,
her overflowing youth
is drenched in sweetness.

Beauty Is Forlorn

When the beauty is filled with sorrow, everything around her takes a turn for the worse. Fear walks in, the breeze halts its movement, and there is a shakeup in the spiritual realm. Such is the hold of her grief.

afsurda faza p jaise chhaaya ho hiraas
duniya ko koi hava bhi aati nahien raas
duubi jaati ho jaise nabz-e konain
jis baat p husn aaj itna hai udaas

अफ़्सुर्दा फ़ज़ा पे जैसे छाया हो हिरास
दुनिया को कोई हवा भी आती नहीं रास
डूबी जाती हो जैसे नब्ज़-ए-कौनैन
जिस बात पे हुस्न आज इतना है उदास

A shadow of fear
hangs over an ambiance
filled with melancholy.
No breeze suits

the world that we know.
Pulses of the physical
and the spiritual domains
are failing.
Knowing this,
the beauty is forlorn.

Virgin Spring

Any explanation will diminish the splendid elegance of this ruba'i.

doshiiza bahaar muskaraaye jaise
mauj-e tasniim gun-gunaaye jaise
ye shaan-e subuk ravi ye khushbuuye badan
bal khaati hui nasiim gaaye jaise

दोशीज़ा-ए बहार मुस्कुराए जैसे
मौज-ए तसनीम गुनगुनाए जैसे
ये शान-ए सुबुक-रवी ये ख़ुशबू-ए बदन
बल खाती हुई नसीम गाए जैसे

As the virgin spring
spreads its smiles
and the paradisical wave
of water hums.
The majesty
of the quickly traveling
fragrance of the body—
twisting and turning,
the gentle breeze sings.

On Seeing Your Face

Comparing female beauty to the moon is a classic cliché in Urdu poetry. But Firaq twists this metaphor by using *maah-paare* (moon-like particles). Notice also the stars sparkling and then disappearing after her smile.

mukhra dekhein to maah-paare chhup jaayein
khurshiid ki aankh ke sharaare chhup jaayein
rah jaana vo muskara ke tera kal raat
jaise kuchh jhilmila ke taare chhup jaayein

मुखड़ा देखें तो माह-पारे छुप जाएँ
ख़ुर्शीद की आँख के शरारे छुप जाएँ
रह जाना वो मुस्कुरा के तेरा कल रात
जैसे कुछ झिलमिला के तारे छुप जाएँ

If they see your face,
parts of the moon will hide.
The flames from the sun's eye
will conceal too.
Your silence
after that smile last night—
it was like stars disappearing
after a short sparkle.

Minaret of Jewels

Each line in this ruba'i is worth its weight in pearls and jewels!

zulfon se fazaaaon mein uda-hat ka samaan
mukhra hai k aag mein tara-vat ka samaan
ye soz o gudaaz-e qad-e raa'na! jaise
hire ke manaar mein ghulaavat ka samaan

ज़ुल्फ़ों से फ़ज़ाओं में उदाहट का समाँ
मुखड़ा है कि आग में तरावट का समाँ
ये सोज़ ओ गुदाज़-ए क़द-ए र'अना! जैसे
हीरे के मिनार में घुलावट का समाँ

An ecstasy of purpleness
due to the fear of black tresses.
Is this your face
or a state of flowing substance
facing fire?
As if passion is mixed
with pathos, the beautiful,
gentle height!
A time for dissolving oneself
in a minaret of jewels!

Magic of Eros

The Kama or Eros, the god of sexual pleasure and longing, is working his magic. Her beauty's exposition reminds one that something enchanting, beyond the ordinary, is happening. It seems that the god himself is flaming the fire of loveliness. The word *suhaag* clarifies that this occurs within the boundaries of married bliss.

ye ruup ki lakhshmi ye jalvon ka raag
ye jaadu-e kaam-ruup ye husn ki aag
khair o barkat jahaan mein tere dam se
teri komal hansi mohabbat ka suhaag

ऐ रूप की लक्ष्मी ये जल्वों का राग
ये जादू-ए-काम-रूप ये हुस्न की आग
ख़ैर ओ बरकत जहान में तेरे दम से
तेरी कोमल हँसी मोहब्बत का सुहाग

The musical notes
of the goddess of beauty's luster
and splendor!
This is the magic of Eros,
and this is the flame of beauty.
Safety and beneficence are your gifts.
Your tender smile
is the marital bliss of love.

Spirit of Jesus

What is happening may be lacking in Jesus's divination—a silent and slow-moving miracle. The earth breathes synchronously with the movement of her feet as she walks.

'iisa' ke nafas mein bhi ye iijaaz nahien
tujh se chamak uth-ti hai a'naasar ki jabiin
ik mo'jaza-e khaamosh tarz-e raftaar
uth-te hain qadam k saans leti hai zamiin

'ईसा' के नफ़स में भी ये एजाज़ नहीं
तुझ से चमक उठती है अनासिर की जबीं
इक मोजिज़ा-ए ख़मोश तर्ज़-ए रफ़्तार
उठते हैं क़दम कि साँस लेती है ज़मीं

Even the spirit of Jesus
can't claim this marvel.
The forehead of the elements
brightens with your presence.
This is a silent and
slow-moving miracle.
You raise your feet to walk,
or the earth is trying to breathe.

Spring Is Intoxicated

Her entire body is a jukebox of music. There is the sound of someone playing the melodious sitar, and sweet sounds emanate from within her. Her one look makes gardens bloom as if the spring, known for its intoxicated persona, is even tipsier after tasting the elixir of her lips.

ye shola-e husn jaise bajta ho sitar
har khatt-e badan ki lau mein maddham jhankaar
rangiin nigaah se khil uth-te hain chaman
ras honton ka pii ke jhuum uth-ti hai bahaar

ये शोला-ए हुस्न जैसे बजता हो सितार
हर ख़त्त-ए-बदन की लौ में मद्धम झंकार
रंगीन निगाह से खिल उठते हैं चमन
रस होंटों का पी के झूम उठती है बहार

Is this the flame of beauty
or someone playing sitar?
In the shine of each part of the body,
there is a low-sounding jingle.
Your colourful glancc
makes gardens blossom.
The spring is intoxicated
after kissing your lips!

Revelation of Flowers

Here, we find a description of beauty that transcends the realm of our ordinary thinking. The emphasis is on what she does rather than how she looks. Youth blossoming amid thorns can mean how its surroundings or complex tasks challenge the beauty she performs for the benefit of others.

ban-baasiyon mein jalva-e gulshan le kar
taariikiyon mein shola-e aiman le kar
vo hansti hui ruup ki devi aaii
kaanton mein khile phuul sa joban le kar

बन-बासियों में जलवा-ए-गुलशन ले कर
तारीकियों में शोला-ए-ऐमन ले कर
वो हँसती हुई रूप की देवी आई
काँटों में खिले फूल सा जोबन ले कर

She brings a revelation of flowers
to the forest dwellers,
the flame of faith
to those living in darkness.
Look over there,
wrapped in smiles,
arrives the goddess of love,
with youth blossoming
amid thorns.

Water Glides Singing Songs

Each line of this rubai is a marvel of metaphors.

lachka lachka badan mujassam hai nasiim
mahka mahka vo chehra saanson ki shamiim
doshiizgi-e jamaal sub-h-e jannat
gaate hue narm-gaam mauj-e tasniim

लचका लचका बदन मुजस्सम है नसीम
महका महका वो चेहरा साँसों की शमीम
दोशीज़गि-ए जमाल सुब्ह-ए जन्नत
गाते हुए नर्म-गाम मौज-ए-तसनीम

Her supple and pliable body
is like an incarnation

of the gentle breeze,
her fragrant countenance
and perfumed breath,
the purity of her beauty
which is like paradise's morning,
and the waves of streams
that glide singing song.

Beauty in the Grip of Anguish

Beauty is not free from pain and suffering. Her illness perturbs the elements and comes together to send her love and a speedy recovery.

vo chehra suta hua vo husn-e biimaar
bechaini ki ruuh ko bhi aata tha pyaar
dekha hai karb ke bhi aalam mein tujhe
hota tha sukuun laakh jaanon se nisaar

वो चेहरा सुता हुआ वो हुस्न-ए बीमार
बेचैनी की रूह को भी आता था प्यार
देखा है कर्ब के भी आलम में तुझे
होता था सुकून लाख जानों से निसार

The troubled and perturbed face
and the ailing beauty.
Even the spirit of unease
was sending her love.
I have seen you in the grip
of such anguish and affliction.
Millions were sacrificing
their peace for your well-being.

Leaves Bloom in the Garden of Love

A description of the rustic beauty's height that breaks new ground. Generally, Urdu and Persian poets compare the beloved's height to a cypress tree. But Firaq goes truly lyrical here. Notice references to pomegranate, moon, rainbow, Bhairavi raga and leaves blooming!

mahtaab mein surkh anaar jaise chhuute
ya qaus-e quza lachak ke jaise tuute
vo qad hai k bhairviin sunayaaye jab sub-h
gulzaar-e i'shq se narm konpal phuute

महताब में सुर्ख़ अनार जैसे छूटे
या क़ौस-ए क़ुज़ह लचक के जैसे टूटे
वो क़द है कि भैरवीं सुनाए जब सुब्ह
गुलज़ार-ए इश्क़ से नर्म कोंपल फूटे

Imagine blazing a red pomegranate
at the surface of the moon,
or the rainbow malleably breaks
over the sky!
Such a height that when Bhairavi raga
is heard in the morning,
soft leaves bloom
in the garden of love.

Untied Locks and the Intoxicated Clouds

A profound connection exists between beauty and the workings of nature. When she does something (unties her hair), a reaction occurs (clouds get intoxicated) in the atmosphere.

gesu bikhre hue ghataaein be-khud
aanchal latka hua havaaein be-khud

pur-kaif shabaab se adaayein be-khud
gaati hui saans se fazaayein be-khud

गेसू बिखरे हुए घटाएँ बे-ख़ुद
आँचल लटका हुआ हवाएँ बे-ख़ुद
पुर-कैफ़ शबाब से अदाएँ बे-ख़ुद
गाती हुई साँस से फ़ज़ाएँ बे-ख़ुद

With your locks untied,
clouds are intoxicated.
With your scarf falling,
breezes are inebriated.
With your captivating youth,
your style of flirting is elated.
With your song-like breaths,
the ambiance is intoxicated.

String of Pearls

Even heaven is seen standing among the beauty's hopefuls! One can't think of a better compliment than this one.

qatre a'raq-e jism ke moti ki lari
hai paikar-e naaz k phuulon ki chhari
gardish mein nigaah hai k bat-ti hai hayaat
jannat bhi hai aaj umiidvaaron mein khari

क़तरे अरक़-ए जिस्म के गोती की लड़ी
है पैकर-ए नाज़ कि फूलों की छड़ी
गर्दिश में निगाह है कि बटती है हयात
जन्नत भी है आज उमीदवारों में खड़ी

The drops of your body's sweat
are like a string of pearls.
The form of your beauty
is a wand of flowers.

The movement of your eyes
is splitting life into parts.
Even heaven is seen standing
among your hopefuls.

Beauty Sunk in Rapture

When she walks, her feet touch the ground, producing musical notes. When it rains, she is in a state of rapture and even drops of water are sweet-smelling.

komal pad-gaamini ki aahat to suno
gaate qadmon ki gungunaahat to suno
saavan lahra hai mad mein duuba hua ruup
ras ki buundon ki jham-jhamaahat to suno

कोमल पद-गामिनी की आहट तो सुनो
गाते क़दमों की गुनगुनाहट तो सुनो
सावन लहरा है मद में डूबा हुआ रूप
रस की बूँदों की झमझमाहट तो सुनो

Listen to the sound
of someone walking tenderly.
Listen to the humming
of singing feet.
The waves of the rainy month
and the beauty sunk in rapture.
Listen to the roar
of sweet-smelling drops.

Boundaries of Music

The poet shifts the focus to himself and talks about what truly inspires him.

har jalve se ik dars-e namuu leta huun
labrez kaii jam o subu leta huun
parti hai jab aankh tujh par ae jaan-e bahaar
sangiit ki sarhadon ko chhu leta huun

हर जल्वे से इक दर्स-ए नुमू लेता हूँ
लबरेज़ कई जाम ओ सुबू लेता हूँ
पड़ती है जब आँख तुझ पर ऐ जान-ए-बहार
संगीत की सरहदों को छू लेता हूँ

From each spectacle,
I draw a lesson of growth.
From overflowing stocks of wine,
I fill my drink glasses.
When my eyes fall on you,
my life of the spring,
I touch the boundaries of music.

Half-Opened Narcissus

The drunken body is like a half-opened narcissus!

sar-ta-ba qadam rukh-e nigariin hai k tan
hain uzv-e hasiin k bol uthne ko dahan
ye masti o kaif ye jamaahi ye jhapak
ik adh-khuli nargis-e khumaariin hai badan

सर-ता-ब क़दम रुख़-ए निगारीं है कि तन
हैं उज़्व-ए हसीं कि बोल उठने को दहन
ये मस्ती ओ कैफ़ ये जमाही ये झपक
इक अध-खुली नर्गिस-ए ख़ुमारीं है बदन

From head to foot,
a beautiful face,
a lovely body.
Each part of her beauty

is making her figure
come alive.
This intoxication,
this yawn, and her use
of a narrowed eye.
The drunken body
is like a half-opened
narcissus.

Hair-Parting of the Rainbow

This ruba'i reminds the reader of beauty's marital status. Even rainbow tries to copy her style. A lot of poetry is written about unmarried, uncommitted women. Firaq is perhaps the only Urdu poet who has written extensively about married women and those who have children, portraying them in their roles as mothers and wives. Their beauty is worthy of lyrical celebration as well.

jab raat gaye suhaag karti hai nigaah
dil mein shab-e maah ke utarti hai nigaah
ratnaar nain se phuut-ti hain kirnein
ya kahkashaan ki maang bharti hai nigaah

जब रात गए सुहाग करती है निगाह
दिल में शब-ए माह के उतरती है निगाह
रतनार नैन से फूटती हैं किरनें
या कहकशाँ की माँग भरती है निगाह

When late in the night,
her eye seeks marital bliss,
and it goes deep into the heart
on a moonlit evening.
While its brightness makes
the rays arise,

it is nothing but an act
of filling the hair-parting
of the rainbow.

Youth's Essence Singing

This ruba'i has the feel of a portrait, something like a photographic shot at a particular moment.

nikhre badan ka muskaraana hai hai
ras ke joban ka gun-gunaana hai hai
kaanon ki lavon ka thartharaana kam kam
chehre ke til ka jagmagaana hai hai

निखरे बदन का मुस्कुराना है है
रस के जोबन का गुनगुनाना है है
कानों की लवों का थरथराना कम कम
चेहरे के तिल का जगमगाना है है

The smile of the newly harvested body
yes, that's what it is –
youth's essence singing.
Her earlobes shiver less.
The brightness of a mole on her face
yes, that's what it is.

Beauty Is Changing Everything

Each line of this ruba'i has a definitional word that makes the associated metaphors come alive: *bijli* (lightning), *amrit* (nectar), *pavan* (air), and *baadal* (cloud).

vo paing hai ruup mein k bijli lahraaye
vo ras aavaaz mein k amrit lalchaaye
raftaar mein vo lachak pavan ras bal khaaye
gesu mein vo latak k baadal mandlaaye

वो पेंग है रूप में कि बिजली लहराए
वो रस आवाज़ में कि अमृत ललचाए
रफ़्तार में वो लचक पवन रस बल खाए
गेसू में वो लटक कि बादल मँडलाये

There's a wave of lightning
due to beauty's intoxicating tale.
There's such essence in beauty's voice
that nectar has turned greedy.
There's such softness in her speed
that the air's core is twisting.
There's such a swing in her locks
that the clouds start to hover.

The Spectacle and the Veil

This is a beautiful play of words about the veil. Is it meant to hide something? Or does the very act of hiding lead to a situation where the beauty is revealed?

khulta hi nahien husn hai pinhaan k aa'yaan
dekhe tujhe kaise koi ae jaan-e jahaan
bandh jaata hai ik jalva o parde ka talism
ye ghaib o shahuud aankh-macholi ka samaan

खुलता ही नहीं हुस्न है पिन्हाँ कि अयाँ
देखे तुझे कैसे कोई ऐ जान-ए-जहाँ
बंध जाता है इक जल्वा ओ परदे का तिलिस्म
ये ग़ैब ओ शुहूद आँख-मिचोली का समाँ

I can't decipher
whether the beauty is concealed
or transparent.
How can anyone look at you,
oh, spirit of existence?

The tension between the spectacle
and the veil arises along with its magic.
O this moment for peekaboo
between the perceptible
and the unnoticeable!

The Stretching

There is a lot of good poetry on *angraii* (stretching). Firaq adds something new by introducing the rainbow, which replicates the act.

qaamat hai k angraaiyaan leti sargam
ho raqs mein jaise rang o buu ka aa'lam
jagmag jagmag hai shabistaan-e iram
ya qaus-e quzah lachak rahi hai paiham

क़ामत है कि अंगड़ाइयाँ लेती सरगम
हो रक़्स में जैसे रंग ओ बू का आलम
जगमग जगमग है शब्नमिस्तान-ए-इरम
या क़ौस-ए-क़ुज़ह लचक रही है पैहम

Is this her majestic figure stretching
or the musical notes elongating?
In every dance,
there is some fragrance hidden.
As if lights are shimmering
in a mythical city.
Or is the rainbow continuously opening
to the moment?

Beautiful Belle or Hafiz's Ghazal

Hafiz, the great Persian poet who lived in the fourteenth century, wrote more than five hundred ghazals celebrating the beloved's beauty. He was a source of inspiration to scores of Persian and Urdu poets. His ghazal is the pinnacle of perfection when Firaq compares the beauty in this ruba'i to Hafiz's ghazal, which is a testimony to her flawlessness and sublimity.

saaghar kaf-e dast mein suraahi b-baghal
kaandhe pe gesuon ke kaale baadal
ye maddh-bhari aankh ye nigaahein chanchal
hai paikar-e naazniin k Hafiz ki ghazal

साग़र कफ़-ए-दस्त में सुराही ब-बग़ल
काँधे पे गेसुओं के काले बादल
ये मध-भरी आँख ये निगाहें चंचल
है पैकर-ए-नाज़नीं कि 'हाफ़िज़' की ग़ज़ल

Goblet in the palm of her hand
and a jug on her side!
On her shoulders,
there are black clouds of her tresses.
Her intoxicating eyes
and her playful glance!
Is this a beautiful belle
or Hafiz's ghazal?

Moon in the Goblet

The mention of saqi and goblet in this ruba'i reminds one of Omar Khayyam's writing style, albeit one big difference. The goblet is filled with the moon and not wine. Since beauty is moon-faced, this act encouraged her to remove her veil—two moons facing each other.

aflaak pe jab parcham-e shab lahraaya
saaqi ne bhara saaghar-e mah chhalkaaya
kuchh soch ke kuchh der ta-ammul kar ke
us ne bhi zara parda-e rukh sarkaaya

अफ़्लाक पे जब परचम-ए शब लहराया
साक़ी ने भरा साग़र-ए-मह छलकाया
कुछ सोच के कुछ देर तअम्मुल कर के
उस ने भी ज़रा पर्दा-ए रुख़ सरकाया

When in the sky,
evening's flag was waved,
Saqi filled the goblet
with the moon and shook it.
After some thinking and hesitation,
she slightly moved her veil
from her face.

Nine

SATYAM (TRUTH)

The pure world of Brahman is attainable by those only who are neither deceitful, nor wicked, nor false.[18]

Prasna Upanishad

TRUTH AS ESSENCE OF LIFE

Satyam is the absolute truth or essence in its simple translation. In some religious traditions (Sikhism), truth is equated with god. In Hinduism, it is one of the five principles that should guide our lives. The other four are *ahimsa* (nonviolence), *asteya* (not stealing), *brahmacharya* (chastity), and *aparigraha* (non-possessiveness). Truth to be absolute must be unchangeable, that which has no distortion, that which is beyond time and space, and that which pervades the whole universe. Satya is also the first word in the mantra *sat-chit-ananda* (absolute truth, consciousness, and bliss), which is the very definition of godhood. According to the *Shanti Parva* of the Mahabharata: 'To speak the truth is meritorious. There is nothing higher than truth. Everything is upheld by truth, and everything rests upon truth. Even the sinful and ferocious swear to keep the truth amongst themselves,

[18]Prabhananda, Swami, and Frederick Manchester, *The Upanishads: Breath of the Eternal.* Vedanta Press, California, 1947, p. 45.

dismiss all grounds of quarrel, and, uniting with one another, set themselves to their (sinful) tasks, depending upon truth. If they behaved falsely towards one another, they would then be destroyed without a doubt.'

Let it Be

The quartets in this chapter are about truths of life—about things that are not left to our judgements. There are many moments of sorrow and bliss in life. It is all bound together. We can't choose one and leave the other.

khote hain agar jaan to kho lene do
aise mein jo ho jaaye vo ho lene do
ek u'mr pari hai sabr bhi kar lein ge
is vaqt to ji bhar ke ro lene do

खोते हैं अगर जान तो खो लेने दे
ऐसे में जो हो जाए वो हो लेने दे
एक उम्र पड़ी हैं सब्र भी कर लेंगे
इस वक़्त तो जी भर के रो लेने दे

If we lose our lives,
let it be.
Whatever happens now,
let it be.
We have life left to spend.
We shall be patient.
At this moment,
please allow us to cry
as much as we wish.

Source of Peace and Tranquility

Companionship is a source of strength. When someone holds our hand, it is a promise that the other will stand by us.

tu haath ko jab haath mein le leti hai
dukh dard zamaane ke mita deti hai
sansaar ke tapte hue viiraane mein
sukh shaant ki goya tu hari kheti hai

तू हाथ को जब हाथ में ले लेती है
दुख दर्द ज़माने के मिटा देती है
संसार के तपते हुए वीराने में
सुख शांत की गोया तू हरी खेती है

When you take my hand
in yours,
you take away
all the pain and worries.
In the boiling wilderness
of this world,
you are the source of peace
and tranquility.

Art of Living

Action is the source of learning, and each failure teaches us how we can succeed.

karte nahien kuchh to kaam karna kaya aaye
jiite-ji jaan se guzarna kaya aaye
ro ro ke maut maangne vaalon ko
jiina nahien aa saka to marna kaya aaye

करते नहीं कुछ तो काम करना क्या आए
जीते-जी जान से गुज़रना क्या आए
रो रो के मौत माँगने वालों को
जीना नहीं आ सका तो मरना क्या आए

Without action,
how do we get the skills?

How do we learn
the art of living?
Those praying for death
while crying should know,
you didn't learn to live
how could you remember
to die?

Message for the Friend

Where there is love, nothing else is needed.

kahti hain yahi teri nigaahein ae dost
nikliin naaii zindagi ki raahein ae dost
kion husn o muhabbat se n uunche uth ke
donon ik duusre ko chaahein ae dost

कहती हैं यही तेरी निगाहें ऐ दोस्त
निकलीं नई ज़िंदगी की राहें ऐ दोस्त
क्यूँ हुस्न ओ मोहब्बत से न ऊँचे उठ के
दोनों इक दूसरे को चाहें ऐ दोस्त

Your eyes,
my friend,
are telling me something.
There are new paths of life,
my friend.
Why don't we rise
above beauty and love,
and start loving each other,
my friend.

When Days Sang Songs

As T.S. Eliot wrote in his famous work *Four Quartets:*

Time present and time past
Are both perhaps present in time future,
And time future contained in time past.
If all time is eternally present
All time is unredeemable.[19]

If something extraordinary happened in the past, it still lives in our consciousness because time is eternally present: past, present and future coalesce.

har saans mein gulzaar khil jaate the
har lamhe mein jannat ki hava khaate the
kaya tujh ko mohabbat ke vo ayyaam hain yaad
jab parda-e shab bajte the din gaate the

हर साँस में गुलज़ार से खिल जाते थे
हर लम्हे में जन्नत की हवा खाते थे
क्या तुझ को मोहब्बत के वो अय्याम हैं याद
जब पर्दा-ए शब बजते थे दिन गाते थे

In every breath we took,
flowers blossomed.
At each moment,
we breathed
paradisiacal breeze.
Do you remember
those points in time
when the evening's veil
played music
and days sang songs?

---

[19]Eliot, T.S., *Four Quartets* Faber Editions, London, p. 13.

Time for Solitude

A memory is made special with the presence of a doe who witnesses the love unfolding.

ye raaz o niyaaz aur ye samaan khalvat ka
ye aankh mein aankh daal dena tera
hirni hai dari dari si aur kuchh maanuus
ye narm jhijak su-purdagi ki ye ada

ये राज़ ओ नियाज़ और ये समाँ ख़ल्वत का
ये आँख में आँख डाल देना तेरा
हिरनी है डरी डरी सी और कुछ मानूस
ये नर्म झिजक सुपुर्दगी की ये अदा

These secret deliberations
and this time for solitude.
Your eyes are dipping
into my eyes.
There is a doe
that is frightened
and is somewhat familiar.
This soft hesitation and
the manner of making over.

Rakhi on the Brother's Wrist

Being a doting sister and honouring a long-standing tradition in which the brother swears to uphold his sister's honour at all costs is another facet of beauty. Weaving Hindu traditions and rituals into his poetic work is the hallmark of Firaq's poetry.

raksha-bandhan ki sub-h ras ki putli
chhaaii hai ghata gagan pe halki halki

bijli ki tarh lachak rahe hain lachhey
bhai ke hai baandhi chamkti raakhi

रक्षा-बंधन की सुब्ह रस की पुतली
छाई है घटा गगन पे हल्की हल्की
बिजली की तरह लचक रहे हैं लच्छे
भाई के है बाँधी चमकती राखी

On a festive morning,
full of essence,
a willowy figure.
The sky is lightly filled
with black clouds.
Like lightning,
skeins of thread
swing softly.
She ties a shining Rakhi
on her brother's wrist.

Sparks of Melodies

Most memories are visual, but many are auditory. We often fill our memories with details of past events by remembering someone by the associated sound (instead of an image).

kya tere khayal ne bhi chhera hai sitaar
siine mein ur rahe hain naghmon ke sharaar
dhyaan aate hi saaf bajne lagte hain kaan
hai yaad teri vo khanak vo jhankaar

क्या तेरे ख़याल ने भी छेड़ा है सितार
सीने में उड़ रहे हैं नग़मों के शरार
ध्यान आते ही साफ़ बजने लगते हैं कान
है याद तेरी वो खनक वो झंकार

Has your thought triggered
a play of a sitar?
Sparks of melodies are rising
from the bosom.
This mental image
has made my ears receptive.
Your memory is an amalgam
of sounds.

Heat of Love

Dewdrops can hide the beauty of a flower. But when they evaporate, the flower is seen more clearly—an ordinary observation turned into a subtle poetic thought.

yuun i'shq ki aanch kha ke rang aur khile
yuun soz-e daruun se ruu-e rangiin chamke
jaise kuchh din charhe gulistaanon mein
shabnam suukhe to gul ka chehra nikhre

यूँ इ'श्क़ की आँच खा के रंग और खिले
यूँ सोज़-ए-दरूँ से रू-ए-रंगीं चमके
जैसे कुछ दिन चढ़े गुलिस्तानों में
शबनम सूखे तो गुल का चेहरा निखरे

With the heat of love,
the complexion blossoms.
The warmth of the inner passion
makes the colourful face brighter.
As if a new day rises
in blooming gardens.
When dewdrops dry up,
the flower's face becomes
more translucent.

Quintessence of Womanhood

A woman can play many roles: a mother, sister and life partner. While modesty encompasses all other facets of her life, a woman can please her partner when she falls into his arms.

maan aur behan bhi aur chaheti beti
ghar ki raani bhi aur jiivan saathi
phir bhi vo kaamini saraasar devi
aur sej pe besava vo ras ki putli

माँ और बहन भी और चहेती बेटी
घर की रानी भी और जीवन साथी
फिर भी वो कामनी सरासर देवी
और सेज पे बेसवा वो रस की पुतली

A mother and a sister
and the little darling.
The majesty of the home
and a life partner.
Even then,
the bundle-of-affection
is like a goddess.
In bed,
she is a harlot,
the quintessence
of womanhood.

Tough Love

'I won't speak with you.' What a beautiful way to express anger!

kis pyaar se hoti hai khafa bachche se
kuchh tevri charhaaye hue munh phere hue

is ruuthne par prem ka sansaar nisaar
kahti hai k ja tujh se nahien bolein ge

किस प्यार से होती है ख़फ़ा बच्चे से
कुछ तेवरी चढ़ाए हुए मुँह फेरे हुए
इस रूठने पर प्रेम का संसार निसार
कहती है कि जा तुझ से नहीं बोलेंगे

She is unhappy
with her child
but still affectionate.
With a frown on her face
she looks away.
For this tantrum,
we can sacrifice
the whole world,
as she says,
'I won't speak with you'.

Thinking of You

Firaq explores three incredibly moving ways to express the magic of a beloved's memory returning to the lover: a star's reflection in a stream, light inside black clouds, and moon rays illuminating the atmosphere.

jis tarah naddi mein ek taara lahraaye
jis tarah ghata mein ek kaunda bal khaaye
barmaaye faza ko jaise ik chander kiran
yuunhi shaam-e firaq teri yaad aaye

जिस तरह नद्दी में एक तारा लहराए
जिस तरह घटा में एक कौंदा बल खाए
बर्माए फ़ज़ा को जैसे इक चंद्र किरन
यूँही शाम-ए-फ़िराक़ तेरी याद आए

Just as a star's reflection
flutters in a stream.
Just as a flash makes a move
inside black clouds.
Just as rays of the moon
pierce the atmosphere.
In the same way,
during separation,
I think of you.

Like the Rising Stream

Nature and beauty are in perfect harmony in this rub'ai.

charhti hui naddi hai k lahraati hai
pighli hui bijli hai k bal khaati hai
pahlu mein lahak ke bhench leti hai vo jab
kaya jaane kahaan baha le jaati hai

चढ़ती हुई नद्दी है कि लहराती है
पिघली हुई बिजली है कि बल खाती है
पहलू में लहक के भेंच लेती है वो जब
क्या जाने कहाँ बहा ले जाती है

Is the stream rising?
Or is it swaying?
Is it molten electricity
or something that quivers
and rolls?
She quickly grasps everything
in her grip.
No one knows
where she goes,
flowing.

Many Facets of Love

Managing a child can be difficult. When a child throws a tantrum, only the mother understands how to respond. It's not just love but love combined with a warning. Children learn to become adults in this way as they grow.

gul hain k rukh-e garm ke hain angaare
baalak ke nain se tuut-te hain taare
rahmat ka farishta ban ke deti hai saza
maan hi ko pukaare aur maan hi maare

गुल हैं कि रुख़-ए गर्म के हैं अंगारे
बालक के नैन से टूटते हैं तारे
रहमत का फ़रिश्ता बन के देती है सज़ा
माँ ही को पुकारे और माँ ही मारे

Are these flowers
or cinders
of your sizzling face?
The child cries,
as if losing stars of his eyes.
An angel
of compassion,
she punishes the child.
He calls for mom,
and mom is the one
who chastises.

Strolling with a Platter in Hand

Treating the husband as a divine being and showing ritualistic obedience to him is part of the tradition and the Hindu way of life, and this aspect is so beautifully captured in this ruba'i.

kis darja sukuun-numa hain abru ke hilaal
khair o barkat ke dhan lutaati hui chaal
jiivan-saathi ke aage devi ban kar
aati hai suhaani sajaaye hue thaal

किस दर्जा सकूँ-नुमा हैं अबरू के हिलाल
ख़ैर ओ बरकत के धन लुटाती हुई चाल
जीवन-साथी के आगे देवी बन कर
आती है सुहागनी सजाए हुए थाल

How tranquil are
her crescent-like eyebrows!
She walks,
dispensing well-being
and beneficence.
In front of her partner,
she emerges as a goddess.
Blessed in matrimony,
she strolls with an ornate platter
in her hand.

The Virgin Relationship

The reference to virginity is about purity, sincerity and devotion to the family and the sanctity of the relationship between the husband and wife.

sun yug o yug ki kahaani n utha
paani mein bhiigte kanval ko dekha
biiti hon gi suhaag raatein kitni
lekin hai aaj tak kanvaara naata

सुन युग ओ युग की कहानी न उठा
पानी में भीगते कँवल को देखा
बीती होंगी सुहाग रातें कितनी
लेकिन है आज तक कँवारा नाता

Don't narrate age-old stories.
Did you see the lotus
drenched in water?
Although many nights
of marital bliss
have come and gone,
the relationship is still
that of a virgin.

Magical Days

The little girl, who was so loved and cherished by her parents, is going to grow into a woman in her own right. There is a play on the word *nain* (eyes).

sote jaadu jagaane vaale din hain
umron ki hadein milaane vaale din hain
kanya ab kamini hai hone vaali
aankhon ko naiyan banaane vaale din hain

सोते जादू जगाने वाले दिन हैं
उम्रों की हदें मिलाने वाले दिन हैं
कन्या अब कामनी है होने वाली
आँखों को नैन बनाने वाले दिन हैं

These are sleepy
and magical days
days that bring all ages
together.
She is going to become
an enchanting beauty
the days when eyes allure
and entice.

Like a Paradise Waving

This is a beautiful representation of intimacy in a marital relationship.

phuulon ki suhaag-sej ye jauban ras
sote mein suhagani lutati hui jas
karvat karvat hai lahlahaati jannat
ye raat ye kuchh hilte hue ruup-kalas

फूलों की सुहाग सेज ये जोबन रस
सोते में सुहागनी लुटाती हुई जस
करवट करवट है लहलहाती जन्नत
ये रात ये कुछ हिलते हुए रूप-कलस

Embellished with flowers,
the marital bed
is the essence of youth.
In her sleep,
the bride is like a celebrity.
On this side and that side,
a paradise is waving.
The night
and a slightly moving crest
on the top of a dome.

When...

This ruba'i is a beautiful symbiosis of nature's beauty and the arrival of the beloved's memory.

jab kirnein himalaaya ki choti guundhein
soe hue aabshaar aankhein kholein
jab kanchan niir si jhalakti ho faza
aise mein kaash teri aahat paayein

जब किरनें हिमालिया की चोटी गूँधें
सोए हुए आबशार आँखें खोलें
जब कंचन नीर सी झलकती हो फ़ज़ा
ऐसे में काश तिरी आहट पाएँ

When the rays knead
the highest peak of the Himalayas,
when sleeping waterfalls
open their eyes,
when the surroundings show
a shine of gold,
I wish, at that time,
I could hear the tinkling
of your footsteps!

At the Riverbank

Before the invention of more modern water supply methods, the village had a single well where young girls and women would come to fetch water. This was also the place where village news was shared, besides laughter about the lighter side of rural life, and in some cases, loving glances were exchanged with boys hovering close to the well. No wonder some girls returned from the well with 'longing in the bosom'.

panghat pe gagariya chhalakne ka ye rang
paani hichkole le ke bharta hai tarang
kaandhon pe siron pe donon haathon mein kalas
mad ankhriyon mein siinon mein bharpuur umang

पनघट पे गगरियाँ छलकने का ये रंग
पानी हचकोले ले के भरता है तरंग
काँधों पे सरों पे दोनों हाथों में कलस
मद अँखड़ियों में सीनों में भरपूर उमंग

The colour of the water spilling
in the pitcher
at the riverbank.
The water adds waves
of emotions when it ebbs and flows.
There is a spire on the shoulders,
on the head,
and in both hands.
Rapture in the eyes
and wholesome longing
in the bosom.

Ten

Shivam (Ultimate Reality)

> *Hindu heritage has made me realize that the relationship between the lover and the beloved, family life, social life, natural scenic beauty, earth, rivers, oceans, fluttering green crops, orchards, gardens, forests, fire, air, sun, moon, stars and changing seasons are far more divine and pious than any religious scripture, or any place of pilgrimage such as Ka'ba or Kashi.*[20]
>
> —Firaq

UNDERSTANDING ULTIMATE REALITY

Based on the threefold conception of Hindu gods, there is a general impression that Shiva is the god of destruction or dissolution. This characterization is simplistic because categorizing Shiva into one box is challenging. The range of functions he performs is vast and covers everything from creation to maintenance, dissolution, concealment, and the bestowal of grace (also known as the five acts of Shiva). This means that Shiva is deeply involved in everything in the universe and within every being. What occurs in the universe also manifests in our personal experiences. As pointed out by Kshemaraja, 'Those who always ponder

[20]Shauq, Prakash Sumant, *Thus Spoke Firaq: A Collection of Interviews* (1959–1976).

over this (the above-mentioned five acts of Shiva), knowing the universe as an unfoldment of the essential nature (of consciousness), become liberated in this very life. This is what the sacred tradition maintains. Those who do not ponder this, seeing all objects of experience as essentially different, remain forever bound.'[21] Shiva is, therefore, all reality, the ultimate reality.

How do we describe ultimate reality? According to Dr S. Radhakrishnan, we need to be aware of six dimensions of ultimate reality. First, there is unbroken continuity in nature. Everything in the cosmos is interconnected. Second, the relatedness encompasses all beings, from the smallest particles to the most extensive systems, from the smallest creatures to the most enormous beasts. There are no exceptions. Third, nature is one large whole with matter, life, mind, and values as its constituents. Although these elements remain utterly unlike each other, they intermingle and coexist. Fourth, nature always aspires to reach higher levels. There is a continuous emergence of new qualities. Unpredictable novelties occur. Fifth, the changes are not meaningless. There is a constant drift towards better things. Sixth and last, the highest kind of experiences are always all-inclusive. Great souls and extraordinary teachers embrace the whole reality, the oneness of being, and unity in diversity.[22]

Firaq is conscious and is respectful of changes that occur over long periods. Great civilizations rise and fall. The same goes for great empires. There is no permanence in life; birth and death are inextricably linked, but we can adapt

---

[21]Shantananda, Swami, and Peggy Bendel, *The Splendor of Recognition*. SYDA Foundation, New York, 2003, p. 206.

[22]Radhakrishnan, S., *An Idealist View of Life*, George Allen & Unwin, 1932, pp. 248–249.

to change. Instead of resisting it, we can learn to survive and thrive. While external challenges are formidable, what happens within us is no less critical. Learning to imbibe higher values is the key to our spiritual evolution. While all higher values are transformative, nothing is more transformative than love. While we can't ignore small things that occur daily, focusing on the bigger picture will always be more rewarding. Firaq was open for his unbridled love for his motherland, but his nationalism and patriotism were not based on blind adoration. He was conscious of things that required change. We need to balance; he felt that our love of the land should be combined with humanistic values, including love for all beings, actions that protect nature, and the need for global peace and harmony.

How Civilizations Die

Civilizations arise, achieving heights of power, creating great cultures and arts, spreading their influence, and then decline, slowly die, and disappear. Starting with the Roman Empire, this history has been repeated too many times. At its zenith, the Mughal Empire created awe-inspiring architecture and fostered the emergence of new languages. However, when the British forces entered Delhi in 1857, there were not enough soldiers to defend it. Firaq raises the question about the rise and fall of civilizations, but doesn't provide an answer. The answer lies in our thinking and our understanding of the causes.

sahra mein zamaan makaan ke kho jaati hain
sadiyon bedaar rah ke so jaati hain
aksar socha kiya huun khalvat mein
tehziibein kyon gharuub ho jaati hain

सहरा में ज़माँ मकाँ के खो जाती हैं
सदियों बेदार रह के सो जाती हैं
अक्सर सोचा किया हूँ ख़ल्वत में 'फ़िराक़'
तहज़ीबें क्यूँ ग़ुरूब हो जाती हैं

Like time and space,
centuries are lost in the desert.
Active for hundreds of years,
they go to eternal sleep.
Firaq, I do think in my solitude.
Why do civilizations dwindle
and disappear?

Life Balance

This ruba'i reads like a meditation on the ups and downs of life. Learning anything new requires great patience. It is hard work that doesn't promise success in the end, and life skills don't come cheap. There are lessons to be learnt from our personal experiences and, more broadly, from the currents of history. Ultimately, it is crucial to strike a balance that fosters peace and stability.

har saaz se hoti nahien ye dhun paida
hota hai bare jatan se ye gun paida
miizaan-e nashaat o gham mein sadiyon tul kar
hota hai hayaat mein tavazun paida

हर साज़ से होती नहीं ये धुन पैदा
होता है बड़े जतन से ये गुन पैदा
मीज़ान-ए-नशात-ओ-ग़म में सदियों तुल कर
होता है हयात में तवाज़ुन पैदा

Every musical instrument
can't produce this sound.

You acquire this skill
with great effort.
Centuries are weighed
in the scales of happy and sad
and that's how we obtain
balance in our lives.

Developing Our Human Nature

How do we become human and achieve our humanness? What seems easy is actually quite challenging. It is a lifelong struggle. We spend a lot of time counting our gains and losses. When we are happy, we forget the days of grief. All this is a part of our daily routine. The critical question, however, is whether we are developing our human nature with lasting values, such as love, empathy, compassion, correct thinking, and right action, essential for a life well-lived.

paate jaana hai aur n khote jaana
hanste jaana hai aur n rote jaana
avval aur aakhri pyaam-e tahziib
insaan ko insaan hai hote jaana

पाते जाना है और न खोते जाना
हँसते जाना है और न रोते जाना
अव्वल और आख़िरी पयाम-ए तहज़ीब
इंसान को इंसान है होते जाना

You gain some,
and you lose some.
Always smiling,
never crying.
It is the first
and the last message

of civilizing oneself.
Humans should continue
to develop
their human nature.

Come to Me

This ruba'i is an invitation to what is best in life. What we seek determines our destiny. We can seek objects that give us pleasure or we can focus on things that matter: the meaning of life and who we are at the core of our being.

ae maa'ni-e kaayenaat mujh mein aa ja
ae raaz-e sifaat o zaat mujh mein aa ja
sota sansaar jhilmilaate taare
ab bhiig chali hai raat mujh me aa ja

ऐ मअनी-ए काइनात मुझ में आ जा
ऐ राज़-ए सिफ़ात-ओ-ज़ात मुझ में आ जा
सोता संसार झिलमिलाते तारे
अब भीग चली है रात मुझ में आ जा

The meaning of this universe,
come to me.
The secret attributes of the selfhood,
come to me.
The world is asleep,
and the stars are shimmering.
Now, the night is drenched,
come to me.

Closer to My Beloved

Our ability to love someone deeply is a fundamental aspect of humanity. It is love that demands less and gives more, and love that doesn't place any limits. Love makes the person you love a part of your being, which lives within you and breathes in the same rhythm as you do.

jis tarah ragon mein khuun-e saaleh ho ravaan
jis tarah hayaat ka hai markaz rag-e jaan
jis tarah juda nahien vujuud o maujuud
kuchh is se ziyaada qurb-e jaan-e jahaan

जिस तरह रगों में ख़ून-ए सालेह हो रवाँ
जिस तरह हयात का है मरकज़ रग-ए-जाँ
जिस तरह जुदा नहीं वजूद ओ मौजूद
कुछ इस से ज़्यादा क़ुर्ब-ए जान-ए जहाँ

Just as the blood of the pious
runs through the veins,
just as the centre of life
lies in the jugular vein,
just as the present
is not separate from the absence,
I'm closer to my beloved
than all the above.

Mother India

This ruba'i shows Firaq's Indianness at its best. Numerous poets have penned homilies for Mother India but the last two lines of this ruba'i brilliantly sum up what is unique about India.

ae maadar-e hind sub-h teri shaam teri
hai saaqi-e dauraan ke chhalakate hue jaam
lamhon mein tere raaz-e abad pinhaan hain
teri har saans ek paighaam-e davaam

ऐ मादरे-हिन्द सुबह तेरी शाम तेरी
हैं साक़ी-ए दौरां के छलकते हुए जाम

लम्हों में तेरे राज़-ए अबद पिन्हाँ हैं
तेरी हर सांस एक पैग़ामे-दवाम

O Mother India,
your glorious morning,
and your spectacular evening!
You are like the overflowing goblets
of the Saqi of our time.
In your moments are hidden
the secrets of eternity.
Every breath of yours
is everlasting.

The Patient's Care

There is a facet of womanhood that is often overlooked and rarely talked of. As a wife, she is the protector of her life partner's well-being. When the husband is sick, she nurses him, being by his bedside. Her touch transmits the positive energy that heals him. She is not doing this as a marital duty; she does it with love and compassion for the inseparable part of her being.

premi ko bukhaar uth nahien sakti hai palak
baithi hai sarhaane maand mukhre ki damak
jalti hai peshaani pe rakh deti hai haath
par jaati hai biimaar ke dil mein thandak

प्रेमी को बुख़ार उठ नहीं सकती है पलक
बैठी है सिरहाने माँद मुखड़े की दमक
जलती हुई पेशानी पे रख देती है हाथ
पड़ जाती है बीमार के दिल में ठंडक

When the lover has a fever,
he can't raise his eyelids.

She sits by the bedside,
dimming the glitter of her face.
On the burning forehead,
she keeps her hand.
With this, the patient's heart
finds solace.

Get Completely Engrossed

How do we make a deep-seated connection with our lives? It depends on the quality of our engagement. Do we act as if the assigned task is to be completed, or do we thoroughly soak up what we are doing? Do we suffer the pain of an action, or do we show excitement at what the prospect of completing a job well done will bring? Is our heart immersed in our actions? That is a critical difference between accepting action as an affliction and performing at a level where everything flows, making it an unending source of enjoyment.

ik raaz se kar raha huun tujh ko aagaah
mamnuun o haraam kuchh nahien hai vallah!
jis kaam mein mahviyat-e kaamil n ho shaamil
ae dost samajh le k hai vo kaam haram

इक राज़ से कर रहा हूँ तुझ को आगाह
ममनून ओ हराम कुछ नहीं है वल्लाह
जिस काम में महवियत-ए कामिल न रहे
ऐ दोस्त समझ ले कि है वो काम गुनाह

I'm making you aware
of a secret.
Nothing in this world
is virtuous or wrong,
good lord!

If you are not
completely engrossed
in a task, my friend,
treat that task as sin.

Luck and Fate

Firaq forces us to pay attention to bigger things. Looking at the big picture is always a rewarding experience. A chain is more significant than its parts, and a portrait is much more than the minuscule dots its made of. Instead of putting ourselves first and always thinking of our self-interest, we should realize that our fate is juxtaposed with the collective—our community, our nation, and the planet.

ik halqa-e zanjiir to zanjiir nahien
ik halqa-e tasviir to tasviir nahien
taqdiir to qomon ki hua karti hai
ik shakhs ki qismat koi taqdiir nahien

इक हलका-ए ज़ंजीर तो ज़ंजीर नहीं
इक हलका-ए तस्वीर तो तस्वीर नहीं
तक़दीर तो क़ौमों की हुआ करती है
इक शख़्स की क़िस्मत कोई तक़दीर नहीं

One circle of the chain
is no chain.
One circle of the portrait
is no portrait.
Fate belongs to nations.
One person's luck
does not equal fate.

An Ocean of Essence

In conclusion, we have an excellent taste of the first and most critical *sringara rasa*, that is, attractiveness—the celebration of the female body. It is a mine of pearls, an ocean of essence, a swan opening its feathers, and a sacred lake filled with milk.

moti ki kaan ras ka saagar hai badan
darpan aakaash ka sarasar hai badan
angadaaii mein rajhans tole hue par
ya duudh bhara maansarovar hai badan

मोती की कान रस का सागर है बदन
दर्पन आकाश का सरासर है बदन
अंगड़ाई में राजहंस तोले हुए पर
या दूध भरा मानसरोवर है बदन

A mine of pearls,
the body is an ocean of essence.
It is a full mirror of the sky.
In your stretch,
a swan is weighing its feathers
or is your Mansarovar-like body
filled with milk?

BIBLIOGRAPHY

Aa'lam, Mahtab. 1995. *Firaq Ka Jaaiza.* Purnia: Dr. Mahtan Aa'lam.

Ali, Navazish. 1991. *Firaq Gorakhpuri: Katabiyaat.* Islamabad: Maqtadarah Qomi Zabaan.

Arifi, Amir. 1997. *Firaq aur Naii Nasal.* Delhi: Saqi Book Depot.

Aziz, Abdul, ed. 2005. Zaaviye: *Firaq Ki Nadar Tehriirein.* New Delhi: M.R. Publications

Farooqi, Suhail Ahmad, and Shamim Hanafi. 1996. *Firaq: Dyaar-e Shab Ka Musafir.* New Delhi: Maktaba Jamia Limited.

Fatmi, Ali Ahmad, ed. 2010. *Firaq Gorakhpuri: Selected Writings.* New Delhi: National Book Trust.

Fatmi, Ali. 2007. *Firaq Gorakhpuri: Shaa'yir aur Daanishvar.* New Delhi: M.R. Publications.

Gorakhpuri, Firaq. 1945. *Shola-e Saaz.* Lahore: Maktaba Urdu.

Gorakhpuri, Firaq. 1945. *Tagore: Anarkali aur duusri kahaniyaan.* Lahore: Azad Book Depot.

Gorakhpuri, Firaq. 1946. *Mash'al.* Badayun: Nizami Press.

Gorakhpuri, Firaq. 1947. *Ramz o Kinayaat.* Allahabad: Sangam Publishing House.

Gorakhpuri, Firaq. 1947. *Roop.* Allahabad: Sangam Publishing House.

Gorakhpuri, Firaq. 1959. *Gul-e Naghma.* Adaraah Aniis Urdu.

Gorakhpuri, Firaq. 1962. *Rabindranath Tagore: Ek Sau Nazmein.* New Delhi: Sahitya Akademi.

Gorakhpuri, Firaq. 1965. *Ghazalistaan*. Allahabad: Sahitya Kala Bhavan.

Gorakhpuri, Firaq. 1966. *Charaaghaan*. Allahabad: Sahitya Kala Bhavan.

Gorakhpuri, Firaq. 1966. *Dharti Ki Karvat*. Allahabad: Sahitya Kala Bhavan.

Gorakhpuri, Firaq. 1966. *Sh'eristaan*. Allahabad: Sahitya Kala Bhavan.

Gorakhpuri, Firaq. 1967. *Gulbaang*. Allahabad: Sahitya Kala Bhavan.

Gorakhpuri, Firaq. 1969. *Bazm-e Zindagi Rang-e Shaa'yiri*. New Delhi: Bhartiya Jananapith.

Gorakhpuri, Firaq. 1976. *Shakespeare's Hamlet:* Urdu Translation. New Delhi: Sahitya Akademi.

Gorakhpuri, Firaq. 1992. *Ruh-e Kaayenaat*. Allahabad: Ram Narain Lal Arun Kumar.

Gorakhpuri, Firaq. 1997. *Man Aanam*. Delhi: Saqi Book Depot.

Gorakhpuri, Firaq. 2011. *Pichhli Raat*. New Delhi: Maktaba Jaam'ia Ltd.

Gorakhpuri, Firaq. Mohammad Tufail, ed. 1956. *Andaze*. Lahore: Adara Farogh-e Urdu.

Gorakhpuri, Majnun. 1930. *Introduction of Ibrat's Masnavi Husn-e Fitrat*. No publisher information.

Gorakhpuri, Majnun. 1983. *Raghupati* in *Firaq: Shaa'yir aur Sakhsiat,* Shamim Hanafi, ed. New Delhi: Mahnama Kitab Nama.

Hanafi, Shamim, ed. 1983. *Firaq: Shaa'yir aur Shakhsiat*. Lahore: Book Traders.

Hanafi, Shamim, Suhail Ahmad Faruqi, eds. 1992. *Firaq: Dayar-e Shab Ka Musafir.* New Delhi: Maktaba Jamia Ltd.

Hasan, Mohammad. 1992. *Thus Spoke Firaq: A Collection of Interviews (1959-1976)*. New Delhi: Allied Publishers.

Hunar, Mahmood Ahmad and Mumtazul Haq, eds. 1965. *Shaahkaar: Firaq Number.* Allahabad.

Husain, Syed Amjad, ed. *Firaq: Sadi Ki Aavaaz.* Lucknow: Department of Information & Communications.

Jafar, Sayyada. 1996. *Firaq Gorakhpuri.* New Delhi: Sahitya Akademi.

Mansingh, Ajai. 2015. *Firaq Gorakhpuri: The Poet of Pain & Ecstasy.* New Delhi: Roli Books Pvt. Ltd.

Nabil, Aziz, ed. 2014. *Firaq Gorakhpuri: Shakhsiat, Shaa'yiri aur Shanaakhat.* Bahrain: Majlis Fakhar Baraae Farogh-e Urdu.

Narang, Gopi Chand. 2008. *Firaq Gorakhpuri: Shaa'yir, Naqqaad, Daanishvar* (Papers presented at the International Seminar organized by the Sahitya Akademi) New Delhi: Sahitya Akademi.

Narang, Gopi Chand. Trans. Surinder Deol. 2020. *The Urdu Ghazal: A Gift of India's Composite Culture.* New Delhi: Oxford University Press.

Narang, Gopi Chand. 2022. Trans. Surinder Deol. *India's Freedom Struggle and the Urdu Poetry: Awakening.* New Delhi: Routledge–Taylor and Francis Group.

Nizami, Mutrib. 1987. *Firaq Gorakhpuri: Yaadon Ke Jharoke Se.* Lucknow: Fakhruddin Ali Ahmad Memorial Committee.

Prasad, Vishwa Ranjan. 1996. *The Poet Who Balanced Irrevocable Contradiction* in *Times of India*, Patna. 27 October 1996.

Quraishi, Kamil, ed. 1967. *Firaq Gorakhpuri.* Delhi: Bazm-e Adab.

Raza, Kalidas Gupta. 1998. *Intikhaab-e Ghazliaat-e Firaq.* (Kalidas Gupta Raza arranged Firaq's ghazals as per their timeline) Mumbai: Sakar Publishers Pvt. Ltd.

Saeedi, Makhmoor, ed. 1997. *Aiwaan-e Urdu. Firaq Number.* Delhi: Urdu Academy.

Saeedi, Makhmoor. 1998. *Firaq Gorakhpuri: Zaat aur Safaat.* Delhi: Urdu Academy.

Siddiqi, Amir Ahmad, ed. 1982. *Naya Daur Firaq Numbers 1 & 2.* Lucknow: Gangadhar Prasad Shukla Publishers.

Yogananda, Paramahansa. 1994. *Wine of the Mystic: The Rubaiyat of Omar Khayyam, A Spiritual Interpretation.* Los Angeles: Self-Realization Fellowship.

INDEX

RUBA'IS

premko [illegible] 362
[illegible] 353
[illegible] 347
rakshā-bandhan [illegible] 361
[illegible] 354
[illegible] 351
[illegible]
[illegible] 340
sote [illegible] 349
[illegible]
[illegible] 357
[illegible]
[illegible]
[illegible]
ye [illegible]
ye shor [illegible]
[illegible] 355
zulfon se [illegible]